Project Procurement Management
A Guide to Structured Procurements

Based on the *PMBOK® Guide*—Sixth Edition

Stephen Guth

This book is dedicated to my sweetheart, the love of my life, my best friend, and partner—Carrie Guth.

Sixth Edition

Copyright © 2009 – 2018 Stephen Guth

Cover Art: Copyright © Wojciech Gajda

ISBN: 978-1717881595

Library of Congress Control Number: 2018908203

About the Author

Stephen Guth is a seasoned supply management professional with extensive procurement, negotiation, contracting, and vendor management experience. He has worked for Aflac Insurance, Dell Computer, and Ryder System as well as proudly serving with the armed forces as part of the United States Special Operations Command. He is a licensed attorney, member of the District of Columbia Bar, and served as Chief Corporate Counsel of the National Rural Electric Cooperative Association. In his career, Stephen personally negotiated or oversaw the negotiation of over 9,000 contracts with a combined total value of over $10 billion dollars, resulting in negotiated savings of over $100 million dollars.

Stephen is a graduate of the University of Miami School of Law (J.D.), University of Maryland University College (M.S., Procurement and Contract Management), and Saint Leo University (*summa cum laude*, B.A., Computer Information Systems). He has also taught procurement-related courses as an adjunct professor with the University of Maryland University College's Graduate School of Management and Technology. Stephen received a Master's Certificate in Commercial Contract Management from George Washington University and is a Certified Commercial Contract Manager, Certified Professional in Supply Management, Florida Certified Contract Negotiator, and Florida Certified Contract Manager.

Stephen served as a member of the Professional Standards and Ethics Committee of the National Contract Management Association Board of Directors, Executive Sponsor of the Institute for Supply Management–Northern Virginia, Director of Professional Development of the Institute for Supply Management–Florida's First Coast, member of the Oracle Procurement Customer Advisory Board, and an expert witness in contract law matters. He is the creator of the *Procurement Maturity Model*® and received the Member of the Year award from the Association of Technology Procurement Professionals.

Stephen is a frequent speaker at supply management industry events and he has authored numerous articles on contracting, procurement, vendor management, and patent law in periodicals such as *CIO Magazine*, *Journal of Contract Management*, *Management Quarterly*, and *Inside Supply Management*. He is the author of numerous books, including *The Contract Negotiation Handbook: Software as a Service*, *The Contract Negotiation Handbook: An Indispensable Guide for Contract Professionals*, and *The Vendor Management Office: Unleashing the Power of Strategic Sourcing*.

Contents at a Glance

Table of Contents

LIST OF FIGURES

LIST OF TABLES

Preface to the Sixth Edition

This Sixth Edition of *Project Procurement Management: A Guide to Structured Procurements* has been updated to correspond to the Project Management Institute's (PMI®) *A Guide to the Project Management Body of Knowledge (PMBOK® Guide)*—Sixth Edition. While this edition represents a third revision, based on feedback from readers, I correlated the edition of this book to that of the *PMBOK Guide*—Sixth Edition. Additionally, I expanded and elaborated on certain areas to ensure that the content is current and relevant. My original purpose for writing this book continues to be reflected in this edition, which is to provide a bridge between the value represented by the PMI's Project Management Procurement Knowledge Area and the need of project managers and procurement practitioners for a structured procurement methodology that can be put to practical use. This book, therefore, focuses on the application of the *PMBOK Guide* and the Project Procurement Management Knowledge Area to a practitioner's world.

As a part of bridging the gap between the ideals of the *PMBOK Guide* and practical realities, an objective of this book is to familiarize procurement practitioners with Project Procurement Management Knowledge Area terminology and, similarly, project managers with procurement-specific terminology. The Project Procurement Management Knowledge Area imposes a structured procurement methodology on the procurement practitioner that at first may seem foreign. This is made particularly obvious by the project management-oriented terminology used by the *PMBOK Guide* and the Project Procurement Management Knowledge Area, which may seem somewhat odd or confusing to a procurement practitioner. Thus, where appropriate, I strive to "translate" project management lexicon through the use of explanatory narrative.

A final reason for me in writing and updating this book is to weave together my other books, which focus on very specific and targeted areas of supply management. I wrote *The Vendor Management Office: Unleashing the Power of Strategic Sourcing* to provide a structured step-by-step approach for building a strategic sourcing and vendor management organization. My other books, such as the *Contract Negotiation Handbook: An Indispensable Guide for Contract Professionals* and the *Contract Negotiation Handbook: Software as a Service*, were written to help procurement practitioners recognize seller negotiation ploys and to leverage buyer negotiation tactics. This book adds to those other books by examining what lies between the procurement function and a procurement practitioner's skills: a structured and disciplined procurement methodology.

Ultimately, my goal for this book is that project managers and procurement practitioners find the information helpful in implementing a mutually beneficial and real-world structured procurement methodology that stays true to the value that the Project Procurement Management Knowledge Area can provide.

Stephen Guth
stephenguth@outlook.com
www.stephenguth.com

1 – Introduction

Procurement is an essential part of many projects as a result of project teams needing products, services, or results that cannot be obtained internally. Unfortunately, procurement is frequently an afterthought in the context of project management and scant time is spent performing the most fundamental of procurement activities to ensure project success: developing requirements; qualifying prospective sellers; conducting a competitive procurement; negotiating a contract; and, making a contract award—all on the most favorable terms and conditions possible. As a consequence of procurements being ill-planned and rushed, the project team is saddled with a product, service, or result that fails to meet requirements, is procured under inflated prices, or is delivered under an unfavorable contract.

As organizations become more sophisticated and disciplined in managing projects, procurement is becoming recognized as a key and integral part of project plans. However, there is a natural tension between the project manager and the individual or function responsible for procurement (the "buyer"). The project manager needs whatever products, services, or results that are required as quickly as possible to proceed with the project. On the other hand, the buyer has the obligation to achieve the best value for the project and the project organization (which does take time). In an effort to minimize that natural tension and to achieve the best results for a project, both the project manager and buyer must have an appreciation for each other's role within the project. It is incumbent upon the buyer to recognize that procurement is an early part of an overall project and not the only part; the project team members want to get through the procurement quickly so that they can have access to the products, services, or results that they need for their project. On the other hand, the project manager must recognize that the method by which a procurement is conducted can shape the outcome of the project. In short, a buyer must understand the time sensitivities of the project and the project manager must have a basic understanding of, and appreciation for, the procurement process.

To facilitate these reciprocal understandings, efficient yet formalized (meaning documented and structured) procurement processes must be established. While many procurement functions likely do have their own formalized—or at least documented—processes, it is almost certain that those processes are stand-alone and not viable in the broader context of a project management methodology. A pivotal question for any project organization is whether its procurement processes are integrated with its project management methodology such that the procurement processes recognize project management inputs and then produce the right outputs for the project team. The answer to that question will determine whether existing procurement processes can be a value-adding part of a project management methodology or not. If the existing procurement processes need to be over-hauled to intersect and integrate with an organization's project management methodology, the difficulty is in figuring out how.

The Project Management Institute (PMI®), the world's leading not-for-profit professional membership association for the project, program, and portfolio management profession, includes what it terms "Project Procurement Management" as one of the ten Knowledge Areas in the Sixth Edition of the PMI's premier publication, *A Guide to the Project Management Body of Knowledge (PMBOK® Guide*[1]). Throughout the various editions of the *PMBOK Guide*, the PMI has included procurement activities in one form or another, refining the activities with each edition. In the current edition, the PMI succinctly defines the Project Procurement Management Knowledge Area as including the management and control processes necessary to procure products, services, or results needed from outside the project team.

As a procurement methodology, the Project Procurement Management Knowledge Area represents a structured and efficient framework to achieve project results that meet the needs of the project organization, project manager, buyer, and contract manager. If the processes, inputs, tools & techniques, and outputs—as further described in this book—of the Project Procurement Management Knowledge Area are translated into phases, activities, and tasks as a part of a project plan and schedule, a project will be well positioned to procure the required products, services, or results at the lowest possible cost and at the requisite level of quality and performance.

To aid in achieving the goal of establishing efficient and value-adding procurement activities within the framework of a project management methodology, this book explores and explains the Project Procurement Management Knowledge Area in a commercial procurement context. The PMI succinctly explains the Project Procurement Management Knowledge Area and its related processes in the *PMBOK Guide*; however, there is limited explanation as to how to implement or actually use the Project Procurement Management Knowledge Area. In practice, the simplicity of limited explanation is part of the benefit of the *PMBOK Guide*: Project organizations have the flexibility to integrate their unique processes with a structured and disciplined approach to procurement. While this book does not describe the detailed how-to of procurement, as a companion to the *PMBOK Guide*, this book seeks to provide a real-life perspective of the Project Procurement Management Knowledge Area as it is described by the PMI.

To facilitate the necessary mutual understandings between buyers and project managers, this book describes procurement activities and related considerations—such as procurement ethics—in the context of the Project Procurement Management Knowledge Area. Further, there is enough of an exposure to procurement terminology and methods in this book such that a project manager can have informed discussions with the buyer and contract manager assigned to the project. Thus, a project manager is equipped to do what he or she does best, and that is to manage a project efficiently and effectively to achieve the desired results.

---

[1] Unless otherwise indicated, all references hereafter to the *PMBOK Guide* mean and include the Sixth Edition.

2 – Project Procurement Management Overview

In 1987, the PMI published *The Project Management Body of Knowledge* as a white paper to document and standardize generally accepted project management practices. At that time, procurement-related processes were clustered under what was entitled "Contract/Procurement Management."

In 1996, after significant revisions by the PMI Standards Committee, the white paper was transformed into the First Edition of what is known today as the *PMBOK Guide*. At that time, the PMI re-named Contract/Procurement Management to the Project Procurement Management Knowledge Area. This new nomenclature removed the distinction between "Contract" and "Procurement," and made the nomenclature consistent with the other Knowledge Areas (which all started with the word "Project" to clarify that the Knowledge Areas are unique or nearly unique to the project context). The Second Edition of the *PMBOK Guide* was published in 2000, using the same six processes for the Project Procurement Management Knowledge Area from the First Edition. The term "supplier" was changed throughout that version of the *PMBOK Guide* to "seller." No other major changes were made to the Project Procurement Management Knowledge Area.

The PMI published the Third Edition of the *PMBOK Guide* in 2004 and renamed all but one (*Contract Administration*) of the six Project Procurement Management Knowledge Area processes. A significant change to the content was identifying the project team as the buyer of products, services, and results, reflecting the important point that the buyer needs to be an integral part of the project and project team, and not an ancillary support function. Seller performance evaluation was added to the *Contract Administration* process and various inputs, tools & techniques, and outputs were clarified. Additionally, the content was changed to reflect a consistent use of the terms "buyer" and "seller." That same nomenclature will be used from this point forward, with "buyer" meaning the individual or function responsible for acquiring products, services, or results and "seller" meaning a provider or supplier of products, services, or results.

The Fourth Edition of the *PMBOK Guide*, published in 2008, included a consolidation of the processes contained within the Project Procurement Management Knowledge Area. More significant updates came in 2013 with the Fifth Edition of the *PMBOK Guide*, including several process name changes made across the Knowledge Areas to improve consistency and clarity. All Planning Process Group processes that created a subsidiary plan were renamed using the form of *Plan* [name of *Process*] *Management*; for example, *Plan Procurement Management*. Certain Monitoring and Controlling Process Group processes were renamed using the form of *Control* [name of *Process*]; for example, *Control Procurements*. Accordingly, and as alluded to in the prior two examples, specific to the Project Procurement Management Knowledge Area, the PMI renamed two of the four processes: The *Plan Procurements* process was renamed *Plan Procurement Management* and the *Administer Procurements* process was renamed *Control Procurements*. Other changes to the Project Procurement Management Knowledge Area included renaming and aligning various inputs and outputs with changes from other Knowledge Areas and to reflect information flow during the execution of project work.

The PMI published the most recent edition of the *PMBOK Guide*, the Sixth Edition, in 2017. In this edition, the PMI made numerous enhancements and refinements, including the incorporation of agile-specific tools and techniques such as sprint and iteration planning.[2] Specific to the Project Procurement Management Knowledge Area, the PMI acknowledged the continued global adoption of the *PMBOK Guide* and that procurements more frequently involve stakeholders located around the world. This acknowledgement is mostly manifested in the PMI's discussion of the impact of culture and local law on procurement agreements. The PMI also eliminated *Close Procurements*, which was a process in the Closing Process Group, from the Project Procurement Management Knowledge Area based on the recognition that it is typically a procurement, contract management, or legal function—and not a project manager—that actually closes out procurements. In place of *Close Procurements*, *Control Procurements* absorbed information about the evaluation of completed deliverables and *Close Project or Phase*, which is a process within the Project Integration Management Knowledge Area, absorbed information about administrative, communications, and records related to contract close-out. Figure 2-1 illustrates the differences between the Second, Third, Fourth, Fifth, and Sixth Editions of the *PMBOK Guide* Project Procurement Management Knowledge Area.

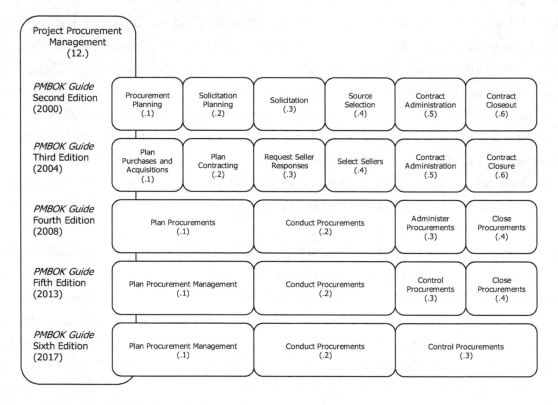

Figure 2-1. *PMBOK Guide* Edition Project Procurement Management Comparison

---

[2] Agile originated as a software development methodology under which requirements and solutions iteratively evolve as the result of collaborative efforts between self-organizing delivery teams and their customers. Through the division of tasks into short phases of work, the agile methodology advocates adaptive planning, evolutionary development, early delivery, continuous improvement, and rapid and flexible response to change. The use of agile and related frameworks, such as the Scaled Agile Framework® which is intended to guide enterprises in scaling agile practices, are more frequently being applied to projects having other than an information technology scope.

As depicted in Figure 2-1, the *PMBOK Guide*—Sixth Edition segments the Project Procurement Management Knowledge Area into three processes:

- 12.1 *Plan Procurement Management* – The process of documenting project procurement decisions, determining the procurement approach, and identifying prospective sellers.
- 12.2 *Conduct Procurements* – The process of obtaining responses from prospective sellers, selecting a seller, and awarding a procurement agreement.[3]
- 12.3 *Control Procurements* – The process of managing seller relationships, monitoring contract performance, managing change, and closing out contracts.

The *PMBOK Guide* explains that the Project Procurement Management Knowledge Area includes the processes necessary to procure products, services, or *results* needed from outside the project to perform the work of the project. By *results*, the PMI means an output from performing project management processes and activities, such as outcomes and work product such as documents. It may seem somewhat confusing that results are distinguished to be something different from a product or service, but the Project Procurement Management Knowledge Area contemplates that its processes may apply to not only traditional buyer-seller arrangements but also to both non-contractual and contractual agreements entered into between the project team and other units or parts of a project organization. Thus, a *result* could be viewed in terms of what is delivered—a product or a service—to the project team by the project organization. Using the example of a cloud application (such as software as a service) procured externally from a seller, an "outcome" could be an integration developed by a project organization's information technology function necessary to implement the application and a "document" could be a change management strategy developed by the project organization's organizational change management function.

It is also important to note that the Project Procurement Management Knowledge Area presents two perspectives of procurement: The project organization can be the buyer *or* seller of the products, services, or results under a project. The processes used by a seller to provide the products, services, or results under a project—that will result in a sale or delivery to another party (either internal to a project organization or external)—are nearly identical to the processes undertaken by a buyer. In this book's examination of the Project Procurement Management Knowledge Area, the context will be primarily from a buyer's perspective seeking to procure products, services, or results from an *external* seller in a commercial setting.

---

[3] In the Project Procurement Management Knowledge Area, the *PMBOK Guide* and this book use the terms "contract," "procurement agreement," and "Agreements" (see Sections 12.2.3.2 and 12.3.1.3) to mean the same thing: the agreement between the project organization and the seller to provide the agreed-upon products, services, or results. Additionally, unless noted otherwise, references to seller "responses" and "proposals" herein shall mean the same thing: a seller's response to a request for information or a competitive solicitation issued by a project organization.

Another consideration is that the processes and activities of the Project Procurement Management Knowledge Area must be performed for *each* project need that is to be procured. For complex or multi-national projects, the Project Procurement Management Knowledge Area may require multiple yet separate procurements and contracts, beginning and ending at different times during the project lifecycle, and involving both external sellers and results being delivered by the project organization to the project. While certain activities associated with procurements can be combined to create efficiencies, there are certain other activities that must be performed distinctly separate from one procurement to the next. For example, while an overall Procurement Management Plan (12.1.3.1) can be developed for all procurements under a project, more than one type of Bid Documents (12.1.3.3) and more than one type of Agreements (12.2.3.2)[4] will likely be required. The ability to combine the Project Procurement Management Knowledge Area inputs and outputs for multiple procurements will be project organization-specific.

Project Procurement Management Structure

Using the format illustrated below, the *PMBOK Guide* is structured by Knowledge Area, processes within a Knowledge Area, and then inputs, tools & techniques, and outputs (each, an "activity") within a process.

x.   [name of Knowledge Area]

      x.x   [name of *Process*]

            x.x.1   [name of *Process*:] [Inputs]
                  x.x.1.x   [name of Input]

            x.x.2   [name of *Process*:] [Tools & Techniques]
                  x.x.2.x   [name of Tool or Technique]

            x.x.3   [name of *Process*:] [Outputs]
                  x.x.3.x   [name of Output]

Within each process contained in a Knowledge Area (such as Project Procurement Management), the *PMBOK Guide* describes each of the inputs, tools & techniques, and outputs. Inputs are any key documentable or documented item, either internal or external to a project, that is required by a process before that process can proceed. To be considered internal to a project, an input must map as an output from another process. Tools are something tangible, such as a template, used to perform an activity and produce a product or result. Techniques are defined procedures employing one or more tools which are used by a project team member to perform an activity that produces a product, service, or result. Combined, tools & techniques are those mechanisms that, when applied to inputs, produce outputs.

---

[4] See also Section 12.1.1.6 regarding contract types.

Outputs are a product, service, or result generated by a process and, unless a terminal output or embedded within another input, serve as an input to a successor process. That same *PMBOK Guide* nomenclature will be used by this book in examining the Project Procurement Management Knowledge Area processes and their inputs, tools & techniques, and outputs.

As illustrated in the structure immediately following this paragraph, the Project Procurement Management Knowledge Area is enumerated as Section 12 in the *PMBOK Guide* and sub-sections are referred to using a "12.x" to "12.x.x.x" numerical reference. Wherever appropriate, this book follows the numerical reference framework used by the *PMBOK Guide* to facilitate an easy correlation between this book, its chapters and sections, and the *PMBOK Guide*. Each Project Procurement Management Knowledge Area process, input, tool, technique, and output are examined in detail in later chapters within this book.

12. Project Procurement Management

    12.1 *Plan Procurement Management*

        12.1.1 *Plan Procurement Management*: Inputs
            12.1.1.1   Project Charter
            12.1.1.2   Business Documents
            12.1.1.3   Project Management Plan
            12.1.1.4   Project Documents
            12.1.1.5   Enterprise Environmental Factors
            12.1.1.6   Organizational Process Assets

        12.1.2 *Plan Procurement Management*: Tools & Techniques
            12.1.2.1   Expert Judgment
            12.1.2.2   Data Gathering
            12.1.2.3   Data Analysis
            12.1.2.4   Source Selection Analysis
            12.1.2.5   Meetings

        12.1.3 *Plan Procurement Management*: Outputs
            12.1.3.1   Procurement Management Plan
            12.1.3.2   Procurement Strategy
            12.1.3.3   Bid Documents
            12.1.3.4   Procurement Statement of Work
            12.1.3.5   Source Selection Criteria
            12.1.3.6   Make-or-Buy Decisions
            12.1.3.7   Independent Cost Estimates
            12.1.3.8   Change Requests

12.3.2 *Control Procurements*: Tools & Techniques
    12.3.2.1   Expert Judgment
    12.3.2.2   Claims Administration
    12.3.2.3   Data Analysis
    12.3.2.4   Inspection
    12.3.2.5   Audits

12.3.3 *Control Procurements*: Outputs
    12.3.3.1   Closed Procurements
    12.3.3.2   Work Performance Information
    12.3.3.3   Procurement Documentation Updates
    12.3.3.4   Change Requests
    12.3.3.5   Project Management Plan Updates
    12.3.3.6   Project Documents Updates
    12.3.3.7   Organizational Process Assets Updates

Numerous inputs, tools & techniques, and outputs within the Project Procurement Management Knowledge Area originate or are described in other Knowledge Areas; for example, the input of the Project Charter to the *Plan Procurement Management* (12.1) process under the Project Procurement Management Knowledge Area is described as an output of the *Develop Project Charter* (4.1) process under the Project Integration Management Knowledge Area. These interrelationships are also examined in later chapters.

Processes contained within a Knowledge Area in the *PMBOK Guide* are grouped into five categories of processes known as Project Management Process Groups:

- Initiating
- Planning
- Executing
- Monitoring and Controlling
- Closing

Of the ten Knowledge Areas, Project Integration Management is the only one that contains all five of the Project Management Process Groups. Specific to the Project Procurement Management Knowledge Area, the processes represent the Planning, Executing, and Monitoring and Controlling Process Groups:

- *Plan Procurement Management* – Planning
- *Conduct Procurements* – Executing
- *Control Procurements* – Monitoring and Controlling

As indicated by this book's table of contents, the examination of the Project Procurement Management Knowledge Area herein is sequential, from beginning to end, process to process. Significant elaboration will be devoted to certain elements of a Project Procurement Management Knowledge Area process that are particularly important. Additionally, there are certain key topics related to the Project Procurement Management Knowledge Area, such as legal considerations and procurement ethics, which will be examined in separate chapters.

PMBOK Guide and Procurement Terminology

The Project Procurement Management Knowledge Area describes procurement and contract management through the lens of project management terminology—that terminology is very different from what a buyer or a contract manager would likely use. Certain *PMBOK Guide* terminology[5] used in this book may seem foreign to those readers who have a commercial procurement or contract management background. For example, most buyers use "vendor" or "supplier" to refer to what the *PMBOK Guide* terms "seller" and use "solicitation" to refer to what the *PMBOK Guide* terms Bid Documents. Since it would be impractical and difficult for a project manager to impose the use of *PMBOK Guide* terminology on a seasoned buyer, the project manager must have an understanding of common commercial procurement terms in order to more effectively communicate project requirements relating to a procurement. Figure 2-2 serves to assist in bridging the gap between broad terms used by the *PMBOK Guide* to describe the Knowledge Area processes and those terms commonly used by buyers in the context of commercial procurements.

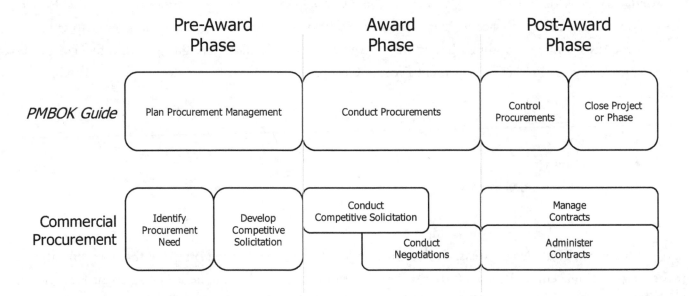

Figure 2-2. *PMBOK Guide* **and Commercial Procurement Terminology Comparison**

---

[5] To differentiate between Project Procurement Management as a Knowledge Area and the processes contained within the Knowledge Area, processes are italicized in the text.

Regardless of how the PMI describes the Project Procurement Management Knowledge Area, one concept of the Knowledge Area is clear: It represents a structured procurement methodology regardless of job role, perspective, or terminology. Consequently, any project organization can benefit from the structure of the Project Procurement Management Knowledge Area and—provided that the underlying processes are followed—can use whatever terminology that is preferred or desired.

Figure 2-2 also indicates certain overlaps between processes. While the Project Procurement Management Knowledge Area implies a sequential activity or "end-to-end" order, there are certain processes and activities within processes that overlap. These overlaps do not represent inefficiencies or redundant work but are instead an intentional result of an effective procurement process. In the Award Phase described above, the Conduct Competitive Solicitation and Conduct Negotiations activities intentionally overlap to achieve a procurement negotiation strategy typically referred to as "pre-negotiations." Pre-negotiations are examined further under the *Conduct Procurements* (12.2) process (see Section 12.2.2.5), but a brief explanation here is that pre-negotiations involve sellers negotiating against themselves in a "best and final offer" scenario. Another reason for the overlap is that negotiations begin at the onset of a procurement—both the project organization[6] and the sellers attempt to learn as much as possible about each other to advantage their negotiations.

In the Post-Award Phase, the Project Procurement Management Knowledge Area combines the sometimes separate activities of contract administration and contract management into the *Control Procurements* (12.3) process. In Figure 2-2, Contract Administration and Contract Management activities are shown as parallel and somewhat overlapping. In practice, organizational functions or individuals may separately but simultaneously administer contracts (such as record retention, monitoring expiration dates, and tracking seller progress to trigger payment releases) and manage contracts (such as measuring seller performance to service level agreements, managing contract changes, and resolving contract disputes). The overlap primarily results from the necessity to share data between the two organizational functions or individuals.

---

[6] As used in this book, the "project organization" shall be the buying entity.

3 – 12.1 Plan Procurement Management

The first process within the Project Procurement Management Knowledge Area is *Plan Procurement Management*, which is a part of the Planning Process Group. The Planning Process Group is comprised of those processes which are required to establish the project scope, refine project objectives, and define the course of action required to achieve project objectives. The *Plan Procurement Management* process encompasses three broad activities: (1) documenting project procurement decisions; (2) specifying the procurement approach; and, (3) identifying prospective sellers. If project needs cannot be fulfilled from within the project organization, this process includes developing the method to procure the product, service, or result from a seller external to the project organization. Assuming the need to externally procure a product, service, or result, the *Plan Procurement Management* process documents project needs, identifies procurement risks, specifies the procurement approach, and identifies qualified prospective sellers. Since a primary precept of project management is advance and thoughtful planning to avoid problems in the execution of future processes, it is no surprise that a significant amount of preparatory work and analysis are performed in the *Plan Procurement Management* process. There is also a significant amount of documentation created in this process, with the outputs being a critical component in facilitating a potential procurement as a part of the *Conduct Procurements* (12.2) process.

Once it is established that a project team is in need of a product, service, or result, that need is documented in the form of detailed requirements as the Requirements Documentation component of the Project Documents (12.1.1.4). Upon completion of the requirements, the project team has not yet fully determined whether the product, service, or result can be obtained internally within the project organization or must be obtained externally from sellers. That decision—the Make-or-Buy Decisions (12.1.3.6)—results from the make-or-buy analysis that is conducted as a part of Data Analysis (12.1.2.3). Assuming that the decision is to "buy," the project team (with the buyer being a primary contributor) creates—in addition to other outputs—a Procurement Management Plan (12.1.3.1), Procurement Statement of Work (12.1.3.4), and, the vehicle that is ultimately used to solicit seller responses, Bid Documents (12.1.3.3).

Tables 3-1, 3-2, and 3-3 describe the inputs, tools & techniques, outputs and who is primarily responsible for a particular activity. For each input, tool or technique, and output, the Project Procurement Management Knowledge Area section reference is listed first and, if applicable, the originating Knowledge Area reference is listed second within parentheses.

Table 3-1. Plan Procurement Management: Inputs

Inputs	Responsibility
12.1.1.1 Project Charter (4.1.3.1)	Project Sponsor
12.1.1.2 Business Documents (1.2.6) – Business Case (1.2.6.1) – Benefits Management Plan (1.2.6.2)	 – Project Sponsor – Project Manager
12.1.1.3 Project Management Plan (4.2.3.1) – Scope Management Plan (5.1.3.1) – Quality Management Plan (8.1.3.1) – Resource Management Plan (9.1.3.1) – Scope Baseline (5.4.3.1)	 – Project Manager – Project Manager – Project Manager – Project Manager
12.1.1.4 Project Documents – Milestone List (6.2.3.3) – Project Team Assignments (9.3.3.2) – Requirements Documentation (5.2.3.1) – Requirements Traceability Matrix (5.2.3.2) – Resource Requirements (9.2.3.1) – Risk Register (11.2.3.1) – Stakeholder Register (13.1.3.1)	 – Project Manager – Project Manager – Project Manager – Project Manager – Project Manager – Buyer – Project Manager
12.1.1.5 Enterprise Environmental Factors	Buyer
12.1.1.6 Organizational Process Assets	Buyer

Table 3-2. Plan Procurement Management: Tools & Techniques

Tools & Techniques	Responsibility
12.1.2.1 Expert Judgment (4.1.2.1)	Buyer
12.1.2.2 Data Gathering – Market Research	 – Buyer
12.1.2.3 Data Analysis – Make-or-Buy Analysis	 – Project Manager

Tools & Techniques	Responsibility
12.1.2.4 Source Selection Analysis	Buyer
12.1.2.5 Meetings	Buyer

Table 3-3. Plan Procurement Management: Outputs

Outputs	Responsibility
12.1.3.1 Procurement Management Plan	Buyer
12.1.3.2 Procurement Strategy	Buyer
12.1.3.3 Bid Documents	Buyer
12.1.3.4 Procurement Statement of Work	Buyer
12.1.3.5 Source Selection Criteria	Buyer
12.1.3.6 Make-or-Buy Decisions	Project Manager
12.1.3.7 Independent Cost Estimates	Buyer
12.1.3.8 Change Requests (4.3.3.4)	Project Manager
12.1.3.9 Project Documents Updates – Lessons Learned Register (4.4.3.1) – Milestone List (6.2.3.3) – Requirements Documentation (5.2.3.1) – Requirements Traceability Matrix (5.2.3.2) – Risk Register (11.2.3.1) – Stakeholder Register (13.1.3.1)	 – Project Manager – Project Manager – Project Manager – Project Manager – Buyer – Project Manager
12.1.3.10 Organizational Process Assets Updates	Buyer

12.1.1 Plan Procurement Management: Inputs

At this point in the *Plan Procurement Management* process, when the inputs are being gathered or developed, the decision as to whether to externally procure the project need has not yet been made. The project manager must conduct the make-or-buy analysis as a part of the Data Analysis (12.1.2.3), which will result in the Make-or-Buy Decisions (12.1.3.6) and a determination as to whether an external procurement will be required.[7] The rationale for involving the buyer before the need for an external procurement is determined is so that the buyer can assist in developing some of the inputs of the *Plan Procurement Management* process that serve to identify costs (for example, by quantifying possible procurement risks) that can be used in conducting the make-or-buy analysis.

12.1.1.1 Project Charter

The Project Charter, an output (4.1.3.1) resulting from the *Develop Project Charter* (4.1) process of the Project Integration Management Knowledge Area, documents the authorization and initiation of a project as well as to provide the project manager with the necessary authority to apply organizational resources to the project's activities. Using the Business Case (1.2.6.1) and Benefits Management Plan (1.2.6.2) as inputs, the Project Charter is typically developed by a project manager with input from the project sponsor and is then approved by the project sponsor. An approved Project Charter serves as notification to a buyer that he or she has the authority to proceed with aligning the resources necessary to conduct a procurement. The buyer should carefully review the Project Charter as it contains key high-level information such as the project purpose, objectives, requirements, milestone schedule, and deliverables. Upon review of a Project Charter, a buyer should confirm his or her understanding of the project needs with the Project Manager to ensure alignment.

12.1.1.2 Business Documents

Business Documents, described in Section 1.2.6 of the *PMBOK Guide*, include the Business Case (1.2.6.1) and the Benefits Management Plan (1.2.6.2). These two interdependent documents are created as a part of pre-project work and are iteratively maintained throughout the project lifecycle. The Business Documents precede the development of, and are used as input to, the Project Charter (12.1.1.1).

Business Case (1.2.6.1)

The Business Case (1.2.6.1), generally developed by the project sponsor with input from the project manager, documents the economic feasibility of a project and is intended to demonstrate the expected benefits or business value to be created as a result of the project. In short, the Business Case is a decision-making tool that assists project organization managers and executives in determining whether the expected outcomes of the project justify the investment required by the project. The Business Case is also used as the basis to measure project progress as well as the success of a project by comparing results with identified objectives and success criteria. A Business Case is frequently used before project initiation as input to a go / no-go decision for the project. As a part of the *Plan Procurement Management* process, the Business Case is a key input to the Procurement Strategy (12.1.3.2) and is used by the buyer to ensure alignment of a

---

[7] If the Make-or-Buy Decisions (12.1.3.6) resulting from the make-or-buy analysis is to "make" rather than "buy," the buyer may still be involved in the project on the basis that, in some cases, "make" decisions require a certain amount of externally procured products, services, or results to support the "make."

procurement with the business needs, expected benefits, and success measures of the project. Where there is a gap of alignment between the Business Case and the Procurement Strategy (12.1.3.2), the project manager and buyer must collaborate on any necessary changes to the Business Case and determine how the economic feasibility of the project is impacted. For example, if the Business Case calls for a tightly controlled scope in order to achieve the expected benefits and the buyer determines that the Procurement Strategy (12.1.3.2) is best suited for a time and material contract type—which shifts cost risk from the seller to the project organization—due to requirements contained in the Project Documents (12.1.1.4) that are ambiguous and cannot be made more specific, the project manager may consider adjusting the Business Case to reflect a lesser benefit due to potential cost increases.

Benefits Management Plan (1.2.6.2)

The Benefits Management Plan (1.2.6.2), developed by the project manager, describes how and when the expected benefits created as a result of a project will be delivered and how such benefits will be measured. The Benefits Management Plan includes the target benefits, timeframe for realizing such benefits, metrics to show benefits realized, assumptions, and risks. Using the Business Case (1.2.6.1) as input, the Benefits Management Plan identifies processes that will serve to maximize and sustain the expected benefits or business value necessary to achieve the Business Case (1.2.6.1). While a project exists for only a point in time with a defined start and end, the overarching purpose of the Benefits Management Plan is to ensure the benefits and business value become a part of the project organization's ongoing operations, including associated metrics, such that the benefits and business value are realized after the project is complete. While all inputs under the Project Procurement Management Knowledge Area processes are important to a buyer, the Benefits Management Plan is profoundly significant to the buyer and guides him or her in the tailoring of inputs, tools & techniques, and outputs. While the role of the buyer—and every project team member is to ensure the successful delivery or performance of the product, service, or result with the required features and functions as defined by the project scope, the expected benefits and business value must also be achieved. Where a procurement is required to achieve those ends, elements such as procurement dates and contract language become critical dependencies. The Benefits Management Plan has a pervasive influence on the Project Procurement Management Knowledge Area processes; for example, driving how a buyer: (1) tailors contract types under Organizational Process Assets (12.1.1.6); (2) aligns the timetable of procurement activities described in the Procurement Management Plan (12.1.3.1); (3) selects the contract payment types under the Procurement Strategy (12.1.3.2); and, (4) negotiates procurement agreements with Selected Sellers (12.2.3.1) under Agreements (12.2.3.2).

12.1.1.3 Project Management Plan

The Project Management Plan, an output (4.2.3.1) resulting from the *Develop Project Management Plan* (4.2) process of the Project Integration Management Knowledge Area, broadly describes how a project will be executed, monitored, controlled, and closed. Specifically, it describes the need, justification, high-level requirements, and boundaries for the project. The Project Management Plan also serves to integrate and consolidate subsidiary plans and baselines from other processes within the Planning Process Group that are key to the project procurement, including the: Scope Management Plan (5.1.3.1); Quality Management Plan (8.1.3.1); Resource Management Plan (9.1.3.1); and, Scope Baseline (5.4.3.1).

Scope Management Plan (5.1.3.1)

The Scope Management Plan, an output (5.1.3.1) resulting from the *Plan Scope Management* (5.1) process of the Project Scope Management Knowledge Area, contains a description of how a project's scope will be defined, developed, monitored, controlled, and validated. Should contracted resources, such as contingent workers or contractors, be procured for the project, the Scope Management Plan describes how the scope of work being provided by the seller will be managed by the project organization and by the seller through the execution phase of the project.

Quality Management Plan (8.1.3.1)

The Quality Management Plan, an output (8.1.3.1) resulting from the *Plan Quality Management* (8.1) process of the Project Quality Management Knowledge Area, establishes how a project organization's quality policies, methodologies, and standards will be implemented to support a project and to achieve the desired expectations of quality. It includes the resources and activities necessary for the project team to achieve the quality objectives of the project and describes the policies, procedures, and guidelines that must be implemented to drive quality. Depending on the scope, size, and complexity of a project, the Quality Management Plan may range in formality and detail. For example, for certain projects there may be detailed industry standards or codes which apply (such as those standards promulgated by the International Organization for Standardization or the Safe Quality Food Code established by the Food Marketing Institute) or there may be broad standards or duties of care required (such as a "professional standard of care" or a "duty of reasonable care"). Any standards, codes, or duties related to the quality of a seller's delivery or performance should be described by the buyer in the Bid Documents (12.1.3.3) to facilitate seller responses and included as a part of the Source Selection Criteria (12.1.3.5) to assist in proposal evaluations conducted through Data Analysis (12.2.2.4). Standards, codes, or duties can also be utilized to develop prequalified seller lists as a part of Organizational Process Assets (12.1.1.6). Agreements (12.2.3.2) should specifically require contractual compliance to standards, codes, or duties through, for example, representations, warranties, service levels, performance measures, and acceptance criteria.

Resource Management Plan (9.1.3.1)

The Resource Management Plan, an output (9.1.3.1) resulting from the *Plan Resource Management* (9.1) process of the Project Resource Management Knowledge Area, has information on which project needs will be purchased or leased, any estimated contingent worker rates and any associated travel costs, and how inventory, equipment, and the seller will be managed throughout the project's lifecycle. A buyer should take note of any resource assumptions or constraints (such as requiring onshore versus offshore resources) that could influence the procurement.

Scope Baseline (5.4.3.1)

The Scope Baseline, an output (5.4.3.1) resulting from the *Create WBS* (5.4) process of the Project Scope Management Knowledge Area, includes a project scope statement and work breakdown structure (WBS) which contain a basic description of the required products, services, or results as well as associated deliverables and acceptance criteria. Any constraints such as required delivery or completion dates, resource availability, or project organization policies are also identified and included. Depending on the Scope Baseline and its project scope statement, this component of the Project Management Plan (12.1.13) is essentially a "trigger" for a potential[8] procurement identified by a project, and would describe the basic need, high-level justification, and any project-specific boundaries. The basic need, estimated delivery and completion dates, high-level acceptance criteria, and other information not yet fully developed will serve as integral input to numerous *Plan Procurement Management* process outputs, including the Procurement Management Plan (12.1.3.1), Procurement Strategy (12.1.3.2), Bid Documents (12.1.3.3), and Procurement Statement of Work (12.1.3.4).

12.1.1.4 Project Documents

Whereas the Project Management Plan (12.1.1.3) describes how a project will be executed, monitored, controlled, and closed, Project Documents are those documents not included as a part of the Project Management Plan but that are nevertheless necessary to manage the project effectively. Project Documents contain the level of detail needed by the project manager, buyer, contract manager, and other project team members to satisfactorily fulfill their duties and responsibilities under the project. For purposes of a *Plan Procurement Management* process input, integral Project Documents include the: Milestone List (6.2.3.3); Project Team Assignments (9.3.3.2); Requirements Documentation (5.2.3.1); Requirements Traceability Matrix (5.2.3.2); Resource Requirements (9.2.3.1); Risk Register (11.2.3.1); and, Stakeholder Register (13.1.3.1).

Milestone List (6.2.3.3)

The Milestone List, an output (6.2.3.3) resulting from the *Define Activities* (6.2) process of the Project Schedule Management Knowledge Area, describes significant points or events in a project and the associated schedule dates. Initially, the milestones are developed by the project manager with input from the project team. This list serves as input to the buyer and informs the buyer as to what milestones must be achieved by the buyer as a part of the project as well as those milestones that are expected to be achieved by a seller, such as providing products, services, or results. Upon review of the milestones, the buyer should provide feedback to the project team as to what additional milestones should be considered, with common events for a procurement being release of the Bid Documents (12.1.3.3) to prospective sellers, occurrence of the Bidder Conferences (12.2.2.3), the determination of Selected Sellers (12.2.3.1), and the award of

---

[8] "Potential" in the sense that a procurement *may* be necessary. As previously indicated, it is not until after the Make-or-Buy Decisions (12.1.3.6) resulting from the make-or-buy analysis that the need to conduct a procurement is determined. The Scope Baseline is, however, a strong indicator of the possibility for a procurement.

Agreements (12.2.3.2) to the Selected Sellers (12.2.3.1). See Sections 12.2.1.2, 12.1.3.1, and 12.1.3.2 for additional procurement phases and activities that may be considered for inclusion on the Milestone List.

Project Team Assignments (9.3.3.2)

Project Team Assignments, an output (9.3.3.2) resulting from the *Acquire Resources* (9.3) process of the Project Resource Management Knowledge Area, documents the project team members, their skills and abilities, their specific roles and responsibilities, and their availability. Ideally, those on the project team supporting the procurement, such as the buyer, will have specific knowledge of the products, services, or results to be procured. Where there is a knowledge gap, research or training may need to be obtained. If the products, services, or results are highly specialized, external expertise (such as from a consulting firm) may need to be procured to augment the buyer's expertise.

Requirements Documentation (5.2.3.1)

Requirements Documentation, an output (5.2.3.1) resulting from the *Collect Requirements* (5.2) process of the Project Scope Management Knowledge Area, is an extremely critical input to the *Plan Procurement Management* process in that it describes—either generally or specifically to the extent possible—what products, services, or results are required. It is also a key part of generating two critical *Plan Procurement Management* process outputs: the Bid Documents (12.1.3.3) and the Procurement Statement of Work (12.1.3.4). The substantive and procedural requirements of the Requirements Documentation, via the Procurement Statement of Work (12.1.3.4), are ultimately incorporated as seller responsibilities and obligations in the associated procurement agreement when awarded (see Section 12.2.3.2).

Broadly, there are two types of requirements that can be contained in the Requirements Documentation: substantive and procedural. Substantive requirements are those that describe the "what" of a procurement, that is, the products, services, or results that the project needs. Procedural requirements are those that describe the "how" of a procurement, such as legal or business constraints in conducting the procurement or managing the subsequent contract. While there may be some overlap, the project manager focuses on the substantive requirements ("what") and the buyer focuses on the procedural requirements ("how"). For example, where a project requires unique research services, the project manager may determine that the to-be-procured research services will need to be re-published on the project organization's fee-based website (substantive). To facilitate this need and the desired result, the buyer must ensure that the project organization has the proprietary rights from the seller, either through outright ownership or a license, to republish the research (procedural). Substantive requirements are comprised of various classifications of technical, non-technical, functional, and non-functional requirements—such as business, stakeholder, solution, transition, quality—which meet the scope and needs of the project. The classifications enable a cascading hierarchy of requirements and allow the initial broad coverage of requirements with a business focus to be traced to detailed requirements with a technical focus. Certain requirements may have legal or contractual implications that must be identified, such as licensing and permitting, security and privacy, intellectual property, performance, health and safety, and other non-technical requirements. Additionally, the project itself will likely have its own requirements in the form of actions, processes, or other conditions that must be met such as milestone dates, contractual obligations, and constraints.

The business requirements represent the high-level needs of the project organization as a whole—not of groups or stakeholders within it—and the reasons why the project has been undertaken. The stakeholder requirements, which represent the needs of a specific stakeholder or class of stakeholders, are derived from the business requirements and define how those stakeholders will interact with or utilize the project solution. Once the business and stakeholder requirements—that is, the business and people needs—are known, the solution that meets those requirements can then be defined. Those solution requirements which describe the features, functions, and characteristics of the desired product, service, or result are grouped into functional and non-functional requirements. Functional requirements are capabilities or behaviors that the product, service, or result must achieve to satisfy stakeholder needs whereas non-functional requirements describe required qualities and environmental conditions such as performance, reliability, service levels, security and privacy, and safety. Temporary capabilities which may be needed to transition from the current state to the desired future state, such as data conversion, training, and organizational change management, comprise what are known as transition and readiness requirements. Quality requirements include any condition or criteria needed to test, certify, or validate the successful completion of a project deliverable or fulfillment of other project requirements.

Requirements Documentation may start out at a high-level but become more detailed and refined as the project progresses and more information becomes known. Ideally, and to the extent possible, the Requirements Documentation should be unambiguous, traceable, complete, and consistent—as well as acceptable to stakeholders. While the inputs, tools & techniques, and outputs of other Project Procurement Management Knowledge Area processes have a high degree of importance, insufficient Requirements Documentation could result in the procurement of products, services, or results that fail to meet the needs of the project—in this way Requirements Documentation can be the single point of failure for the entire procurement effort. This failure can be devastating to a project and the project organization in a number of ways, and present financial, operational, and even reputational risks. However, Requirements Documentation can be incomplete to a certain point yet *not* be considered insufficient for purposes of a procurement. For example, a buyer may have an understanding of the project's basic needs for products, services, or results but be unfamiliar with the capabilities in the marketplace. As a result, the buyer's Requirements Documentation and subsequent Procurement Statement of Work (12.1.3.4) may be vague or lack specificity. As described under the *Conduct Procurements* (12.2) process, this acknowledged lack of complete Requirements Documentation is a factor in determining which procurement approach to undertake. The potential for failure to procure the needed products, services, or results is highest when the project team neglects to acknowledge that the Requirements Documentation is incomplete and then, consequently, the buyer creates a poor-quality Procurement Statement of Work (12.1.3.4) and uses an inappropriate procurement approach. It is important to attempt to drive to the most complete and specific

Requirements Documentation as possible so that subsequent inputs, tools & techniques, and outputs are enabled and not adversely impacted.

Requirements Traceability Matrix (5.2.3.2)

The Requirements Traceability Matrix, an output (5.2.3.2) resulting from the *Collect Requirements* (5.2) process of the Project Scope Management Knowledge Area, links project requirements from their origin to the deliverables that will fulfill them and, as a result of the linkage, facilitates the assessment of the potential impact of any scope changes or deviations as the project proceeds. Additionally, the Requirements Traceability Matrix traces requirements throughout the project life cycle, helping to ensure that requirements approved in the Requirements Documentation component of the Project Documents are delivered at the end of the project. The Requirements Traceability Matrix is typically in the form of a table or grid that aligns the described requirements to the associated business need and project objectives. Common attributes of a Requirements Traceability Matrix include a description of the requirement, the related business need, the project objective that will fulfill the requirement, the associated deliverable, the strategy for testing whether the requirement has been met by the associated deliverable, and attributes such as a unique identifier, owner, source, priority, version, status, and status date. For purposes of the Project Procurement Management Knowledge Area, the Requirements Traceability Matrix can be utilized by a buyer in ensuring that all requirements to be addressed by sellers are properly documented in the Bid Documents (12.1.3.3).

Resource Requirements (9.2.3.1)

Resource Requirements, an output (9.2.3.1) resulting from the *Estimate Activity Resources* (9.2) process of the Project Resource Management Knowledge Area, identify the types and quantities of resources (such as people, equipment, or materials) needed to perform the activities required by the Project Procurement Management Knowledge Area processes. For people needed by a project, Resource Requirements describe the number of resources for each project activity and the knowledge, skills, and abilities required for each resource. Resource Requirements are typically described at the work package level, which is the work of the project described at the lowest level of the WBS for which cost and duration can be estimated and managed. It is helpful to include specifics and assumptions in support of estimates for each activity. Table 3-4 depicts a basic, abbreviated example of a Resource Requirements form in the context of a potential software as a service procurement.

Table 3-4. Resource Requirements Example

WBS ID	Resource	Quantity	Activity Requirement
4.2	Buyer	Six weeks	Need technology-specific procurement experience
4.3	Competitive solicitation template	N/A	Need request for proposal (RFP) competitive solicitation template and related materials such as seller proposal evaluation matrix
4.4	Contract template	N/A	Need software as a service contract template for inclusion in competitive solicitation
4.5	Meeting space	Six weeks	Must have ten-person capacity and video-conference capabilities
5.3	Subject matter experts	Three at one week each	One representing each of the three lines of business, to describe required functionality
5.6	Business analysts	Two at two weeks each	Develop requirements for RFP based on subject matter expert input
5.9	Contract manager[9]	Three days	Review RFP and provide service level input
6.3	Seller selection committee	Three at two weeks each	Subject matter experts will comprise seller selection committee
7.7	Seller negotiation committee	Four at four weeks each	Subject matter experts and buyer will comprise seller negotiation committee
8.1	Legal counsel	One week	Consult with buyer on contract negotiations and contract drafting

Assumptions

- Project will likely involve procurement of software as a service versus on-premises software
- Outside legal counsel may be required as in-house counsel do not have requisite software as a service contracting experience

---

[9] While contract management activities do not begin until the *Control Procurements* (12.3) process, it is helpful for the contract manager, if named and time permitting, to be engaged in certain *Plan Procurement Management* and *Conduct Procurements* (12.2) processes so as to provide input relevant to ensuring future seller performance (such as drafting service levels) and to obtain familiarity with the project history to inform the *Control Procurements* (12.3) process activities.

Risk Register (11.2.3.1)

The Risk Register, an output (11.2.3.1) resulting from the *Identify Risks* (11.2) process of the Project Risk Management Knowledge Area, is a risk identification, analysis, and response planning repository. More specifically, the Risk Register identifies possible risks, the likelihood and impact of possible risks, the "owners" of those risks areas, measures to prevent a risk from occurring, and actions in response to risks should they occur. Once a buyer identifies and assesses possible risks, the project team can respond to the risk by avoiding it completely, transferring the risk to another party such as the seller, devising a method to mitigate the risk, or accepting the risk. Likely risks in conducting a procurement and selecting a seller include:

- Multiple procurements under the same project that must be conducted simultaneously or in sequence
- Inability to procure products, services, or results because they do not currently exist in the marketplace
- Increased cost due to products, services, or results being in short supply or by the project organization being in competition with other buyers for the same products, services, or results
- Long lead-times and flow of materials associated with providing products, services, or results
- Demand uncertainty
- Need for scalability
- Failure to source qualified sellers
- Sole source risk (meaning that there is only one viable seller in the marketplace)
- Laws, regulations, or ordinances relating to the products, services, or results that complicate the procurement
- Financial, social, and environmental factors associated with international procurements such as import rules, tariffs, customs, duties, taxes, governmental stability, bribery and corruption, confiscation, and regional conflicts
- Lengthy "switch-over" in moving from an incumbent seller to a successor seller
- Business culture fit between the project organization and seller
- Information security and data privacy concerns
- Seller-based business continuity concerns (for example, a seller with its facility in an earthquake-prone area)

For procurement-related risks identified in the Risk Register, the buyer—in close collaboration with the project manager and the project team—would be responsible for addressing the likelihood of occurrence and impact as well as the most expeditious and cost-effective means of mitigating a risk or in responding to a risk that does occur. An important point to reiterate is that risk can be transferred from a project organization to a seller. The primary vehicle to transfer risk is the agreement associated with the procurement. Generally, the transfer of risk to the seller does not come without some amount of additional cost to the project organization: A seller may be willing to accept more risk but will likely want to be compensated for that acceptance. As explored under Organizational Process Assets (12.1.1.6), an example of risk transfer is a firm fixed price contract type, where a seller must perform the procurement agreement for the agreed-upon price. This contract type presents risk to the seller's profit margin should cost overruns occur. Therefore, with a firm fixed price contract type, a seller will likely build a financial "margin of error" or contingency reserve into its price. On the other hand, with a time and material contract type, a seller shoulders less price risk and the seller's price will reflect that. Other risk transfers will likely affect price as well; for example, if a buyer requires a robust indemnification provision, which means more potential risk for the seller, the price will more than likely reflect any legal risk perceived by the seller. Figure 3-1 illustrates an excerpt of a basic Risk Register with example procurement-related risks.

Risk #	Risk Breakdown Structure (T)echnical (M)anagement (C)ommercial (E)xternal	Risk Description	Consequences	Likelihood 1 - Very Unlikely 2 - Unlikely 3 - Likely 4 - Very Likely	Impact 1 - Very Limited 2 - Limited 3 - Moderate 4 - High	Risk Response (M)itigate a(V)oid (A)ccept (T)ransfer	Possible Mitigating Measures
21	C	Unauthorized disclosure of company's confidential information by seller's offshore resources	~ Reputational harm to company resulting from seller's unauthorized disclosure of customer data ~ Financial harm to company resulting from resolving any customer claims (such as credit monitoring services)	3	4	M	~ As part of solicitation, require response to IT Security questionnaire and require sellers to provide SOC 2 Type II reports ~ As part of contracting, include standard information security and data privacy contract terms and conditions; require selected seller to provide annual SOC 2 Type II report and to provide cybersecurity insurance ~ As a part of contracting, include required actions by selected seller and appropriate remedies, such as immediate notice upon suspicion of unauthorized disclosure and provisioning of credit monitoring services to affected customers ~ As a part of implementation, require selected seller to obfuscate production data
22	C	Inability of seller to deliver application using agile methodology	Operational harm to company resulting from seller's inability to deliver story points / incremental value based on two-week sprints	3	3	V	~ As part of solicitation, include mandatory requirement for sellers to comply with agile methodology and respond with capabilities ~ As a part of proposal evaluation criteria, include inability to deliver using agile methodology as a disqualifying criteria ~ As a part of contracting, require selected seller to adhere to agile methodology by utilizing a firm fixed price contract type with sprint-based milestone payments

Figure 3-1. Example Risk Register

Stakeholder Register (13.1.3.1)

The Stakeholder Register, an output (13.1.3.1) resulting from the *Identify Stakeholders* (13.1) process of the Project Stakeholder Management Knowledge Area, describes those persons, groups, and internal or external organizations directly or indirectly involved in the project. Whereas a member of a project team supports the project manager by performing work in furtherance of the project, a stakeholder may or may not influence the project and may be positively or negatively affected by a decision, activity, or outcome of the project. The project manager builds and updates the Stakeholder Register, which typically includes identification information (for example, name, position, and project role) and stakeholder assessment information (for example, expectations, potential influence, and project interests). The Stakeholder Register is an important tool in project planning, defining success criteria, communications, governance, and defining tasks and responsibilities. As a part of developing the Procurement Management Plan (12.1.3.1), a buyer can leverage the Stakeholder Register to select and document potential evaluators for a seller selection committee, negotiators for a seller negotiation committee, and other necessary participants for a competitive procurement.

Prospective Seller Selection Committee Members

A possible role of stakeholders under the Project Procurement Management Knowledge Area is to serve as an evaluator of sellers and seller proposals as a part of the seller selection committee. In brief, the seller selection committee applies Source Selection Criteria (12.1.3.5) using proposal evaluation techniques under Data Analysis (12.2.2.4) to Seller Proposals (12.2.1.4) submitted to the project organization in response to Bid Documents (12.1.3.3) in order to determine Selected Sellers (12.2.3.1). The seller selection committee can be an impactful positive or negative dynamic in a competitive procurement, and, if dysfunctional, can quickly derail the procurement. That dysfunction can be triggered by any number of environmental factors such as too many or too few committee members, overly extroverted or overly introverted committee members, organizational politics, and personal agendas. One important role of the project manager and the buyer is to appropriately influence the size and makeup of the seller selection committee and to closely navigate committee members through the processes of the Project Procurement Management Knowledge Area and competitive procurement activities.

Unless a competitive procurement is anticipated to be extremely complex, ideally, a seller selection committee should have no less than three and no greater than five committee members. A lesser number of committee members may result in an insufficient evaluation and can raise questions of impartiality or undue influence. A greater number of committee members can waste organizational resources (particularly human resources), presents administrative and logistical problems (such as having to coordinate schedules), dilutes the selection process (through over-representation), and creates unnecessary bureaucracy. When considering members for a seller selection committee, a prospective committee member should:

- Have some knowledge (preferably in-depth) of the products, services, or results to be procured
- Have a significant stake (such as a major consumer or primary budget holder) in the products, services, or results to be procured
- Be able to adequately represent a certain organizational component of the project organization and aggregate the "stake" on behalf of his or her department or function (so as to avoid multiple different people representing one department or function)
- Be a decision-maker, empowered to act without having to seek approval related to procurement activities
- Have good verbal, written, organizational, and analytical skills
- Have the time and interest to participate in a competitive procurement process
- Understand the importance of holding competitive procurement materials and seller selection committee materials in strict confidence
- Not have any conflict of interest, actual or apparent, in prospective sellers or the products, services, or results being procured

Guidance for Seller Selection Committee Members

Since some or all of the seller selection committee members may be unfamiliar with a competitive procurement process, it is helpful for a buyer to provide committee members with guidance as to what is expected of them. As an example, the following guidance can be used to advise committee members regarding their role, duties, and cautions.

**SELLER SELECTION COMMITTEE
ROLE, DUTIES, CAUTIONS**

ROLE

Your role as a Seller Selection Committee member is to materially contribute to the competitive procurement process, to perform an unbiased, objective evaluation of seller responses, and, ultimately, to recommend a seller for contract award. Committee members are frequently required to devote considerable time to responding to seller questions, reading seller responses, attending seller conferences, scoring responses, and meeting as a committee to discuss sellers and their responses with other committee members. Participation on the Seller Selection Committee should be construed as a commitment, within reasonable limits, to expend the time necessary to complete the entire competitive procurement process and to perform a thorough and objective evaluation of sellers and their responses.

DUTIES

To materially contribute to the Seller Selection Committee, a committee member must:

- Attend all Seller Selection Committee meetings. A timeline will be established for the entire competitive procurement process. This timeline will include the number and dates of future meetings, if seller conferences will be held and, if so, when. Because of difficulties in coordinating schedules, it is the responsibility of the individual committee members to arrange their work schedules to allow for full and complete participation.
- Participate in identifying prospective sellers.

- Assist in developing responses to seller written questions (by actually writing responses) and reviewing other committee members' responses.
- Attend and participate, if appropriate, in the pre-proposal bidder conference.
- Assist in developing proposal evaluation criteria and weighting.
- Read all responses received and make appropriate notations directly in or on the proposal evaluation matrix.
- Formulate seller-oriented questions regarding parts of responses needing explanation or clarifications, and / or comments regarding those sections of a response that are regarded as having deficiencies or weaknesses that could be cured.
- If conducted, attend all post-proposal bidder conferences, demonstrations, and / or proof-of-concept sessions.
- Conduct due diligence on sellers (by actually conducting research), as requested by the buyer.
- Openly and objectively discuss individual findings / scoring at the appropriate Seller Selection Committee meeting.
- Identify sellers to continue in the competitive procurement process (i.e., the "shortlist") and those sellers to "de-select" from the process.
- Participate in developing negotiation strategies, such as best and final offers, as requested by the buyer.
- Re-direct sellers that do not follow the communication protocol to the buyer.
- Be available for, and participate in, debriefing (if conducted) of unsuccessful sellers.

CAUTIONS
- You must maintain the confidence of Seller Selection Committee's work. Unless otherwise determined by the buyer, no one outside of the Seller Selection Committee needs to know the composition of the committee or other information pertaining to the committee members.
- At any seller conferences, Seller Selection Committee members will be introduced to sellers, but no contact information should be disclosed. Any attempts at communication or contact with any committee members by a seller or other interested party regarding the competitive procurement should be reported promptly to the buyer.
- You must immediately recuse yourself in the case of an actual or apparent conflict of interest.

12.1.1.5 Enterprise Environmental Factors

Enterprise Environmental Factors are conditions beyond the full control of the project team that can enhance, constrain, or positively or negatively influence the *Plan Procurement Management* process activities. Where the impact of Enterprise Environmental Factors is perceived to be or actually is negative, the *Plan Procurement Management* process activities may require modification to mitigate or lessen the impact. While the Project Procurement Management Knowledge Area contains a very structured procurement process, the *PMBOK Guide* recognizes that "real world" factors affect how a competitive procurement is conducted. Identification and awareness of Enterprise Environmental Factors allow a procurement to be shaped to the marketplace and industry conditions for a particular product, service, or result at a given point in time. An assessment of these factors may also result in updates to the Risk Register (see Section 12.1.3.9) and risk-related contract decisions included as a part of the Project Documents (12.2.1.2). Enterprise Environmental Factors that merit consideration include:

- Current economic conditions
- Marketplace conditions that affect the price, availability, or lead-times for the required products, services, or results
- Legal or regulatory requirements impacting the procurement
- Project organization attributes such as size, financial strength, and potential revenue to sellers resulting from the procurement, any of which can impact negotiation leverage for both business and contractual terms and conditions
- Sellers previously used by the project organization or that have indicated an interest in participating in future procurements conducted by the project organization
- Seller attributes such as past performance, position in the marketplace, market innovation, and market share
- Geographic factors including local, national, or international constraints and requirements
- Advice from subject matter experts and legal counsel
- Industry-specific procurement "traditions" such as the method of procurement (for example, direct from a manufacturer versus indirect via a distributor) and typical terms and conditions
- Systems used by the project organization such as finance and accounting, source-to-settle, seller management, contract management and contract change control, and project management and project change control
- Strengths and weaknesses of the procurement function within the project organization

12.1.1.6 Organizational Process Assets

Project organizations generally have some number of policies, procedures, processes, practices, standards, guidelines, templates, job aids, knowledge bases, and other resources that are used to perform and optimize the work of those organizations. As project organizations perform work, they create data, knowledge, historical information, artifacts, and lessons learned. The *PMBOK Guide* broadly categorizes all of the foregoing as "Organizational Process Assets" and groups them into: (1) policies, processes, and procedures; and, (2) organizational knowledge bases (also referred to in the *PMBOK Guide* as "organizational knowledge repositories").

Policies, processes, and procedures are used for conducting project work. The *PMBOK Guide* segments policies, processes, and procedures that are part of the Organizational Process Assets into the Process Groups that they are most closely associated with: (1) Initiating; (2) Planning; (3) Executing; (4) Monitoring and Controlling; and, (5) Closing. In the context of the *Plan Procurement Management* process, which is contained within the Planning Process Group, policies, processes, and procedures could include:

- Procurement policy and related procedures and guidelines
- Competitive solicitation templates
- Seller qualification criteria

- Seller proposal evaluation matrix templates
- Contract templates and types
- Prequalified seller lists (also referred to as "qualified," "preapproved," or "approved" sellers)
- Procurement record retention policy

The organizational knowledge base serves as a repository or system for the retention and retrieval of information. Unlike policies, processes, and procedures, an organizational knowledge base that is a part of the Organizational Process Assets is not segmented by Process Group. In the context of the *Plan Procurement Management* process, such repositories and systems could include:

- Seller tracking list (for tracking of competitive solicitations)
- Finance and accounting (to include budgets, project costs including labor, and variances)
- Source-to-settle
- Seller management
- Contract management and contract change control
- Project management and project change control
- Records management
- Project file (including project artifacts and lessons learned)
- Contract file
- Configuration management (containing, for example, a baseline of assets such as technology components, standards, policies, and procedures)
- Issue and defect management
- Enterprise data warehouse
- Metrics

Procurement Maturity

To effectively utilize the Project Procurement Management Knowledge Area as a structured procurement methodology, a project organization must have an appropriate degree of sophistication as well as the associated Organizational Process Assets. That sophistication and ability to perform is dependent upon the maturity level of the procurement function contained within the project organization. The *Procurement Maturity Model*[10] is an analytical tool which gauges the performance and maturity level of a procurement function and helps to define where there are gaps in Organizational Process Assets. Figure 3-2 describes the levels of procurement maturity described in the *Procurement Maturity Model* and basic attributes of each level.

---

[10] The *Procurement Maturity Model* was developed by the National Rural Electric Cooperative Association and is available for download at www.stephenguth.com.

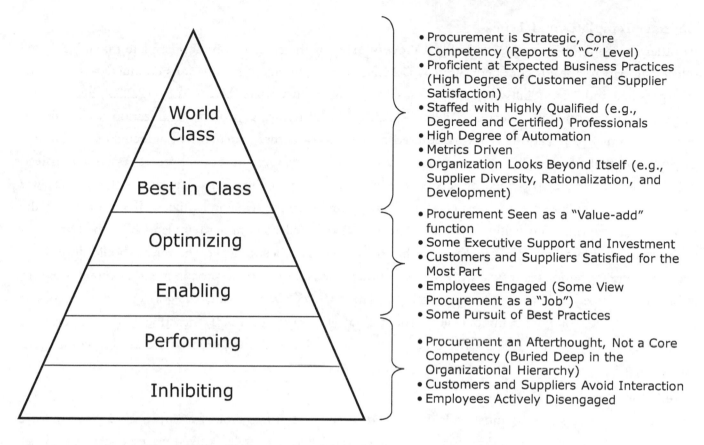

Figure 3-2. *Procurement Maturity Model* – **Levels of Maturity**

Prequalified Seller List

An important component of Organizational Process Assets is a prequalified seller list. As a result of prior procurements, buyers commonly maintain a list of sellers that have the technical, functional, and financial capabilities to provide certain products, services, or results (the "prequalified seller list"). It should be recognized that "prequalified" does not mean "qualified" or "approved" at this point in the Project Procurement Management Knowledge Area, and that a buyer may later conclude from a seller's subsequent proposal that the seller is not qualified or approved to provide the required products, services, or results. The prequalified seller list may include incumbent sellers (those satisfactorily performing sellers already doing business with a project organization) and sellers that had a prior business relationship with a project organization (that performed satisfactorily). Buyers frequently receive unsolicited inquiries from various sellers interested in doing business with a project organization and, consequently, buyers commonly maintain a list or database of those inquiries for future procurements. A project organization may also permit prospective sellers to electronically register with the project organization to express interest in being considered for future procurements. While such sellers have no prior business relationship with the project organization and buyers typically do not pre-approve or qualify them to any extensive degree, buyers do routinely include such sellers as a part of a prequalified seller list for purposes of inviting them to respond to a competitive solicitation.

Contract Templates and Types

Another key component of Organizational Process Assets is the type of contract template that a buyer will select as a part of the Procurement Strategy (12.1.3.2) for procurement negotiations conducted as a part of Interpersonal and Team Skills (12.2.2.5) and use to create any necessary Agreements (12.2.3.2) between the project organization and Selected Sellers (12.2.3.1). Commonly, a project organization will maintain contract templates of various types to be used as a basis for future procurement agreements. A project organization that does not have contract templates as a part of its Organizational Process Assets and instead uses contract templates provided by sellers is disadvantaged for two reasons. The first is that a seller will use a contract template that is almost certainly more favorable to the seller and which shifts more risk to the project organization. The second reason is that the use of a seller's contract template shifts the burden of review (commonly called "redlining") to the buyer. Rather, as a best practice, the buyer should develop or procure contract templates to use with sellers in order to ensure favorable procurement agreements and to shift the resource burden of redlining to sellers. The *PMBOK Guide* broadly categorizes contract types as either fixed price or cost reimbursable. The following paragraphs briefly describe both categories of contract types and then examines specific contract types within each category that are used in commercial contracting.

Fixed Price Contracts Overview

Fixed price contracts are the most widely used and preferred contract types for buyers because they place the greatest amount of price and performance risk on the seller. Generally, a fixed priced contract provides for a price that is not subject to any adjustment on the basis of a seller's cost experience in performing the contract. Thus, under fixed price contracts, a seller must perform the contract for the stated price and, if there are any unanticipated complications, the seller is required to bear any financial impact of additionally incurred expenses. In their strictest form, fixed price contracts place maximum risk on a seller and full responsibility for all costs as well as the resulting profit or loss. However, even though the seller may be responsible for absorbing increases in costs, the seller is not responsible for any unplanned costs resulting from or due to the project organization; for example, where a project delay results from the project organization's inability to provide its own committed resources to a project. Therefore, a project organization must diligently manage its own performance under the contract in a way that avoids seller claims for significant price adjustments (for example, resulting from "scope creep" or delays caused by the project organization). In some cases, fixed price payments are made by a buyer on a scheduled or periodic basis rather than at the end of the contract. In those cases, there is typically a milestone-based or periodic payment schedule described in the associated procurement agreement. There are certain variations of fixed price contracts that shift a reasonable amount of acceptable risk to a buyer and that provide for price adjustments based on clearly defined criteria. The following sections describe the most common fixed price contract types.

Firm Fixed Price Contract

The firm fixed price (FFP) contract type, also referred to as a "lump sum" contract, is an arrangement where a seller agrees to provide the products, services, or results at a price that is fixed and not subject to adjustment. Under FFP contracts, assuming that a seller performs the contract in a satisfactory manner, the seller receives the agreed upon price regardless of what the seller's costs ultimately are. Thus, the seller is motivated to provide the required products, services, or results in the most cost-effective manner since the seller is the sole and direct beneficiary of controlling the costs (which, if controlled, result in a greater profit). An FFP contract is the most common yet most stringent type of contract in the category of fixed price contracts and is best suited for use when the products, services, or results requirements are well defined or clearly specified by the project organization. Additionally, since this contract type places the greatest amount of risk and control with the seller, the seller should be experienced in providing the required products, services, or results. This contract type should not be used in volatile market conditions or where the financial risks are significant; there are other contract types, such as the fixed price with economic price adjustment reviewed later in this chapter, that better address such conditions and risks.

Buyers prefer to use the FFP contract type because—with few exceptions—the agreed-upon price is not subject to change unless the scope of work changes. Any cost increases are generally the responsibility of the seller (not the project organization), who is obligated to perform the contract at the agreed-upon price. Since a seller bears the greatest risk under this contract type, sellers can be tempted to inflate their price for contingencies that may occur when performing the contract. An additional consideration for buyers is that the project organization will not receive complete price protection when the project organization is the cause of any cost increases. For example, incomplete requirements, changes in scope, and project organization delays will likely result in increased costs being passed to the organization. However, neither the potential of inflated pricing or lack of complete price protection is significant in diluting the business value that an FFP contract type can bring to a project organization.

Fixed Price Incentive Firm

The fixed price incentive (firm target) (FPIF) contract type is a fixed price contract that provides for adjusting profit and establishing the final contract price by a formula based on the relationship of final negotiated total cost to total target cost. An FPIF contract type specifies a target cost, a target profit, a ceiling price (that does *not* represent a ceiling or floor profit), and a profit adjustment formula. These elements are all negotiated at the outset of the contract. The ceiling price is the maximum to be paid to the seller, except for any adjustments permitted under other provisions contained in the contract.

When the seller completes performance, the parties negotiate the final cost, and the final price is established by applying the profit adjustment formula. When the final cost is less than the target cost, application of the profit adjustment formula results in a final profit greater than the target profit; conversely, when the final cost is more than the target cost, application of the profit adjustment formula results in a final profit less than the target profit or even a net loss. Because the profit varies inversely with the cost, this contract type provides a positive, calculable profit incentive for the seller to control costs. In short, the project organization is reasonably protected by the ceiling price, which covers the most probable risks inherent under the contract and the seller can realize a higher profit by satisfactorily delivering or performing below the ceiling price.

The profit adjustment formula is typically represented as a ratio, such as 70 / 30, with the antecedent representing the buyer (70 in this example) and the consequent representing the seller (30 in this example). Using that ratio as an example, for cost underruns, the buyer will "save" 70-cents and the seller will "gain" 30-cents of each dollar of cost underrun and, for cost overruns, the buyer will "spend" an extra 70-cents and the seller will "lose" 30-cents of each dollar of cost overrun. The profit adjustment formula is sometimes bifurcated, with an "under target" ratio and an "over target" ratio (for example, respectively, 40 / 60 and 70 / 30), with the intent being to further motivate a seller to achieve cost underruns. If bifurcated, the under target ratio is applied when the final cost is below the target cost and the over target ratio is applied when the final cost is above the target cost but below the price ceiling. Regardless of using a single or bifurcated profit adjustment formula, ultimately, if the final negotiated cost exceeds the ceiling price, the seller absorbs the difference as a loss.

This contract type serves to mitigate the risk associated with uncertainty of labor or material requirements. However, an FPIF contract type is only appropriate if the parties can negotiate at the outset a firm target cost, target profit, and profit adjustment formula that will provide a fair and reasonable incentive and a ceiling price that provides for the seller to assume an appropriate share of the risk. Since the target cost and target profit are negotiated at the onset of delivery or performance by the seller, there must be adequate cost or pricing information available at the time of initial contract negotiation for establishing reasonable yet firm targets. When the seller assumes a considerable or major share of the cost responsibility under the adjustment formula, the seller will likely demand that the target profit reflect that responsibility. The use of an FPIF contract type is also dependent upon adequate data available at the completion of the contract: Because of the need to negotiate cost at a point that follows delivery or performance by the seller, the seller's accounting system must be adequate for providing data to support negotiation of the final cost.

As an example, assume a one-year contract with a target cost of $1,000,000, target profit of $100,000, ceiling price of $1,500,000, and a profit adjustment formula of 40 / 60 as an under target ratio and 70 / 30 as an over target ratio. If the seller has a final cost of $900,000, there is a cost underrun because the final cost is $100,000 less than the target cost of $1,000,000. In this case, the seller is due the final cost of $900,000, the seller's target profit of $100,000, and an incentive of $60,000 (60% of the $100,000 cost underrun) for a final price of $1,060,000. The seller benefits because it received an additional $60,000 profit and the project organization benefits because it achieved a "savings" of $440,000 (the ceiling price of $1,500,000 less the final price of $1,060,000).

If the seller has a final cost of $1,100,000, there is a cost overrun because the final cost is $100,000 more than the target cost of $1,000,000. In this case, the seller is due the final cost of $1,100,000, the seller's target profit of $100,000, and a reduction of $30,000 (30% of the $100,000 cost overrun) for a final price of $1,170,000. The seller benefits because its costs are covered but its profit is diminished and the project organization benefits because it achieved a savings of $330,000 (the ceiling price of $1,500,000 less the final price of $1,170,000).

If the seller has a final cost of $2,000,000, which is greater than the ceiling price of $1,500,000, the seller absorbs the difference and the project organization is only liable for paying the ceiling price.

Fixed Price Award Fee

The fixed price award fee (FPAF) contract type is a fixed price contract that establishes a ceiling price (the fixed price, which includes normal profit—but that does *not* represent a ceiling or floor profit) that will be paid to the seller for its satisfactory delivery or performance and that includes an award fee plan under which a seller can earn an award fee based on its delivery or performance. The ceiling price is the maximum to be paid to the seller, except for any adjustments permitted under other contract provisions. All costs incurred by the seller above the ceiling price are the responsibility of the seller and costs that are below the ceiling price represent profit (as determined by the award fee rating and pool amount) to the seller.

This contract type is used when a project organization wants the price protection of a fixed price contract and wants to motivate the seller to deliver or perform but where another type of incentive (other than an award fee) cannot be used because the seller's delivery or performance cannot be measured objectively. Even though a quantitative, objective measurement is impractical, the FPAF contract type requires that the seller's delivery or performance be periodically evaluated by the project against a qualitative, adjectival measurement. This measurement—part of the award fee plan included in the contract—then determines if and how much of the award fee pool is earned by the seller. The intervals at which the periodic evaluations are conducted are stated in the contract as well as how the award fee amount is allocated across each evaluation period. The award fee plans, due to their qualitative and adjectival structure, can be complex. Table 3-5 provides an example of a very basic award fee plan for an FPAF contract type.

Table 3-5. Award Fee Plan Example

Award Fee Adjectival Rating	Rating Description	Award Fee Pool Available to Be Earned
Excellent	Seller exceeded all or almost all of the cost, schedule, and technical performance requirements	76% - 100%
Very Good	Seller exceeded many of the cost, schedule, and technical performance requirements	51% - 75%
Good	Seller exceeded some of the cost, schedule, and technical performance requirements	1% - 50%

Award Fee Adjectival Rating	Rating Description	Award Fee Pool Available to Be Earned
Satisfactory	Seller has satisfactorily met overall cost, schedule, and technical performance requirements	Seller receives the fixed price for satisfactory performance but does not earn an award fee

As an example, assume a one-year contract term, a fixed price of $120,000 paid proportionally on a monthly basis in arrears, performance rating occurring at the end of each contract month, an award fee pool amount of $1,200 allocated monthly across the contract term ($100 per month), and an award fee plan using Table 3-5. Assume that, at the end of month 1, the seller's cost was $8,000 and the project organization rated the seller's performance as "Excellent," electing to pay out the award fee pool at 100% for that rating. The seller would receive $10,000 representing the monthly portion of the fixed price, $100 representing the award fee (which is 100% of the $100 monthly award fee pool amount), and, consequently, a profit of $2,100. Assume that, at the end of month 2, the seller's cost was $11,000 and the project organization rated the seller's performance as "Satisfactory." The seller would receive $10,000 representing a portion of the fixed price, no award fee, and, consequently, a loss of $1,000.

Fixed Price with Economic Price Adjustment Contract

The fixed price with economic price adjustment (FP-EPA) contract type is a fixed price contract that establishes a ceiling on upward price adjustment but includes a formula for adjusting the price up or down below the ceiling based on actual labor or material costs, labor or material indices, or established prices. This contract type is used when economic uncertainties exist that threaten long-term fixed price arrangements. The economic price adjustment provisions contained within an FP-EPA contract provide for both price increases and decreases to protect the project organization and the seller from the effects of economic changes. This contract type is normally not used for short-term contracts and is only used when there is serious doubt between the contracting parties about the stability of market or labor conditions that will exist during the extended period of contract performance. In fact, if the markets for labor or material are volatile, many sellers may be unwilling to enter into a fixed price contract type other than an FP-EPA contract. Thus, an FP-EPA contract facilitates a long-term business relationship where the project organization is advantaged by a fixed price arrangement while at the same time protecting the seller against external conditions that are beyond its control. While it is a fixed price contract type, the project organization and seller agree on pre-defined adjustments to the contract price due to changed conditions. Typically, the price adjustment is tied to recognized, reliable, and acceptable market indices that can be used to appropriately adjust the contract price. However, if a cost variance is not tied to an economic price adjustment, the seller will absorb that cost as a change in its profit (or loss).

Cost Reimbursable Contracts Overview

The cost reimbursable category of contract types involves payments by a project organization to the seller for all legitimate actual costs incurred (cost reimbursement) plus a fee representing the seller's profit for completed work. Cost reimbursable contracts are suitable for use by project organizations when it is difficult to determine the cost of the products, services, or results with sufficient accuracy or there are other project uncertainties that preclude the use of a fixed price contract type. A cost reimbursable contract also gives the project organization the needed flexibility to redirect a seller whenever the scope of the products, services, or results cannot be clearly defined at the project start and as the scope is then subsequently altered during the progression of the project. Despite the difficulty in determining total contract cost or scope, a buyer should require that the seller provide some sort of estimated total cost for budgeting purposes. The most significant risk to a project organization when using a cost reimbursable contract type is that the seller is reimbursed for all allowable costs and therefore the seller has no incentive to control its costs. To drive a cost controlling behavior with a seller, similar to fixed price contracts, cost reimbursable contracts may include seller incentives. The following sections describe the most common cost reimbursable contract types.

Cost Plus Fixed Fee Contract

A cost plus fixed fee (CPFF) contract type provides for payments to a seller based on allowable costs in performing the contract and specifies a negotiated fee that is fixed at the inception of the contract. Thus, the seller is reimbursed for its costs and receives a fixed fee payment (which is typically calculated as a percentage of the initially estimated costs). The fixed fee component does not vary with the actual cost, but may be adjusted as a result of changes in the products, services, or results to be provided under the contract. There is no ceiling price under a CPFF contract type; therefore, the seller does not absorb any cost variance (the project organization absorbs all allowable cost variances) and is due the fixed fee regardless of the amount of allowable cost. This contract type permits contracting for products, services, or results that might otherwise present too great of a financial risk to a seller due to cost variability, but it provides no financial protection to the project organization as the seller has no incentive to control costs.

Cost Plus Incentive Fee Contract

A cost plus incentive fee (CPIF) contract type provides for the initially negotiated fee to be later adjusted by a formula based on the relationship of allowable cost to target cost. This contract type specifies a target cost, a target fee (which is *not* a price ceiling), a minimum fee, a maximum fee, and a fee adjustment formula. Similar to an FPIF contract type, the fee adjustment formula reflects the degree of uncertainty each party bears under the contract. However, unlike the FPIF contract type, the CPIF contract type has no ceiling price: All allowable costs are reimbursed by the project organization.

     After contract performance, the fee payable to the seller is determined in accordance with the fee adjustment formula. The difference between the minimum fee and maximum fee, in combination with the fee adjustment formula, defines the contract range of incentive effectiveness (RIE) within which the fee adjustment formula applies. When the allowable cost is below the RIE (a cost underrun), the seller is paid the allowable cost plus the maximum fee. Conversely, when the allowable cost is above the RIE (a cost overrun), the seller is paid the allowable cost plus the minimum fee. Within the RIE, the fee to the seller increases when allowable cost is less than the target cost and the fee to the seller decreases when the allowable cost is more than the target cost. This increase or decrease in fee is intended to provide an incentive for the seller to manage the contract and costs effectively. This contract type is best suited for use by a project organization when the products, services, or results requirements are not well defined or clearly specified by the project organization and where the seller does not have the experience to bridge the gaps created by the project organization's lack of definition or specificity.

As with the FPIF contract type's *profit* adjustment formula, the CPIF contract type's *fee* adjustment formula is typically represented as a ratio, such as 70 / 30, with the antecedent representing the buyer (70 in this example) and the consequent representing the seller (30 in this example). The fee adjustment ratio is sometimes bifurcated, with an "under target" ratio and an "over target" ratio (for example, respectively, 40 / 60 and 70 / 30), with the intent being to further motivate a seller to achieve cost underruns. If bifurcated, the under target ratio is applied when the allowable cost is below the target cost and the over target ratio is applied when the allowable cost is above the target cost. This contract type is best suited for use by a project organization when the products, services, or results requirements are not well defined or clearly specified by the project organization and where the seller does not have the experience to bridge the gaps created by the project organization's lack of definition or specificity.

As an example, assume a one-year contract with a target cost of $1,000,000, target fee of $100,000, a minimum fee of $50,000, a maximum fee of $150,000, and a fee adjustment formula of 40 / 60 as an under target ratio and 70 / 30 as an over target ratio. The upper end of the RIE is calculated by using the following formula: [((target fee - minimum fee) / seller over target ratio) + target cost]. Using the example data, the upper end of the RIE is $1,166,667 [((target fee of $100,000 - minimum fee of $50,000) / seller over target ratio of 30%) + target cost of $1,000,000]. The lower end of the RIE is calculated using the following formula: [target cost – ((maximum fee – target fee) / seller under target ratio)]. Using the example data, the lower end of the RIE is $916,667 [target cost of $1,000,000 – ((maximum fee of $150,000 – target fee of $100,000) / seller under target ratio of 60%)]. Therefore, the seller has the greatest incentive to achieve an allowable cost within the range of $916,667 to $1,166,667. If the seller achieves an allowable cost of $916,667 or lower, it will receive the maximum fee of $150,000 and will not receive any additional incentive for a lower cost; therefore, theoretically, the seller has no reason to strive for a lower allowable cost. If the seller realizes an allowable cost of $1,166,667 or higher, it will receive the minimum fee of $50,000 and will not be subject to any further diminishment of the incentive resulting from a higher cost; therefore, theoretically, the seller has no reason to strive to control costs any further.

If the seller has an allowable cost of $950,000, there is a cost underrun because the allowable cost is $50,000 less than the target cost of $1,000,000. In this case, the seller is due the allowable cost of $950,000, the seller's target fee of $100,000, and an incentive of $30,000 (60% of the $50,000 cost underrun) for a final price of $1,080,000. The seller benefits because it received an additional $30,000 in fees and the project organization benefits because it achieved a "savings" of $70,000 (the target cost of $1,000,000 and the maximum fee of $150,000 less the final price of $1,080,000).

If the seller has an allowable cost of $700,000, there is a cost underrun because the allowable cost is $300,000 less than the target cost of $1,000,000. Applying the fee adjustment formula of 40 / 60 would result in a fee of $280,000 (60% of the $300,000 cost underrun and the target fee of $100,000); however, the seller is only due the maximum fee of $150,000. The seller is due the allowable cost of $700,000 and the maximum fee of $150,000 for a final price of $850,000. The seller benefits because it received an additional $50,000 in fees as a result of achieving its maximum fee and the project organization benefits because it achieved a "savings" of $300,000 (the target cost of $1,000,000 and the maximum fee of $150,000 less the final price of $850,000).

The following two scenarios examine the effect of a cost underrun using the example figures. As described in the scenarios, the project organization paid less than the combined target cost and maximum fee and the seller benefited by receiving greater than the target fee.

If the seller has an allowable cost of $700,000, there is a cost underrun because the allowable cost is $300,000 less than the target cost of $1,000,000. Applying the fee adjustment formula of 40 / 60 would result in a calculated fee of $280,000 (the target fee of $100,000 plus 60% of the $300,000 cost underrun) which is greater than the maximum fee of $150,000. The seller is due the allowable cost of $700,000 and the maximum fee of $150,000 for a final price of $850,000. The project organization paid $300,000 less than the combined target cost of $1,000,000 and the maximum fee of $150,000 (total of $1,150,000).

If the seller has an allowable cost of $950,000, there is a cost underrun because the allowable cost is $50,000 less than the target cost of $1,000,000. Applying the fee adjustment formula of 40 / 60 would result in a calculated fee of $130,000 (the target fee of $100,000 plus 60% of the $50,000 cost underrun) which is less than the maximum fee of $150,000 but greater than the minimum fee of $50,000. The seller is due the allowable cost of $950,000 and the calculated fee of $130,000 for a final price of $1,080,000. The project organization paid $70,000 less than the combined target cost of $1,000,000 and the maximum fee of $150,000 (total of $1,150,000).

The following two scenarios examine the effect of a cost overrun using the example figures. As described in the scenarios, while the project organization paid more than the combined target cost and maximum fee, the project organization's costs were controlled and contributed to by the seller through a reduction in the seller's fee. The amount paid by the project organization could have been greater had it not been for the fee adjustment formula associated with this contract type.

If the seller has an allowable cost of $1,100,000, there is a cost overrun because the allowable cost is $100,000 more than the target cost of $1,000,000. Applying the fee adjustment formula of 70 / 30 would result in a calculated fee of $70,000 (the target fee of $100,000 less 30% of the $100,000 cost overrun) which is greater than the minimum fee of $50,000. The seller is due the allowable cost of $1,100,000 and the calculated fee of $70,000 for a final price of $1,170,000. The project organization paid $20,000 more than the combined target cost of $1,000,000 and the maximum fee of $150,000 (total of $1,150,000).

If the seller has an allowable cost of $1,200,000, there is a cost overrun because the allowable cost is $200,000 more than the target cost of $1,000,000. Applying the fee adjustment formula of 70 / 30 would result in a calculated fee of $40,000 (the target fee of $100,000 less 30% of the $200,000 cost overrun) which is less than the minimum fee of $50,000. The seller is due the allowable cost of $1,200,000 and the minimum fee of $50,000 for a final price of $1,250,000. The project organization paid $100,000 more than the combined target cost of $1,000,000 and the maximum fee of $150,000 (total of $1,150,000).

Cost Plus Award Fee Contract

A cost plus award fee (CPAF) contract type provides for a fee consisting of a base amount fixed at the inception of the contract and an award amount negotiated by the parties which is intended to provide an incentive for the seller to perform at a high-level in terms of cost, schedule, and performance. This contract type is very similar to an FPAF contract type, using a qualitative, adjectival measurement as a part of an award fee plan included in the contract to determine if and how much of the award fee pool is earned by the seller. A CPAF contract type typically includes a target cost, which, if exceeded, results in no award fee. However, the seller is due all allowable costs, even if the target cost is exceeded and no award fee is paid.

Cost Sharing Contract

A cost sharing (CS) contract type is one in which a seller does not receive a fee and is reimbursed only for an agreed-upon portion of its allowable costs. It is typically used when a seller agrees to absorb a portion of the costs in the expectation of substantial compensating benefits. An example would be where a seller is developing new products, services, or results for the project organization that the project organization agrees the seller can take to market and sell to other project organizations. Since the seller intends on receiving the benefit from future sales, it is reasonable for the project organization to not solely fund the seller's development efforts.

Cost Plus Percentage of Cost Contract

The cost plus percentage of cost (CPPC) contract type allows a seller to charge a predetermined percentage representing profit calculated on total allowable costs. Like cost reimbursable contracts in general, there is no incentive (unless specified) for a seller to control costs. Further, with CPPC contracts, a seller has a built-in incentive to *increase* costs since its profits are based on a percentage of costs. For this reason, this contract type is prohibited for use within the federal government and most state and local governments. There is no legitimate business purpose from a buyer's perspective for the use of a CPPC contract.

Time and Material Contracts Overview

The *PMBOK Guide* considers time and material (T&M) contracts to be a hybrid of both fixed price and cost reimbursable contract types. T&M contract types are used for services, such as staff augmentation, when it is not possible to accurately estimate the extent or duration of the services to be performed. In its base form, where a seller charges a unit rate such as an hourly rate, a T&M contract type includes the seller's cost and profit as a part of the unit rate and allows for cost reimbursement of any materials provided (which are typically minor and incidental to the services performed) or any allowable travel expenses incurred.

Buyers sometimes attempt to control T&M costs by developing or using "rate cards" which are used to specify the maximum rates that a project organization is willing to pay for a certain type of resource. Rate cards are commonly used in the procurement of technology services, distinguishing between job function and skill sets. Buyers also sometimes seek to control the open-ended cost nature of the T&M contract type by including a "not-to-exceed" (NTE) price, meaning that the total of the unit rate, material costs, and allowable travel expenses charged by the seller are subject to a ceiling. If the ceiling price is reached, the seller absorbs any additional costs beyond that ceiling price. Essentially, a T&M-NTE contract type is a cost reimbursable contract that converts to a fixed price contract when the ceiling price is reached. The concept of this contract type seems attractive to both parties: The buyer is protected by the ceiling price and the seller is not subject to a fixed fee until the ceiling price is exceeded. However, unlike a fixed price contract type where a seller is rewarded if it closely manages the margin between its costs and the fixed price so as to maximize its profit, a T&M-NTE contract type provides no such reward if the seller manages its costs; rather, the seller is penalized if it did not accurately scope the effort and, consequently, agreed to an insufficient NTE amount. In other terms, there is no seller incentive and nearly the same seller risk as a fixed price contract type. Often, there is confusion between buyers and sellers as to the exact meaning of a T&M-NTE contract type. Buyers generally understand the correct definition and meaning of T&M-NTE (as described above) while many sellers have a different and incorrect interpretation. The incorrect interpretation held by many sellers is that a seller is *not* required to perform the contract at or below the NTE price, but that the NTE amount instead provides an implied price target that the buyer and seller agree to *attempt* to achieve. If the seller exceeds the NTE amount, the seller incorrectly believes that it can still continue to charge the unit rate, the cost of materials, and allowable travel expenses. Therefore, if a T&M-NTE contract type is used, the buyer should ensure that the seller clearly understands the definition of T&M-NTE and that the contract clearly describes the structure of the T&M-NTE arrangement.

As with other cost reimbursable contract types, the T&M contract type is not optimal for a buyer and can be avoided through the development of detailed requirements that can then be delivered or performed by a seller under a fixed price contract type or a cost reimbursable contract type that has better cost protection for a project organization. In some cases, the project organization lacks confidence in its requirements and is focused on the number of resources provided by a seller (such as the number of developers on a software project) instead of focusing on results. In these cases, the project organization will specify the quantity of resources (either in number of staff or hours) it requires from the seller. This is a mistaken perspective. Instead, the buyer should specify the *results*, not resources, that the project organization requires and then negotiate the price that the project organization is willing to pay—it should be irrelevant to the project organization whether the seller can achieve the desired results with one staff member or one hundred staff members as long as the results are achieved. While there are legitimate purposes for the use of a T&M contract type, the selection of this contract type should be examined as a possible symptom of ill-defined project requirements.

12.1.2 Plan Procurement Management: Tools & Techniques

12.1.2.1 Expert Judgment

Expert Judgment, a tool & technique (4.1.2.1) used in the *Develop Project Charter* (4.1) process of the Project Integration Management Knowledge Area, is judgment based on expertise—such as an industry, a discipline, a knowledge area, or an application—that is provided by an individual or group with specialized education, training, knowledge, skill, ability, or experience. Expert Judgment in the *Plan Procurement Management* process is heavily focused on stakeholders in terms of their subject matter expertise needed to develop the Requirements Documentation component of the Project Documents (12.1.1.4) and the Procurement Statement of Work (12.1.3.4). As would be expected, a significant amount of Expert Judgment is required from the buyer assigned to the project team to develop the Procurement Management Plan (12.1.3.1), the Bid Documents (12.1.3.3), and the Source Selection Criteria (12.1.3.5). The buyer must also use Expert Judgment in considering the risk-related contract decisions associated with the Risk Register component of the Project Documents (12.1.1.4) and when selecting or drafting the contract template and appropriate contract type (see Section 12.1.1.6) as part of the Procurement Strategy (12.1.3.2). Where the buyer does not have the requisite expertise, Expert Judgment from legal professionals may be required for identifying and resolving contractual matters and legal issues including regulatory and compliance topics.

For complex or high-value procurements where project team members have limited or no Expert Judgment, a buyer may recommend that the project team engage an industry expert who has a unique understanding of the marketplace for the required products, services, or results (and the sellers within that marketplace) to provide the needed Expert Judgment. An industry expert can help guide—likely for a fee—a project team and the seller selection committee through a procurement and competitive solicitation. As an example, there are boutique consulting firms which can guide a project team through the very technical and detailed aspects of procuring an enterprise resource planning system, acquiring healthcare benefits for employees, or leasing commercial office space. This type of Expert Judgment from an industry expert inherently includes, as a result of his or her expertise, access to market research as a part of Data Gathering (12.1.2.2).

12.1.2.2 Data Gathering

Data Gathering—most frequently in the form of market research—is conducted by a buyer (and shared with others, such as the seller selection committee) to gain a better understanding of the marketplace for the required products, services, or results and to obtain knowledge of marketplace sellers and their capabilities. The results of Data Gathering can have far-reaching and beneficial effects for a procurement and how the procurement is conducted. As is the case with many other business activities, "knowledge is power" and that truism is particularly relevant to procurement and negotiation. A seller sells its products, services, or results more often than a buyer buys them. A seller knows its products, services, or results intimately, has likely encountered every possible buyer objection or negotiation tactic, and has honed its sales process—resulting in an imbalance of knowledge / power and unequal bargaining positions between buyer and seller.

Data Gathering is a critical, albeit not complete or total, equalizing strategy that a buyer can use to improve the project organization's bargaining power. Using Data Gathering, a better understanding by a project organization of a particular marketplace and its sellers can result in:

- More robust requirements and specifications – Requirements Documentation component of the Project Documents (12.1.1.4)
- Clearer scope of work – Procurement Statement of Work (12.1.3.4)
- Better definition of possible risks – Risk Register component of the Project Documents (12.1.1.4)
- Comprehensive contract template – Organizational Process Assets (12.1.1.6)
- More complete understanding of costs – Independent Cost Estimates (12.1.3.7)
- Clearer sense of influencing factors – Enterprise Environmental Factors (12.1.1.5)
- Specific and tailored evaluation criteria – Source Selection Criteria (12.1.3.5)
- Clearer and more targeted competitive solicitation – Bid Documents (12.1.3.3)

Data Gathering can be conducted through a variety of different methods and manners. Internet research is the most obvious, and, in many cases, at no cost. Fee-based services or subscriptions from market research firms—such as Gartner, Inc. or Forrester Research in the technology marketplace—can provide extremely valuable insight. Industry conferences, user and special interest groups, trade associations, and trade journals are other sources of information. Another very effective and common method of Data Gathering is to use a "request for information" in advance of a competitive solicitation (see Section 12.1.3.3). Alternatively, rather than a request for information, a buyer may arrange meetings with prospective sellers to gain knowledge prior to developing a competitive solicitation (see Section 12.1.2.5).

12.1.2.3 Data Analysis

Data Analysis in the context of the Project Procurement Management Knowledge Area commonly involves a make-or-buy analysis, which is a method of determining whether project needs can be created by the project team or must be obtained outside of the project team. The *PMBOK Guide* views "outside of the project team" to include other functions within the same project organization as well as sellers external to the organization. The *PMBOK Guide* make-or-buy analysis is conducted solely within the context of the project team as to whether it makes sense for the project team to make the products, services, or results and, if not, to acquire them from another function within the same project organization or procure them from an external seller. The context used to frame the make-or-buy analysis herein is whether the project organization as a whole should make the project need or buy it from an external seller. When the make-or-buy analysis has been conducted, the results are documented as a part of the Make-or-Buy Decisions (12.1.3.6).

While simple in concept, a make-or-buy analysis assesses a variety of factors to determine whether it is more effective and efficient to make or buy. The manner in which a make-or-buy analysis is performed may vary based on the project organization and that organization's industry. However, one aspect is nearly universal—to perform the analysis, it is necessary to quantify all of the relevant factors into costs or values and to weight each factor based on the likelihood of occurrence. That is where the complexity arises in the analysis. While one of the *Plan Procurement Management* process outputs, Independent Cost Estimates (12.1.3.7), ties costs to factors that should be included in the analysis, potential costs represented by the Risk Register component of the Project Documents (12.1.1.4) and risk-related contract decisions (see also Section 12.2.1.2), Enterprise Environmental Factors (12.1.1.5), and necessary updates to Organizational Process Assets (12.1.1.6) must be quantified. Common methods relating to the financial aspect of a make-or-buy analysis include discounted cash flow (DCF), net present value (NPV), internal rate of return (IRR), payback period (PB), and cost–benefit analysis (CBA)—sometimes called benefit-cost analysis (BCA). A more robust make-or-buy analysis would include more than one method and, ideally, each method included would indicate a similar decision. Depending on the project organization's preferences and criteria, more emphasis may be put on one method over another. In addition to financial concerns, Table 3-6 describes additional factors, correspondingly organized as "make-side" or "buy-side," that merit consideration for inclusion in the make-or-buy analysis.

Table 3-6. Make-or-Buy Analysis Factors

Make-Side	Buy-Side
Total cost (including direct costs and indirect costs) of making project need is lower	Cost (including any financing or credit costs) of buying project need externally is lower
Seller lead times exceed project organization's "speed to market" requirement and its ability to timely make the project need	Little to no seller lead times
Project organization has available, idle resources	Project organization does not have necessary resources readily available
Core competencies of project organization not diluted by making project need	Project organization cannot deviate from its core competencies focus
Project organization has necessary capability and expertise to make project need	Project need requires capability and expertise that project organization does not have
Project organization has organizational maturity and discipline to make project need	Project organization does not have needed maturity nor discipline to effectively and efficiently make project need
Project organization willing to accept risks associated with making project need	Project organization desires to transfer risk to seller

Make-Side	Buy-Side
Project organization desires competitive advantage via intellectual property related to project need	Ownership of intellectual property related to project need unimportant
Control of making project need important to project organization	Project organization willing to cede control to seller or seller is willing to materially commit to project organization
Project organization has ability to sustain ongoing support of project need	Seller better positioned to provide ongoing support of project need
Lower internal support costs	Support costs lower if procured externally

12.1.2.4 Source Selection Analysis

While the Source Selection Criteria (12.1.3.5) contains the detailed criteria by which Seller Proposals (12.2.1.4) will be evaluated, the result of the Source Selection Analysis will be the determination of a broad method by which prospective sellers will be selected. By including the broad selection method in the Bid Documents (12.1.3.3), a project organization assists prospective sellers in determining whether to make the investment in responding to the Bid Documents (12.1.3.3). For example, if a prospective seller's business model is to provide a premium level of service (at a premium price) and the selection method described in the Bid Documents (12.1.3.3) indicates that the project organization is focused primarily on cost, that seller may elect to "no bid" the competitive solicitation because its business model is inconsistent with the "least cost" focus of the project organization. In that example, the seller avoids the cost of producing what would likely have been a non-selected proposal and the project organization avoids the cost of evaluating a proposal for a seller that it would have likely non-selected.

Where the cost resulting from a procurement is anticipated by a project organization to be low, the buyer may suggest employing the "qualifications only" selection method which allows the project organization and prospective sellers to avoid the time and cost of a more exhaustive selection process. Under this method, the project organization selects the seller—irrespective of cost but at the same time assuming reasonableness—with the best capabilities and that has demonstrated the capacity, reliability, and integrity to perform. A cost-specific selection method is "least cost," which is most likely to be utilized by a buyer when the focus of the project organization is primarily on obtaining the lowest possible cost. Under this method, the project organization selects the seller that responds with its proposal meeting the minimum requirements of the project organization at a cost that is the lowest of all other seller proposals. The "least cost" method is best suited for commoditized products, services, or results for which established practices, standards, specifications, or measurements exist. Another cost-oriented selection method is "fixed budget," which discloses, in the competitive solicitation, the project organization's budget for the desired product, service, or result. The project organization selects the seller having the highest-ranking technical proposal within the constraints of the fixed budget. Because sellers adjust the scope and quality of their proposed product, service, or result to the fixed budget disclosed in the competitive solicitation, it is critical for the project organization to fully and precisely describe the project scope within the Requirements Documentation component of the Project Documents (12.1.1.4) and the Procurement Statement of Work (12.1.3.4). Further, before issuing Bid Documents (12.1.3.3), the buyer should ensure that there is reasonable cost congruency between the project scope and the fixed budget based on the market research resulting from Data Gathering (12.1.2.2), Meetings (12.1.2.5) with prospective sellers, and Independent Cost Estimates (12.1.3.7). If the research indicates that the cost of the desired product, service, or result is significantly greater than the fixed budget, prospective sellers will likely "no bid" the competitive solicitation or submit proposals that exceed the fixed budget of the project organization.

Where cost is less of a concern and the capability of the product, service, or result is paramount, the buyer may elect to employ the "quality-based/ highest technical proposal score" method. Under this method, prospective sellers are initially ranked and selected by the seller selection committee based on the quality of proposed technical capabilities. Those sellers are then invited to negotiate the associated procurement contract. The seller having the highest-ranked technical proposal is selected provided that the negotiated procurement contract meets the requirements of the project organization.

The "quality and cost-based" method, also referred to as the "best value" method, includes quality, cost, and other factors such as design in the seller selection process. In general, when project risk and uncertainty are high, the quality of the product, service, or result should be a key selection criterion when compared to cost. This method blends elements of the "quality-based / highest technical proposal score" method with the "least cost" method. It is generally preferred by buyers as this method permits the project organization to obtain the optimal product, service, or result yet gives the buyer ample negotiation leverage to achieve advantaged pricing.

While not a true selection method, "sole source" involves a project organization requesting a specific seller to prepare technical and financial proposals. Under this method, since there is no competition with other sellers, the ability of the project organization to negotiate reasonable pricing and favorable contract terms and conditions is significantly diminished—the project organization essentially has no negotiation leverage due to the seller knowing that it is the sole source of the desired product, service, or result. The use of the "sole source" method is acceptable only when amply justified. Its use is generally avoided by buyers because of this method's debilitating impact on negotiation leverage.

12.1.2.5 Meetings

If Expert Judgment (12.1.2.1) and market research as a part of Data Gathering (12.1.2.2) do not provide enough information to formulate and refine a negotiation strategy (see Section 12.1.3.1) or a Procurement Strategy (12.1.3.2), the project team or a subset thereof can alternatively meet and collaborate with prospective sellers prior to the *Conduct Procurements* (12.2) process. While this is an alternative, it is fraught with risk and should only be considered if all other avenues to obtain information have been exhausted.

With an unscrupulous seller, one risk is that the seller will attempt to influence how the Bid Documents (12.1.3.3) and Source Selection Criteria (12.1.3.5) are drafted such that the seller is advantaged because the requirements and criteria are biased toward that seller and against other sellers. Another risk with an unscrupulous seller is that it will attempt to develop relationships with the project team and project stakeholders in order to influence a procurement decision or outcome. Even if the prospective sellers involved in any Meetings are of the highest ethical standards, there could be the perception of other prospective sellers not invited to the Meetings that the invited sellers had unequal access to information which will provide them with a competitive advantage or that the project organization is now biased—and, therefore, that it is not worth the effort for the non-invited sellers to respond to a competitive solicitation. Ideally, Meetings are to be avoided and only used as a last resort. Further, the Meetings should only be conducted with the buyer present and never with the project stakeholders alone. With the buyer present, he or she can ensure that the discussion stays on-topic, project organization information not known to non-invited sellers is not inadvertently revealed, and there is no undue influence by the seller. Based on the foregoing reasons, it is common for a project organization's procurement policy to prohibit these types of Meetings with prospective sellers for procurements above a certain monetary threshold but allow such Meetings—only if needed—for smaller size procurements. A "request for information" (see Section 12.1.3.3) would be a more feasible choice to obtain the needed information and it would eliminate the risks presented by Meetings with prospective sellers.

12.1.3 Plan Procurement Management: Outputs

12.1.3.1 Procurement Management Plan

The Procurement Management Plan, which becomes a subsidiary plan of the Project Management Plan (12.1.1.3), is a key output that has two primary purposes: (1) to describe all of the activities to be performed as a part of the procurement process, including a decision roadmap for the impending procurement; and, (2) to function as a "toolbox" for all of the inputs, tools & techniques, and outputs to be used to facilitate the competitive procurement and describing how those tools will be employed and when. The Procurement Management Plan ensures that all project team members agree upon, understand, and commit to how a procurement will be conducted. This is a particularly important aspect to resolve prior to beginning any discussions with prospective sellers so as to mitigate a seller's ability to use "divide and conquer" ploys during negotiations. The Procurement Management Plan must be revised to include relevant materials as the procurement progresses, such as the Source Selection Criteria (12.1.3.5). Depending on project needs and the complexity of the anticipated procurement, the Procurement Management Plan can be informal, formal, broadly written, or highly detailed. Appendix I contains a sample Procurement Management Plan taken from an actual plan and adapted into a template format. In summary, a comprehensive Procurement Management Plan for a competitive procurement would include:

- Identification of funding sources for the products, services, or results to be procured
- In the case of international procurements, the locus—such as international, national, or local—for the competitive solicitation, jurisdiction of the contract for legal matters, and choice of currency for contract payments
- Procedures for conducting the competitive procurement, including the issuance of Bid Documents (12.1.3.3) to prospective sellers and notification to sellers of selection / non-selection
- Roles, if any, that the project team and / or project stakeholders will have in the actual procurement in collaboration with the project organization's procurement function (including the buyer) and the legal function
- Performance metrics for the buyer relating to his or her responsibilities and procurement-specific activities (such as adherence to schedule and target cost savings for the procurement)
- Establishing the use, form, and format of templates and standardized procurement and contracting documents, such as a competitive solicitation template, that are needed to facilitate the procurement and subsequent contracting
- Concise list of the required products, services, or results derived from the Requirements Documentation component of the Project Documents (12.1.1.4) and the Procurement Statement of Work (12.1.3.4)
- Addressing the Make-or-Buy Decisions (12.1.3.6) and ensuring that the decisions are coordinated with the *Develop Schedule* (6.5) process of the Project Schedule Management Knowledge Area and *Estimate Activity Resources* (9.2) process of the Project Resource Management Knowledge Area
- Seller service levels expectations, WBS requirements, and coordinating schedule dates for providing the products, services, or results with the *Develop Schedule* (6.5) and *Control Schedule* (6.6) processes of the Project Schedule Management Knowledge Area
- Risk-related contract decisions (see Section 12.2.1.2) and risk response decisions (such as bonding and insurance requirements) associated with the Risk Register component of the Project Documents (12.1.1.4)
- Procurement assumptions and the impact of constraints, such as Enterprise Environmental Factors (12.1.1.5)
- Preliminary negotiation strategy and approach to prepare the project organization's seller negotiation committee for the actual negotiations to be conducted as a part of Interpersonal and Team Skills (12.2.2.5)
- Benchmarks, such as Independent Cost Estimates (12.1.3.7), to assess Seller Proposals (12.2.1.4)
- Prequalified seller list (see Section 12.1.1.6) to identify prospective sellers and recipients of the Bid Documents (12.1.3.3)

- Coordination of any products, services, or results lead times with non-procurement project activities
- Seller and contract management procedures (see Section 12.3.1.1), including performance metrics monitoring and reporting
- Activities that must be undertaken upon early contract termination or planned contract expiration (see Section 12.3.3.1)

The Procurement Management Plan should also contain a timetable of procurement activities. This timetable—to include associated planned start and finish dates, durations, and milestones—must be incorporated within the Project Schedule, an output (6.5.3.2) resulting from the *Develop Schedule* (6.5) process of the Project Schedule Management Knowledge Area. The development of the timetable in the Procurement Management Plan must be performed concurrently with the creation of the Procurement Strategy (12.1.3.2), which includes information on the sequencing and phasing of procurement activities. Because a buyer has significant expertise with procurements, the project manager must depend on the buyer to provide the detailed list of activities, estimated durations, and activity relationships or dependencies related to a possible procurement. The buyer must estimate the schedule associated with the procurement-related activities with reasonable completeness and accuracy. This necessitates the buyer having a standardized set of activities, ideally from a procurement policy, that is readily available but that can be adjusted for a specific procurement. Tables 3-7, 3-8, and 3-9 contain example procurement and contract management activities (using terminology commonly used by buyers and contract managers) correlated to *PMBOK Guide* inputs, tools & techniques, and outputs. The PMI sequences inputs, tools & techniques, and outputs in the *PMBOK Guide* according to certain stylistic rules, such as Expert Judgment being listed as the first activity in tools & techniques and Meetings being listed as the last activity; therefore, the inputs, tools & techniques, and outputs as enumerated in the *PMBOK Guide* may not always flow in a seemingly obvious or logic sequence. Consequently, the example procurement activities described in Tables 3-7, 3-8, and 3-9 dictate the sequence of the inputs, tools & techniques, and outputs in the order that the example activities would logically occur in a competitive solicitation and the management of a subsequent procurement agreement. Additionally, there may be the Project Procurement Management Knowledge Area inputs, tools & techniques, and outputs not included in Tables 3-7, 3-8, or 3-9 because they are inherently part of, or are embedded in, the example procurement activities.

Table 3-7. Pre-Award Phase Activity Comparison

Procurement Activity	PMBOK Guide Equivalent
Identify stakeholders	12.1.1.4 Stakeholder Register component of the Project Documents
Determine resources required to conduct potential competitive procurement	12.1.1.4 Resource Requirements component of the Project Documents
Develop preliminary competitive solicitation schedule	12.1.3.1 Procurement Management Plan
Research marketplace for desired products, services, or results	12.1.2.2 Market Research component of Data Gathering 12.1.2.5 Meetings
Obtain understanding of marketplace and potential constraints	12.1.1.5 Enterprise Environmental Factors
Conduct make-or-buy analysis	12.1.2.3 Make-or-Buy Analysis component of Data Analysis 12.1.3.6 Make-or-Buy Decisions
Determine appropriate competitive solicitation strategy and approach	12.1.3.1 Procurement Management Plan 12.1.3.2 Procurement Strategy
Research and identify prospective sellers	12.1.2.2 Market Research component of Data Gathering 12.1.2.5 Meetings
Identify prequalified seller list	12.1.1.6 Organizational Process Assets
Develop negotiation strategy	12.1.3.1 Procurement Management Plan 12.2.2.5 Interpersonal and Team Skills
Develop or update procurement policy	12.1.1.6 Organizational Process Assets
Obtain or draft competitive solicitation template	12.1.1.6 Organizational Process Assets 12.1.3.3 Bid Documents
Conduct competitive solicitation kick-off meeting	12.1.3.1 Procurement Management Plan
Identify seller selection committee members	12.1.1.4 Stakeholder Register component of the Project Documents

Procurement Activity	PMBOK Guide Equivalent
Confirm competitive solicitation timetable (to be published in competitive solicitation)	12.1.3.1 Procurement Management Plan
Develop statement of work	12.1.3.4 Procurement Statement of Work
Develop competitive solicitation requirements and specifications	12.1.1.4 Requirements Documentation component of the Project Documents
Estimate marketplace costs for desired products, services, or results	12.1.3.7 Independent Cost Estimates
Select the appropriate contract type	12.1.1.6 Organizational Process Assets
Identify potential risks for purposes of competitive solicitation and / or contract template	12.1.1.4 Risk Register component of the Project Documents
Develop seller selection criteria	12.1.2.4 Source Selection Analysis 12.1.3.5 Source Selection Criteria
Obtain or draft contract template	12.1.1.6 Organizational Process Assets 12.1.3.2 Procurement Strategy
Draft final form of competitive solicitation using timetable, statement of work, requirements and specifications, seller selection criteria, and contract template	12.1.3.3 Bid Documents

Table 3-8. Award Phase Activity Comparison

Procurement Activity	PMBOK Guide Equivalent
Confirm list of sellers to receive competitive solicitation	12.2.1.6 Organizational Process Assets
Issue and / or post competitive solicitation	12.2.2.2 Advertising
Receive responses to intent to bid from sellers	12.2.1.4 Seller Proposals
Refine list of sellers intending to respond	12.2.1.6 Organizational Process Assets

Procurement Activity	PMBOK Guide Equivalent
Receive written questions from sellers	12.2.2.3 Bidder Conferences
Respond to written questions from sellers	12.2.2.3 Bidder Conferences
Distribute written questions to sellers	12.2.2.3 Bidder Conferences
Conduct pre-proposal bidder conference	12.2.2.3 Bidder Conferences
Develop seller proposal evaluation matrix	12.1.3.5 Source Selection Criteria 12.2.2.4 Data Analysis
Receive proposals from sellers	12.2.1.4 Seller Proposals
Conduct responsiveness and qualified seller review	12.2.1.4 Seller Proposals 12.2.2.5 Interpersonal and Team Skills
Disqualify non-responsive and unqualified sellers	12.2.1.4 Seller Proposals
Notify disqualified sellers	12.2.1.1 Procurement Management Plan component of the Project Management Plan
Benchmark and determine sellers' competitive range	12.1.3.7 Independent Cost Estimates 12.2.2.4 Data Analysis
Distribute proposals to seller selection committee	12.2.2.4 Data Analysis
Seller selection committee members individually score responses (for shortlisting purposes)	12.2.2.4 Data Analysis
Select shortlisted sellers	12.2.2.4 Data Analysis
Notify sellers of selection / non-selection for individual post-proposal bidder conferences	12.2.1.1 Procurement Management Plan component of the Project Management Plan
Conduct individual post-proposal bidder conferences	12.2.2.3 Bidder Conferences
Request revised proposals from sellers	12.2.1.4 Seller Proposals
Receive revised proposals from sellers	12.2.1.4 Seller Proposals

Procurement Activity	PMBOK Guide Equivalent
Distribute revised proposals to seller selection committee	12.2.2.4 Data Analysis
Seller selection committee members individually score responses (for finalist purposes)	12.2.2.4 Data Analysis
Select finalist sellers	12.2.2.4 Data Analysis
Notify sellers of selection / non-selection into finalist negotiations	12.2.1.1 Procurement Management Plan component of the Project Management Plan
Request best and final offers from sellers	12.2.2.5 Interpersonal and Team Skills
Receive best and final offers from sellers	12.2.1.4 Seller Proposals
Conduct price and business terms negotiations with finalist sellers (using seller negotiation committee if different from seller selection committee)	12.2.2.5 Interpersonal and Team Skills
Conduct contract and legal terms and conditions negotiations with finalist sellers	12.1.1.6 Organizational Process Assets 12.2.2.5 Interpersonal and Team Skills
Confirm finalist seller(s) and execute contract	12.2.3.1 Selected Sellers 12.2.3.2 Agreements
Notify finalist seller(s) of selection / non-selection of contract award	12.2.3.1 Selected Sellers
Announce contract award	12.2.3.1 Selected Sellers

Table 3-9. Post-Award[11] Phase Activity Comparison

Contract Management Activity	PMBOK Guide Equivalent
Conduct seller kick-off meeting and onboarding	12.3.1.1 Project Management Plan 12.3.1.2 Project Documents 12.3.1.3 Agreements
Develop contract monitoring tool	12.3.1.1 Project Management Plan 12.3.1.2 Project Documents 12.3.1.3 Agreements
Obtain seller-provided performance reports	12.3.1.6 Work Performance Data
Obtain data for measuring quality, timeliness, and costs	12.3.1.4 Procurement Documentation 12.3.1.6 Work Performance Data
Manage seller performance and relationship using contract monitoring tool	12.3.1.3 Agreements 12.3.2.2 Claims Administration 12.3.2.3 Data Analysis 12.3.2.5 Audits 12.3.3.2 Work Performance Information
Receive, inspect, and accept products, services, or results	12.3.2.2 Claims Administration 12.3.2.4 Inspection
Conduct contract audits	12.3.2.5 Audits
Seek seller corrective action for non-performance	12.3.1.4 Procurement Documentation 12.3.1.6 Work Performance Data 12.3.2.2 Claims Administration 12.3.3.2 Work Performance Information
Resolve seller disputes	12.3.2.2 Claims Administration 12.3.3.2 Work Performance Information 12.3.3.4 Change Requests

---

[11] The post-award phase process of *Control Procurements* (12.3), which includes contract management and contract administration activities, is sometimes excluded from the Project Management Plan (12.3.1.1) due to a project manager only considering the pre-award and award phase processes of the *Plan Project Management* and *Conduct Procurements* (12.2) processes as being procurement-oriented. A contract manager, not the project manager, is normally responsible for ongoing seller relationship management, contract management, and contract administration activities (which are generally considered outside the scope of a "procurement" project).

Contract Management Activity	PMBOK Guide Equivalent
Review / approve seller invoices	12.3.1.3 Agreements 12.3.1.4 Procurement Documentation 12.3.1.5 Approved Change Requests 12.3.2.2 Claims Administration 12.3.2.4 Inspection 12.3.2.5 Audits 12.3.3.7 Organizational Process Assets Updates
Manage contract changes	12.3.1.5 Approved Change Requests 12.3.2.2 Claims Administration
Conduct contract administration activities	12.3.3.5 Project Management Plan Updates 12.3.3.6 Project Documents Updates 12.3.3.7 Organizational Process Assets Updates
Upon anticipated contract termination or expiration, prepare for contract close-out	12.3.1.1 Project Management Plan 12.3.1.4 Procurement Documentation 12.3.2.2 Claims Administration
Complete final or true-up payments	12.3.2.2 Claims Administration 12.3.3.1 Closed Procurements 12.3.3.7 Organizational Process Assets Updates 4.7.3.2 Final Product, Service, or Result Transition
Administer record retention activities	12.3.3.1 Closed Procurements 12.3.3.7 Organizational Process Assets Updates 4.7.3.3 Final Report
Ensure organizational assets are returned or destroyed (including data)	12.3.3.1 Closed Procurements 4.7.3.2 Final Product, Service, or Result Transition
Complete other contract close-out and seller off-boarding activities	12.3.3.1 Closed Procurements 12.3.3.6 Project Documents Updates 12.3.3.7 Organizational Process Assets Updates
Terminate contract	12.3.3.1 Closed Procurements
Document lessons learned	12.3.3.5 Project Management Plan Updates 12.3.3.6 Project Documents Updates 12.3.3.7 Organizational Process Assets Updates 4.7.3.3 Final Report

12.1.3.2 Procurement Strategy

Once the make-or-buy analysis as a part of Data Analysis (12.1.2.3) has been conducted, the results have been documented as a part of Make-or-Buy Decisions (12.1.3.6), and the determination has been made that an external procurement will be required, the Procurement Strategy must then be developed by the buyer in collaboration with the project team. The Procurement Strategy includes the: (1) determination of the project delivery method; (2) the selection of the contract template and contract payment type (see Section 12.1.1.6) that will be used to negotiate with sellers during procurement negotiations conducted as a part of Interpersonal and Team Skills (12.2.2.5) and to create any necessary Agreements (12.2.3.2) between the project organization and Selected Sellers (12.2.3.1); and, (3) the development of the procurement phases associated with the timetable described in the Procurement Management Plan (12.1.3.1). The Procurement Strategy does not include the development of a negotiation strategy, which is instead a part of the Procurement Management Plan (12.1.3.1).

Project delivery methods vary significantly based on the product, service, or result that will be procured as well as the business needs of the project organization. It is important to choose a project delivery method that best meets the unique needs of the project and project organization. The determination of the project delivery method is a key decision made by the project team in terms of strategy because the method of delivery establishes or influences critical factors such as ownership, duration, cost, payment method, risk, and project outcomes. Choosing the best project delivery method for any project must start with a good understanding of the choices available, which may require significant Expert Judgment (12.1.2.1) and Data Analysis (12.1.2.3). In the case of a software or software as a service implementation, the project organization may select a more traditional project delivery method such as the "waterfall" methodology—which is a sequential, linear process consisting of discrete phases—or an iterative and adaptive methodology such as agile. In the case of professional services, the project organization may select a project delivery method that is more consultative in nature or that does or does not permit subcontracting. If the project organization is undertaking a construction project, there are a number of project delivery methods to consider such as construction management at risk, design-bid-build, design-build, and integrated project delivery. In some instances, the selection of a project delivery method may result in the need for multiple procurements or multiple procurement agreements; for example, a design-bid-build method for a construction project could result in a single prime agreement or multiple prime agreements. Ultimately, the selected project delivery method is a tool for the project manager to control risks, obtain the desired product, service, or result, and fulfill the project scope.

The selection of the contract type in the *Plan Procurement Management* process could be considered premature and that a more appropriate point in time to select the contract type would be during the *Conduct Procurements* (12.2) process. Why be concerned with the contract type while planning for a procurement when the negotiation of a procurement agreement will occur when the procurement is actually being conducted or finalized? This appears to be a valid question on its face but illustrates a fundamental problem with many competitive procurements: Commonly, but incorrectly, a draft procurement agreement is *not* included as a part of the competitive solicitation. When that is the case, there is no ability for a project organization to determine whether a prospective seller is agreeable or not to the terms and conditions of the procurement agreement. Rather, a prospective seller is evaluated by the seller selection committee based solely on the seller's proposal and responses to the requirements contained in the competitive solicitation. It is very possible that, among two otherwise equally responsive sellers, one seller is reluctant or unwilling to contract under the terms and conditions desired by the project organization. Unfortunately, any reluctance or unwillingness will likely only be determined after a significant amount of time has been invested with what is ultimately a non-responsive seller—instead of that seller having been eliminated early in the competitive procurement process. Therefore, the *Plan Procurement Management* process is the most ideal and efficient time at which to select the appropriate contract type and to include the contract template as an evaluative part of the competitive solicitation.

The fundamental purposes of a procurement agreement in the form of a written contract are to: (1) describe the business relationship between the contracting parties; (2) specify the responsibilities and obligations of the parties; (3) quantify the period of delivery or performance; and, (4) enumerate other key terms and conditions affecting the business relationship. At its core, however, a procurement agreement is a risk-shifting mechanism. Like good fences make for good neighbors, good procurement agreements attempt to achieve a mutually acceptable risk arrangement between the contracting parties. In that sense, another fundamental purpose of a contract is to allocate or apportion financial, legal, and operational risk between the contracting parties. As described under Organizational Process Assets (12.1.1.6), certain contract types are predisposed, because of their construction, to shift more or less risk to one contracting party versus another; therefore, the selection of the contract type for inclusion in the Bid Documents (12.1.3.3) and for the anticipated Agreements (12.2.3.2) is a particularly important and impactful decision. Additionally, the contract type determines the degree of management and oversight that the project organization will need to provide: The greater degree of risk absorbed by a party under a contract generally translates into a greater degree of contract management and oversight that must be provided by that party. Ultimately, while procurement agreements must be built on a formal and legal foundation, they should not be so restrictive that it precludes flexible management of the relationship between the project organization and the seller. It is therefore a goal of the buyer to balance the selection of a contract type with the desired flexibility during the period of contract delivery or performance.

As described under Organizational Process Assets (12.1.1.6), the specific contract types range in project organization risk from firm fixed price (in which a seller has full responsibility for the performance costs and resulting profit or loss) to cost plus percentage of cost (in which a seller has minimal responsibility for the performance costs and the seller's profit actually increases as the seller's costs increase). Within both ends of the range of contract types are the various incentive contracts in which a seller's responsibility for the performance costs and the profit or fee incentives offered are tailored to the uncertainties involved in contract performance. In making the determination as to which contract type to use, a buyer should evaluate the following considerations:

- Project organization's willingness to transfer risk in exchange for money
- Complexity and type of products, services, or results that are being procured
- Marketplace conditions and volatility
- Capacity and maturity of the seller to deliver or perform
- Capacity and maturity of the project organization to manage and oversee the contract
- Project delivery method
- Clarity of delivery or performance acceptance criteria
- Length of the period of delivery or performance
- Possibility of "scope creep" and the ability of the project organization to control it
- Ability of the project organization to determine price and / or cost reasonableness at the onset of a procurement agreement
- Urgency of the project organization to obtain the products, services, or results
- Difficulty in making cost or fee adjustments and validating them (such as through industry indices)

In building out the procurement activities and timetable described in the Procurement Management Plan (12.1.3.1), a buyer must also develop procurement phases as a part of the Procurement Strategy. To ensure clarity and understanding by those both within and outside of the project team, the phases must be logically sequenced to meet the needs of the project and the sub-elements of the phases and level of detail of each must be tailored to the complexity of the procurement. When defining each phase, a description of the specific objectives, performance indicators or milestones, criteria, and any knowledge transfer should be included to ensure that the buyer and project manager can monitor and track progress. Table 3-10 describes basic example procurement phases for a non-complex software as a service procurement utilizing a request for proposal (RFP) competitive solicitation format where proposals are evaluated by a seller selection committee and negotiations are conducted by a seller negotiation committee.

Table 3-10. Example Procurement Phases

Procurement Phase	Objective	Milestone / Exit Criteria
Procurement Stakeholder Identification	Identify key procurement stakeholders and definition of roles and committees	• Solicitation development team identified • Subject matter experts identified • Seller Selection Committee identified • Seller Negotiation Committee identified
Research and Analysis	Conduct market research and analysis in preparation for RFP scope development, software as a service contract template tailoring, prospective seller identification, marketplace leader identification, and pricing benchmarks determination	• Draft RFP scope developed • Contract type and template selected • Pricing benchmarks determined • Prospective sellers identified
RFP Development	Develop RFP scope, form, and contract template	• RFP and associated contract template approved by stakeholders and ready for issuance
Proposal Evaluation Criteria Development	Develop objective and quantitative proposal evaluation criteria and select evaluation method	• Proposal evaluation criteria approved by stakeholders • Proposal evaluation method selected
Prospective Seller Identification	Develop list of all prospective sellers to receive RFP and identify any potential websites for posting RFP	• List of prospective sellers intended to receive RFP developed • Websites to post RFP identified
RFP Issued	Issue / post RFP and receive intent to bid responses from prospective sellers	• RFP issues and posted • Proposal tracking sheet updated to indicate prospective sellers intending to respond
Pre-proposal Bidder Conference	Conduct pre-proposal bidder conference to present RFP to bidders, respond to bidder questions, and ensure bidder understanding of RFP	• Clarifying responses provided to all bidders • Any RFP amendments provided to all bidders

Procurement Phase	Objective	Milestone / Exit Criteria
Proposal Receipt	Receive proposals and conduct assessment to determine responsiveness of proposals as well as bidder financial soundness, capacity, reliability, and integrity to provide the software as a service	• Responsive proposals from qualified bidders received within required timeframe • Rejected bidders notified • Seller Selection Committee initiated
Post-proposal Bidder Conferences	Conduct post-proposal bidder conferences individually with each bidder to ensure an understanding of the software as a service being proposed	• All scheduled bidder conferences completed • Non-selected bidders notified
Proposal Evaluation	Evaluate proposals using previously developed proposal evaluation criteria	• Proposal evaluation forms completed by Seller Selection Committee • Bidders ranked by Seller Selection Committee
Finalists Selection	Select shortlist of finalist bidders based on post-proposal bidder conferences and proposal evaluation forms	• Bidders shortlisted • Selected and non-selected bidders notified • Seller Negotiation Committee initiated • Knowledge transferred from Seller Selection Committee to Seller Negotiation Committee
Bidder Negotiations	Negotiate proposals and request bidder refinement of proposals to ensure all software as a service capabilities, implementation, and integrations are appropriately contracted	• Acceptable deal points achieved by Seller Negotiation Committee • Contracts tailored and require only finalization • Non-selected bidders notified
Best and Final Offers	Using an iterative best and final offer format, further negotiate proposals and request bidder refinement of proposals	• Additional deal points achieved by Seller Negotiation Committee • Best and final offers received within required timeframes

Procurement Phase	Objective	Milestone / Exit Criteria
Contract Award	Award, finalize, and execute contract with selected bidder	• Selected bidder and non-selected bidders notified • Contract executed • Knowledge transferred from Seller Negotiation Committee to Contract Manager

The selection of the project delivery method and contract type may affect the economic feasibility of the project; for example, the selection of a riskier cost reimbursable contract type instead of a more favorable fixed price contract type could result in higher costs to the project organization. Consequently, decisions made as a part of developing the Procurement Strategy must reconciled and aligned with the Business Case component of the Business Documents (12.1.1.2).

12.1.3.3 Bid Documents

Bid Documents are used to communicate the project scope statement contained in the Scope Baseline component of the Project Management Plan (12.1.1.3), the Requirements Documentation component of the Project Documents (12.1.1.4), and the Procurement Statement of Work (12.1.3.4) to prospective sellers in order for the sellers to submit their proposals to the project organization for consideration and evaluation. The project organization may elect to include the results of the Source Selection Analysis (12.1.2.4) in the Bid Documents to assist prospective sellers in determining whether to respond with a proposal. In addition to being used as a vehicle to communicate project needs, some buyers incorporate the Bid Documents and the Seller Proposals (12.2.1.4) of Selected Sellers (12.2.3.1) as a part of subsequent Agreements (12.2.3.2). The purpose behind doing so is to ensure that a seller is contractually obligated, regardless of all subsequent discussions between the project organization and the seller, to complete what the project organization originally communicated to the seller in the Bid Documents.

When the Bid Documents are issued to more than one prospective seller and where those sellers are competing against one another for the award of a procurement agreement, the documents are then considered a "competitive solicitation." In the commercial procurement context, such competitive solicitations most commonly take the form of a request for proposal (RFP) or a request for quotation (RFQ).[12] Where the Bid Documents merely request information from prospective sellers and will not result in the award of a procurement agreement, the documents are considered a "solicitation." In both the

---

[12] An invitation for bids (IFB), invitation to bid (ITB), and an invitation to negotiate (ITN) are less common terms in the commercial context and more common in the public sector. An IFB and ITB are most similar to an RFQ in that the focus is on price; however, an IFB and ITB commonly do not contemplate any subsequent negotiations—a seller's proposal is accepted or not—whereas an RFQ in the commercial context can involve additional negotiation. An ITN is most similar to an RFP, where the focus in on best value and negotiations are permitted.

commercial and governmental procurement contexts, solicitations most commonly take the form of a request for information (RFI). Frequently, the acronym "RFx" is used to generically or collectively to refer an RFP, RFQ, or RFI.

The primary difference between an RFP, RFQ, and RFI centers on a project organization's knowledge of the needed products, services, or results and the project organization's understanding of what the marketplace offers. The clarity of requirements contained in each of the three RFx[13] types varies based on the specificity of the Requirements Documentation component of the Project Documents (12.1.1.4) and the Procurement Statement of Work (12.1.3.4), with an RFI being used when the requirements are the least clear and an RFQ being used when the requirements are the clearest.

An RFI is in many ways an educational and information-seeking tool—used when the project organization does not have an understanding of the marketplace or is otherwise unable to develop a robust scope of the procurement need. Consequently, an RFI is usually very broad in its scope and, if it does contain requirements, the requirements are typically vague. In simple terms, the buyer is testing the marketplace to determine whether sellers exist that can offer what the project organization is seeking. By virtue of a project organization having a limited knowledge of the scope or marketplace (or both), and therefore unable to craft detailed requirements, little effort is required to quickly create an RFI. As described earlier, because an RFI results in sellers providing informational responses rather than sales proposals, an RFI is not a true "competitive" solicitation; however, it is frequently included in the family of competitive solicitation types in that an RFI generally leads to an RFP or RFQ. The term "competitive solicitation" is often used to refer to an RFI but with the understanding that sellers are not truly in competition and that the RFI will not result in a contract award. In an RFI-to-RFP or RFI-to-RFQ competitive procurement, the buyer issues an RFI, obtains knowledge about the products, services, or results, what is available in the marketplace, and what the capabilities are of sellers in that marketplace. The buyer and the project team use the RFI responses to better scope out the procurement need and to develop more comprehensive and detailed Requirements Documentation as a component of the Project Documents (12.1.1.4) and Procurement Statement of Work (12.1.3.4) for the subsequent RFP or RFQ.

While the RFI serves as an informational tool, the RFP is an evaluative tool. An RFP is used when a buyer has: (1) clearer requirements resulting from the Requirements Documentation component of the Project Documents (12.1.1.4); (2) a defined Procurement Statement of Work (12.1.3.4); (3) a better knowledge of the marketplace; and, (4) some knowledge of qualified sellers in the marketplace that can provide the required products, services, or results. More time and effort are required to develop the content of an RFP in order to ensure that the scope and requirements are well-formulated. The formality and structure of an RFP enables the objective and quantitative evaluation of sellers and proposals which meet the requirements stated in the RFP.

---

[13] For the purpose of this book, RFx, competitive solicitation, solicitation, and Bid Documents are used interchangeably and have the same meaning. Similarly, a seller's proposal, bid, or response to an RFI or competitive solicitation are used interchangeably and have the same meaning.

An RFQ is essentially a price comparison tool, commonly used to procure tangible assets, commodity items, and commodity services such as technology hardware, office supplies, materials, or temporary administrative services. An RFQ is used when a buyer has: (1) very detailed requirements resulting from the Requirements Documentation component of the Project Documents (12.1.1.4); (2) a well-defined and clear Procurement Statement of Work (12.1.3.4); (3) a strong knowledge of the marketplace; and, (4) a strong knowledge of qualified sellers in the marketplace (and very likely has a prequalified seller list) that can readily provide the required products, services, or results. With an RFQ, the project organization is simply looking for the lowest possible cost from sellers that can satisfactorily fulfill the Requirements Documentation component of the Project Documents (12.1.1.4) and Procurement Statement of Work (12.1.3.4), and provide the needed products, services, or results at the requisite level of quality based on the schedule of the project organization. The following lists summarize the attributes of an RFI, RFP, and RFQ:

Request for Information (RFI)

- Informational tool
- Focus is on obtaining information
- Used to request information from prospective sellers when the Requirements Documentation component of the Project Documents (12.1.1.4) and the Procurement Statement of Work (12.1.3.4) are vague or cannot be sufficiently completed, and the buyer is seeking to understand what products, services, or results exist in the marketplace
- Can be developed quickly and with relatively little effort
- Can be informal in process and structure
- Enables the efficient collection of significant amounts of information relating to a product, service, or result and to ascertain capabilities within the marketplace
- Can be used as a precursor to an RFP or an RFQ, meaning that responses to an RFI can be used as input to the development of a more detailed and comprehensive RFP or RFQ

Request for Proposal (RFP)

- Evaluation tool
- Focus is on best value
- Used to request responses from prospective sellers when the Requirements Documentation component of the Project Documents (12.1.1.4) and Procurement Statement of Work (12.1.3.4) are well-defined but where the buyer is seeking to understand seller capabilities
- Significant time and effort may be needed to formulate the Requirements Documentation component of the Project Documents (12.1.1.4) and Procurement Statement of Work (12.1.3.4)
- Results from and follows a formal competitive procurement process

- Enables the objective and quantitative evaluation of seller responses that meet the requirements stated in the RFP
- Can be a precursor to an RFQ, meaning that seller responses to an RFP may indicate existing and available products, services, or results that, if the project organization is willing to modify the requirements, will meet the needs of the project organization

Request for Quotation (RFQ)
- Price comparison tool
- Focus is on best price and schedule adherence
- Used to request price quotes from prospective sellers when the Requirements Documentation component of the Project Documents (12.1.1.4) and Procurement Statement of Work (12.1.3.4) are detailed and precise and where the buyer has a strong knowledge of the marketplace and qualified sellers
- Significant time and effort may be needed to formulate the Requirements Documentation component of the Project Documents (12.1.1.4) and Procurement Statement of Work (12.1.3.4); however, an RFQ is frequently used for repetitive procurements—in which case an RFQ can be developed quickly and with relatively little effort
- Results from and follows a formal and usually very rigid competitive procurement process
- Enables simplified evaluation of seller responses to determine whether the seller can provide the required products, services, or results at a competitive price in the timeframe required by the project organization

An RFP or RFQ creates competition simply by virtue of participating sellers vying against each other for a project organization's business. Each seller participating in a competitive procurement knows that its proposal will be measured and compared to other proposals and that its offer should be as competitive as possible, that is, the best possible solution at the best possible price. An RFP or RFQ is also a very powerful competitive tool for a buyer in that a competitive solicitation works to equalize the bargaining power between buyer and seller. Where a seller has an intimate knowledge of its products, services, or results and has a more complete understanding of the marketplace, a buyer will likely have inferior knowledge and understanding because the buyer procures the products, services, or results far less frequently than the seller sells them. Further, sellers commonly have an array of resources aligned to bring a sale to closure and those resources are highly disproportionate to a buyer's resources; for example, sellers typically have extensive sales training, marketers, product managers, business development staff, inside sales representatives, outside sales executives, and account managers at their disposal. Because a procurement and competitive solicitation involve an objective process where sellers must follow a protocol that limits or prohibits interaction with the seller selection committee, sellers have a difficult time using sales ploys and relationship management to influence a procurement decision. Key points for consideration regarding a competitive solicitation (in the form of Bid Documents) is that it:

- Conveys to sellers that the project organization is disciplined and follows a structured and fair competitive procurement process
- Avoids scope creep by requiring project stakeholders to document their needs in a relatively formalized fashion
- Explains, through the Requirements Documentation component of the Project Documents (12.1.1.4) and Procurement Statement of Work (12.1.3.4), how a seller can successfully compete for a project organization's business
- Makes the process of evaluating sellers more efficient because all of the sellers are responding to the same set of requirements in a similar format
- Serves to select a qualified seller that has the ability to timely provide the required products, services, or results at a competitive price
- Provides competitive leverage for a buyer with limited negotiation effort and, at the same, time qualifies sellers on the basis that each seller must provide a coherent response (or, if not, be excluded from the procurement)
- Communicates the expected terms of a formal procurement agreement (via the included contract template) that holds both the buyer and seller responsible for meeting the agreed-upon commitments
- Serves as a historical record for record retention purposes

The Bid Documents represent the project organization to the marketplace and may be the first encounter between the project organization and prospective sellers. Therefore, it is important for a buyer to conduct a final review of the Bid Documents before issuing them to prospective sellers in order to ensure that the competitive solicitation is as complete and accurate as possible. The following competitive solicitation finishing checklist, primarily intended for an RFP or RFQ, can be used by a buyer to spot potential issues requiring correction:

- Appropriate and sufficient narrative describing the business need or problem?
- Adequately describes goals and requirements?
- Areas defined or made clear that a seller should consider as out-of-scope?
- Is the correct name for the procurement need (such as the project name) included?
- Images, if any, are appropriate and legible?
- Requirements are combined closed-ended / open-ended questions (Does seller...? If so, how does seller...?) versus solely closed-ended or open-ended questions?

- Requirements structured into logical components such that a seller can provide logically scoped solutions, timelines, and costs?
- Requirements concise and specific such that they require a seller to provide a narrow and targeted response?
- Requirements detailed and clear such that a seller understands what is required?
- Requirements can each be evaluated and measured?
- Processes, procedures, or standards which must be followed or considered by a seller specified in the requirements?
- Contract template included?
- Necessary attachments embedded as files in the body of the competitive solicitation document?
- Buyer contact information correct?
- Timetable activities and dates correct?
- No conflicting or duplicative content / sections?
- No incorrect content / sections?
- No missing content / sections?
- Contributor and reviewer redlines and comments removed?
- Pages numbered correctly?
- Table of contents correct?
- Simple sentences and short paragraphs?
- Headings and sub-headings used to break up content?
- Same fonts and consistent font formats used throughout?
- Same style (for example, indented paragraphs) used throughout?
- Section, table, and image references and cross-references correct?
- Numbered / bulleted sections sequenced correctly?
- Attachments / appendices named correctly and numbered appropriately?
- Acronyms defined (only once) and used consistently throughout?
- Consistent use of terms throughout (for example, seller versus respondent, supplier, and vendor)?
- Written in third person point of view (for example, no "you" or "us")?
- No use of slang, terms of art (unless otherwise defined), non-business language, or contractions?
- No fragmented, run-on, or other sentence errors?
- No grammatical / typographical errors?
- No misspellings?

The form and format of an RFx can vary greatly based on the project organization and the complexity of the procurement; however, the general composition of an RFx is common from project organization to project organization. A competitive solicitation in the form of Bid Documents is typically comprised of the major sections described in the following paragraphs. An example Request for Information / Proposal template is included in Appendix II for illustrative purposes.

Objective

The objective is a high-level and holistic theme which conveys the main purpose, intent, and goals of the competitive solicitation. Competitive solicitations can be technical and complex, and, without a clearly defined overall objective, sellers may be unable to glean why a project organization is issuing a competitive solicitation. Certainly, the requirements contained in a competitive solicitation should represent the quantitative needs of a project organization; however, the context and qualitative needs are sometimes lost within the bulk of a solicitation. A short, clear objective written in plain language is extremely helpful to sellers in crafting their proposals. For example, if the stated objective of an anticipated procurement is "…to improve the quality of services currently being provided," a seller will likely formulate a very different proposal than it would have if the stated objective is "…to reduce the costs of services currently being provided." If concise, the project scope statement contained in the Scope Baseline component of the Project Management Plan (12.1.1.3) should be included in this section.

Project Organization Overview

While most project organizations have an Internet presence which provides information about the organization—and sellers will certainly research that and more to gain intelligence for purposes of their response to a competitive solicitation—a brief overview of the project organization specific to the required products, services, or results is helpful for sellers to tailor their proposals. Similar to a holistic theme, the overview should generally describe to sellers how the needs and requirements articulated by the competitive solicitation fit into the project organization. For example, describing that the needs and requirements are for a new line of business or for a long-established function within the project organization could inform a seller on how to formulate its proposal.

Timetable

The timetable described in the Procurement Management Plan (12.1.3.1)—also known as the "calendar of events"—specifies key dates relating to the competitive solicitation, such as its release date, the intent to bid date, question and answer period, Bidder Conferences (12.2.2.3) (including pre- and post-proposal bidder conferences, Seller Proposals (12.2.1.4) submission due date, demonstrations or proof-of-concept sessions, shortlisting of sellers, negotiations, contract award, and Selected Sellers (12.2.3.1) start date.

Background

While the theme described in the objective section provides a general basis for the competitive procurement, the background contains deeper insight that supports the theme, such as detailed objectives and project goals. Including the Source Selection Analysis (12.1.2.4) in a summarized form can serve as guidance to sellers on areas of focus. This section may also contain information related to perceived risks (see Section 12.1.1.4) as well as perceived constraints and assumptions (see Section 12.1.1.5). Sellers can include in their proposals how they can address these detailed objectives and mitigate or resolve concerns of the project organization.

Functional and Technical Requirements

The Requirements Documentation component of the Project Documents (12.1.1.4) and the Procurement Statement of Work (12.1.3.4) comprise the requirements section of a competitive solicitation. Any functional and technical requirements, specifications, or other information that detail the responsibilities, deliverables, or activities necessary for the seller to provide the required products, services, or results should be included in this section. Where feasible, a project plan and schedule relating to the expected delivery or performance of a seller's products, services, or results should be included.

Seller Qualifications

In this section, a buyer is requesting information to determine whether a seller is qualified to provide the desired products, services, or results. Some of the information may be redundant in that the buyer may have already prequalified some or all of the prospective sellers. Past performance of a seller is one of the best indicators of future performance, so the questions or requirements in this section should be heavily weighted toward past projects and current or prior references. This section will also typically request a seller to provide an overview of its organization and financial information.

Pricing Information

While not all procurement decisions are based on price alone, price is clearly an important consideration. This section describes the pricing that sellers are required to provide and the format that the pricing must be provided in. To ensure that a seller selection committee has an appropriate period of time to evaluate pricing contained in Seller Proposals (12.2.1.4), this section typically stipulates that the proposed pricing be valid for a specified period of time, such as 180-days, from the date of a seller's proposal submission. Pricing submitted should be as detailed and complete as possible, and in a format that facilitates evaluation by the seller selection committee. Summarized pricing with detailed schedules for such cost components as products, services, or results, implementation, training, and support allows for a quick and thorough analysis.

Response Procedures

The mechanics and logistics of responding to a competitive solicitation should be included within this section. The instructions and directions should be very clear so that a seller knows exactly what it needs to do to participate in the competitive procurement process and to submit a proposal. For example, to ensure a consistent response from sellers that permits the equivalent comparison of proposals, a buyer typically instructs sellers in this section to provide their proposals in a very specific format. In some cases, a buyer may include detailed evaluation criteria as described in the Source Selection Criteria (12.1.3.5), describing exactly how proposals will be evaluated, what will be evaluated, and even the points or scores that may be awarded. In doing so, the buyer is communicating to sellers how they can maximize the possibility of being awarded a contract.

If any Bidder Conferences (12.2.2.3), demonstrations, proof-of-concept sessions, or other meetings involving sellers (such as seller site visits) are included as a part of the competitive procurement process, those meetings and associated logistics should be included in this section. This section also typically includes instructions as to with whom and when a seller should communicate. To prevent attempts by sellers to influence a project organization or a seller selection committee, a buyer may include a communication protocol for prospective sellers which restricts communication to the buyer until a contract award is made and indicates that sellers may be disqualified from the competitive procurement process for violating the communication protocol.

Contract Template

While not necessary for an RFI (which is focused on seeking information—not proposals—from sellers), it is important to include the selected contract template and contract payment type for the Agreements (12.2.3.2) as a part of the Procurement Strategy (12.1.3.2) in the form of a draft procurement agreement within an RFP or RFQ. If a draft procurement agreement is not available at the time the RFx is to be issued, desired key contract terms and conditions should be included in its place. While a project organization's understanding of how a seller can meet the specified requirements is critically important, it is equally as important to gauge a seller's willingness to contract its commitments. Thus, an RFx should include a requirement that sellers provide, as a part of their proposals, a "redline" mark-up to the included draft procurement agreement or included key contract terms and conditions.

12.1.3.4 Procurement Statement of Work

The Procurement Statement of Work describes the products, services, or results that the project team requires from a seller. While the Bid Documents (12.1.3.3) (that is, the form of a competitive solicitation) are the means by which the project needs are communicated to prospective sellers to solicit their proposals, the Procurement Statement of Work is the key component of the Bid Documents (12.1.3.3) used by sellers to base the formulation of their proposals. Thus, a Procurement Statement of Work must be allotted appropriate time and attention by a project team to fully develop. Each project need should be described separately so as to be clearly delineated but multiple products, services, or results can be grouped as one procurement item within a single Procurement Statement of Work. The Procurement Statement of Work is heavily dependent on the Requirements Documentation component of the Project Documents (12.1.1.4) and the project scope statement contained in the Scope Baseline component of the Project Management Plan (12.1.1.3) to derive and describe the project needs that must be procured from a seller. While a Procurement Statement of Work should be clear and concise, it should also be comprehensive and include, as applicable:

- Roles and responsibilities of the project organization and seller
- Technical and functional requirements
- Specifications
- Quantities

- Products, services, or results required to be provided
- Resource requirements (staffing levels, functional titles, skill sets)
- Schedule, period of delivery or performance, milestones, or deadlines
- Inspection, audit, or testing procedures
- Acceptance or approval criteria and review periods
- Quality standards
- Service levels or performance standards
- Performance reporting required of the seller
- Locations and facilities

In the commercial procurement context, the contents of a Procurement Statement of Work are commonly referred to as the "scope of work," "competitive solicitation requirements," "functional and technical requirements," or "specifications." For services, particularly in an international context, a Procurement Statement of Work may be referred to as the "terms of reference" or "TOR." Regardless of nomenclature, requirements and specifications are included as a part of the competitive solicitation—the Bid Documents (12.1.3.3). Referring to these types of requirements and specifications as a "statement of work"—even with the "procurement" qualifier—at this planning point in a structured procurement methodology may create confusion for a buyer. Buyers generally consider a "statement of work" to be part of a procurement agreement, executed between a project organization and seller, which describes the *actual* services, products, or results to be provided by a seller. At this planning point, a "scope of work" would make more sense to a buyer than would "statement of work," with the scope of work being a description of a *desired* need for products, services, or results that would be communicated to sellers as a part of a competitive solicitation. For the purposes of this section and to eliminate confusion between a statement of work and a scope of work (and the timing of either), the contents of a Procurement Statement of Work will be referred to simply as "requirements."

Even though a buyer will format the requirements in such a way that lends itself best to the format of a competitive solicitation, the buyer is heavily dependent upon the project team's and stakeholders' business knowledge in articulating their requirements. A buyer is also responsible for developing more procedurally-oriented requirements (based upon information gleaned from the project team and stakeholders) such as information security, proprietary rights, and seller performance objectives. The breadth and degree of requirements detail may vary based on a project team's knowledge of the project needs. This level of detail will be a factor in determining the type of Bid Documents (12.1.3.3) that will be issued to sellers. At a minimum, the Procurement Statement of Work must describe the requirements in sufficient detail so as to provide prospective sellers with enough information to formulate a response describing their corresponding capabilities. However, the requirements should be structured in such a way that sellers can be flexible in proposing solutions and alternatives. Considerations to aid in the development of requirements contained within a Procurement Statement of Work include:

- Breaking the scope of the project needs into componentized requirements so the sellers can do the same in providing solutions, timelines, and costs (thus making it easier for the seller selection committee to evaluate and compare seller responses)
- Stating requirements clearly and concisely such that a prospective seller knows what is required
- Stating requirements in such a way that they require a prospective seller to respond with a targeted solution and / or a deliverable
- Avoiding vague requirements statements that may hinder the development of seller responses by limiting a prospective seller's understanding of the project organization's critical objectives
- Avoiding incomplete or unclear requirements that may be misinterpreted or inconsistently responded to by sellers
- Avoiding over-specification of requirements and identifying needs without over-complication
- Avoiding unnecessary "how-to" requirements that preclude the ability for sellers to propose their most efficient / innovative operations
- Ensuring that requirements are not unnecessarily constraining so that sellers can suggest creative options; however, being clear at the same time as to what would be absolutely out-of-scope
- Determining whether a requirement can be easily evaluated and measured (if not, the requirement is either at too high of a level or it may not be a valid requirement)
- Using a format that enables efficient but thorough evaluation such as combining closed-ended questions ("yes" or "no") that permit quantitative evaluation with open-ended questions (explanations or descriptions) which allow for qualitative evaluation (for example, "Does the proposed enterprise resource planning system allow for reverse auctions? If so, describe the reverse auction functionality.")
- Giving prospective sellers full responsibility for quality delivery and performance by stating formal, measurable quality and performance standards
- Correctly describing how any project organization processes, procedures, or standards should be followed by a seller
- Stating completion criteria and being explicit in describing how acceptance will be accomplished

The concept of closed-ended and open-ended questions described above is particularly important. Too frequently, upon receipt of seller proposals to a competitive solicitation, a buyer realizes that certain sellers did not respond to one or more requirements in such a way that truly assesses those sellers' capabilities and that those sellers' responses are difficult to compare to other sellers participating in the competitive procurement. As an example, the question of "What are the source-to-settle capabilities of the proposed enterprise resource planning system?" could yield many different forms of responses from prospective sellers: Some of which may describe source-to-settle functionality throughout the system, some of which may indicate that the functionality will be delivered in the very near future, some of which may provide long, rambling responses, and some of which may provide a clear, bulleted list of functionality—and all of which are going to be extremely difficult to compare response-to-response.

Closed-ended questions require a definitive, quantitative response. A question that begins with "Does seller…" is an example of a closed-ended question that forces a binary "yes" or "no" response. Therefore, one seller's response to closed-ended question is easy to evaluate and easy to compare to another seller's response. However, while this question form can provide concise responses that are easy to quantitatively evaluate and because of the tendency of sellers to want to respond "yes" to every requirement, the close-ended question form lacks the information needed to fully evaluate a seller's capabilities. On the other hand, open-ended questions require some sort of explanatory, qualitative response. A question that begins with "How does seller…" is an example of an open-ended question that requires a descriptive response. While this question form can provide significant insight into the information needed to fully evaluate a seller's capabilities, it is difficult to quantitatively evaluate. Formulating requirements using a combination of both question forms is optimal for capturing information necessary to provide for easy quantitative evaluation *and* for fully assessing the qualitative aspects and veracity of a seller's capabilities. As another example, "Using only a 'yes' or 'no' response, does the proposed enterprise resource planning system include a source-to-settle module that is separate and distinct from other system modules? If so, please describe the basic functionality of the source-to-settle module using a concise, bulleted format." This question form is clearer and more precise than the example given in the prior paragraph and facilitates ease of evaluation.

When writing requirements, it is essential for a buyer to consider how the proposal evaluation will be structured and conducted. Without that consideration, translating sellers' responses into a structure or framework that can be easily evaluated may create a formatting dilemma for a buyer. Thus, it is prudent to formulate the Source Selection Criteria (12.1.3.5) at the same time the requirements are being developed. Preferably, requirements should be formatted to allow for an "apples-to-apples" comparison of Seller Proposals (12.2.1.4) on a quantitative basis that also provides for electronic evaluation. For example, a buyer may include a spreadsheet or form as a part of the competitive solicitation requirements section in which the sellers must respond using a scoring schema (such as, 3 – Seller exceeds requirement; 2 – Seller fully meets requirement; 1 – Seller partially meets requirement; 0 – Seller does not meet requirement; or, 1 – Yes, 0 – No) along with an additional column reserved for sellers to provide qualitative responses. The spreadsheet can then be easily manipulated by the buyer and the seller selection committee members for proposal evaluation purposes.

12.1.3.5 Source Selection Criteria

Source Selection Criteria[14] is used by a seller selection committee to evaluate a seller's response and then, in the case of multiple sellers, compare and contrast seller responses. At this point in the *Plan Procurement Management* process, the seller selection committee is not yet evaluating responses; rather, the buyer is instead developing the Source Selection Criteria in preparation of receiving responses. The buyer should develop the Source Selection Criteria, starting from the Source Selection Analysis (12.1.2.4), in conjunction with the Requirements Documentation component of the Project Documents (12.1.1.4) and the Procurement Statement of Work (12.1.3.4) so as to ensure that the selection criteria mirror the requirements contained in the corresponding competitive solicitation. Ultimately, and in summary, a buyer seeks to procure the products, services, or results that meet the stated requirements at the lowest cost consistent with appropriate levels of contractual commitment, quality, and service. To that end, the Source Selection Criteria must have the breadth and depth to adequately evaluate sellers. At the same time, however, the Source Selection Criteria should be developed in such a manner so as to allow for efficient and effective response evaluations. In developing the Source Selection Criteria, a buyer should consider the selection criteria described in the following paragraphs.

Seller's Understanding of Project Needs

While a seller's adherence to requirements contained in the Bid Documents (12.1.3.3) arguably represents the most important criteria for selection, the seller should be evaluated on its overall understanding of the project needs. For example, if a buyer indicates in the Bid Documents (12.1.3.3) that there is a focus on quality, and a seller does not emphasize its capabilities relating to quality, that seller will be deficient when evaluated on that criteria against other sellers.

Management Approach

A culture "fit" between a project organization and a seller is particularly important for cases where the products, services, or results are complex, lengthy in duration in terms of delivery or performance, or require close interaction between the project organization and seller. For those types of procurements, the seller selection committee should evaluate sellers on their approach to managing the delivery or performance of the products, services, or results.

Capability and Approach

The single most important point of evaluation is whether a seller has the required capability, under contract, to satisfactorily provide the required products, services, or results. Thus, a great deal of attention and analysis should be devoted to evaluating prospective sellers on their capabilities and approach. In an international procurement, the specific capabilities of a seller in international locations—such as the seller's ability to source local workers or resources—must be evaluated in addition to that seller's overall capabilities. In some cases, a buyer may be requesting products, services, or results that are not currently

---

[14] Source Selection Criteria are commonly referred to by buyers as "evaluation criteria."

provided by a seller. If so, a seller selection committee may elect to eliminate the seller from further consideration or to evaluate the seller on its ability to obtain the capability necessary to satisfactorily deliver or perform.

Business Capacity and Interest

A seller's business operations must be evaluated by a seller selection committee to determine whether there is adequate capacity for the seller to successfully deliver or perform under the procurement agreement. This part of the evaluation may require site tours of the sellers that are submitting responses. However, evaluating capacity alone is not sufficient—the seller selection committee should also evaluate a seller's interest in the project organization's business. If the project organization represents only a small fraction of a seller's business or requires the products, services, or results that result from a part of the seller's business that the seller is no longer investing in, the seller selection committee should consider whether a business relationship with that seller would be prudent over the long-term.

Financial Capacity and Stability

Even though a seller may have the requisite technical capability, approach, business capacity, and interest, a seller's ongoing ability to provide the products, services, or results is directly related to the seller's financial capacity and stability. Thus, a seller should be carefully evaluated on its financial stability and capacity to obtain, if necessary, financial resources to meet its contractual obligations. This evaluation usually entails a review of a seller's financial statements representing a reasonable period of time and that have been certified by an independent third party such as a certified public accountant.

Diversity Sellers

In some cases, even in a commercial context, project organizations require that a certain percentage of procurements be awarded to diversity sellers such as minority-owned, woman-owned, veteran-owned, or disadvantaged businesses. Mostly, in the commercial context, this requirement is based on the project organization's desire to be viewed in a favorable light by the public as opposed to being mandated by government regulation. In any case, sellers that claim diversity status should be required to submit appropriate credentials in their responses to a competitive solicitation so as to evidence such status.

Acceptance and Warranty

The willingness of a seller to stand behind its products, services, or results is an age-old concern of project organizations. Project organizations typically desire a period of time to evaluate whether the products, services, or results that are provided by a seller conform to a project organization's requirements. If not, a prudent buyer typically would require that the seller correct the deficiency, or, if the seller is unable or unwilling to make corrections, refund any monies paid by the project organization. Thus, sellers should be evaluated on their willingness to provide an acceptance period, the duration of the acceptance period, and the remedies available to the project organization if the seller is unable or unwilling to correct any deficiencies. Similar to an acceptance period, a seller should also be evaluated on its willingness to provide a warranty period and, if provided by the seller, the characteristics of the warranty such as duration and coverage. Sellers that provide both acceptance and warranty periods, and contractually commit to the same, indicate strong confidence in their ability to satisfactorily deliver or perform.

Customer References

Customer references are frequently viewed by both buyers and sellers as a mere administrative part of evaluating responses. In that view, there is not much value in the information derived from a "good" reference that a seller provides because of what is usually overly positive commentary—with very little substance—from an existing customer. In fact, since providing a customer reference consumes that reference's time and effort, certain customers receive consideration from sellers in return for a positive reference; for example, training credits or "free" registration at a seller event. Considering the lack of real value resulting from "good" references, buyers are still reluctant to exclude asking for references as a part of a competitive solicitation: Requesting references seems to be an immutable part of a competitive solicitation. The objective of a buyer in reviewing customer references is to determine if a seller can and will meet the procurement need, and the best means by which to accomplish that objective is to ask questions that truly probe the customer reference. The following list of questions goes beyond the standard "Are you satisfied with the performance of the seller?" type of questions and are oriented to obtaining more informative responses from a customer reference. A buyer can use a reasonable subset of questions from this list to obtain the desired information. For example, in the list below, the question regarding contract changes assists in determining whether a seller can appropriately scope a procurement need: If the customer reference acknowledges some number of change controls, that could be a sign the seller did not appropriately scope the procurement need or did not adequately manage scope creep as the project progressed. Another example is the question regarding whether the customer reference would single source future work to the seller; if not, it could be that the customer reference's procurement rules do not permit single source—or it could be that the seller did not perform as well as the customer expected.

- What type of procurement process did you employ to select the seller?
- Is the seller still providing the products, services, or results?
- On a scale of 1 to 5, with 5 being the highest, how satisfied are you with how the seller delivered or performed on the project or engagement? [Probe if less than 5]
- On a scale of 1 to 5, with 5 being the highest, how satisfied are you with the skills of the seller's staff who worked on the project or engagement? [Probe if less than 5]
- Did the seller fully understand your business needs in providing the products, services, or results? Did the seller miss anything?
- Did the seller maintain clear communication during all phases of the project or engagement? What could the seller have done to better communicate?
- Is the value you received consistent with price or costs charged by the seller? If not, did the seller attempt some sort of resolution?
- Was the project or engagement managed effectively? What could the seller have done better?

- Did you have to make any changes in scope to the contract after the seller began performing, such as change requests? What were the reasons for the change requests?
- Were there any schedule, performance, or delivery slippages?
- Was there a point in the project or engagement where the seller let you down, underperformed, or disappointed you? If so, how did the seller respond?
- Did the seller miss any service levels, key performance measures, key project dates, or critical milestones?
- What one thing could the seller have done to improve your overall experience with the seller?
- If there was one thing you could have changed about the seller in the performance of the project or engagement, what would it be?
- If you needed additional products or services in the future similar to what the seller provided to you, what is the likelihood that you would choose the seller again?
- Would you choose the seller as part of a single source procurement without going through some sort of competitive procurement process or would you still conduct a competitive procurement? If you would conduct a competitive procurement, is that because of your procurement rules?
- Now, after working with the seller, are there any things that you wish you had known in advance before contracting with the seller?
- What advice do you have for me in working with the seller?
- Are there any important questions that I should have asked but did not?

The process of reference checking can also provide significant value when contacting "bad" references—meaning prior references which are no longer customers of a seller. With this type of reference, a buyer is not necessarily attempting to dredge up negative information about a seller; rather, a buyer is attempting to learn what a seller tried to do to retain or salvage the business of a prior customer. Sellers may balk initially at providing this type of reference, but quickly do so when they learn that a material amount of evaluation "points" are allocated to receiving references of prior customers from the sellers. In a competitive solicitation, the requirement may be simply stated as "Provide two (2) references that are existing customers and two (2) references that are no longer customers along with the reasons as to why the references are no longer customers."

Intellectual Property and Proprietary Rights

When a project organization requires products, services, or results unique to that organization, the project organization may require ownership of the intellectual property and proprietary rights associated with the applicable products, services, or results. In such a case, the seller selection committee must evaluate prospective sellers on their willingness to assign all intellectual property and proprietary rights to the project organization. Some sellers may include already owned or licensed intellectual property in their products, services, or results and may be precluded or prohibited from further assigning or transferring those rights. Other sellers are simply unwilling to assign proprietary rights to a project organization even though the organization may be compensating the seller for newly developing the products, services, or results. Thus, where proprietary rights are of concern to a project organization, the buyer must include sufficient information in the Bid Documents (12.1.3.3) such that sellers are made aware of the requirement. As a parallel, a buyer should also include detailed criteria as a part of the Source Selection Criteria in order to evaluate the seller's understanding of, and adherence to, proprietary rights requirements.

Contract Commitments and Risk

Not only must prospective sellers indicate their ability to deliver or perform, they must also show a willingness to contractually stand behind their commitments. Further, a seller must demonstrate (and be evaluated on) its ability to shoulder the risk that a project organization seeks to transfer to the seller. If a seller provides a well-formulated response and competitive pricing, but then substantively modifies the terms and conditions of the included contract template such that the seller's accountability or commitment is diluted or negated, those modifications should be an important part of an evaluation by the seller selection committee.

Pricing

While price is an important evaluation factor—particularly with an RFQ—price should not necessarily be the single most important criteria of evaluation since price is typically negotiable. With an RFP, a project organization is frequently seeking the "best value," which is typically a combination of price and quality as opposed to price alone. However, it is clearly relevant to evaluate a seller on all aspects of price for purposes of comparison to other sellers.

Methods of Evaluation

While there are many different methods and automated tools that exist to facilitate proposal evaluation, there are two broad methods of evaluation: qualitative and quantitative. Bid Documents (12.1.3.3) containing closed-ended questions lend themselves to quantitative evaluation of seller responses whereas open-ended questions lend themselves to qualitative evaluation. Thus, closed-ended questions not used in conjunction with open-ended questions will almost certainly require a qualitative evaluation method and will require the use of word descriptors, such as "acceptable" or "unacceptable." This type of qualitative evaluation method is clearly inefficient and highly subjective. However, it may be appropriate for low-cost or non-complex procurements. Using open-ended questions, or a combination of closed-ended and open-ended questions, in Bid Documents (12.1.3.3) facilitates a more efficient and objective quantitative evaluation method. The quantitative evaluation method requires the use of a rating schema, and, preferably, the application of weighting which results in a scoring schema. The quantitative method with a scoring schema best evaluates a seller's capabilities and places an appropriate degree of importance (via the weighting) on the competitive solicitation's requirements. The key for buyers is to not overcomplicate the evaluation process. A spreadsheet in most cases will be sufficient to evaluate responses to the most complex competitive solicitations. The purpose of the seller proposal evaluation matrix is to evaluate, not impress.

Of the quantitative seller proposal evaluation methods described above, there are two primary types. One type is called the rating method, as exemplified in Figure 3-3 (entitled "Rating"). The other type is called a weighting / rating or scoring method, as exemplified in Figure 3-4 (entitled "Weighting / Rating"). The Rating method is simple to develop and use but lacks the specificity as to the importance of a project organization's criteria. The Weighting / Rating method fills this gap by assigning degrees of importance (the weightings) to the criteria. An example of the difference between methods—and where the Rating method can cause improper results—is illustrated by contrasting Figures 3-3 and 3-4. Even though all of the companies, criteria, and ratings are exactly the same in both examples, a seller selection committee member would have selected Company C in the Rating example. This selection is based on the ratings being applied to all criteria with an equal weighting. Under the Weighting / Rating example, because of the change in scores caused by the added weightings that vary by criteria, a seller selection committee member would select Company B. Thus, with these examples, a seller selection committee member using only the Rating method would have incorrectly selected Company C.

Criteria	Ratings		
	Company A	Company B	Company C
Product meets specified requirements	3	4	3
Can meet delivery schedule	2	2	4
Provides on-site training	1	2	1
Provides product warranty	4	3	1
Conformance to our contract terms and conditions	3	3	2
Customer references	2	2	4
Industry reputation	2	2	4
Totals	17	18	19

Legend
1 - Non-responsive or does not meet requirements
2 - Partially meets requirements
3 - Fully meets requirements
4 - Exceeds requirements

Rating

Figure 3-3. Response Evaluation Method – Rating

Criteria	Weighting	Company A		Company B		Company C	
		Rating	Score	Rating	Score	Rating	Score
Product meets specified requirements	30%	3	0.9	4	1.2	3	0.9
Can meet delivery schedule	20%	2	0.4	2	0.4	4	0.8
Provides on-site training	10%	1	0.1	2	0.2	1	0.1
Provides product warranty	10%	4	0.4	3	0.3	1	0.1
Conformance to our contract terms and conditions	20%	3	0.6	3	0.6	2	0.4
Customer references	5%	2	0.1	2	0.1	4	0.2
Industry reputation	5%	2	0.1	2	0.1	4	0.2
Totals	100%		2.6		2.9		2.7

Legend
1 - Non-responsive or does not meet requirements
2 - Partially meets requirements
3 - Fully meets requirements
4 - Exceeds requirements

Weighting / Rating

Figure 3-4. Response Evaluation Method – Weighting / Rating

As a part of Source Selection Criteria, the project manager and buyer must designate the individuals who will assist in evaluating seller responses (the seller selection committee). In advance of receiving any responses to evaluate, the seller selection committee should be familiarized with the Source Selection Criteria and the selected method to evaluate responses. As described further in the Stakeholder Register component of the Project Documents (12.1.1.4), in order to avoid any seller influence, the seller selection committee should be advised that their role necessitates no communication with sellers unless facilitated by the buyer.

A consideration for buyers is whether to put the evaluation criteria and proposal evaluation method, or a summary such as the Source Selection Analysis (12.1.2.4), in the competitive solicitation itself. The upside is that sellers have a better understanding of what is important to the project organization but the downside is that sellers will know where to build up their strengths and downplay their weaknesses (which may affect the ability to accurately evaluate a seller).

12.1.3.6 Make-or-Buy Decisions

This output documents the decisions resulting from the make-or-buy analysis component of the Data Analysis (12.1.2.3), describing which products, services, or results will be procured from sellers and which project needs will be produced by the project team. If the procurement need is a tangible product, such as a capital asset, and the decision has been made to buy, there needs to be an additional analysis conducted to determine whether it makes better business sense for the project organization to lease versus purchase. This analysis is usually done in collaboration with the buyer and the project organization's finance function. This analysis will not likely shape the process of how the procurement is conducted in any significant way, but the result of the lease versus purchase decision is key information that should be communicated to sellers so that they can develop their proposals accordingly. Make-or-Buy Decisions may also document the decisions to buy insurance policies or bond contracts (such as material or performance bonds) necessary to respond to identified risks. The decisions to make-or-buy may be modified as the project progresses and the need arises to procure products, services, or results that were previously designated to be produced by a project team.

12.1.3.7 Independent Cost Estimates

The primary purpose of the Independent Cost Estimates is to analyze and benchmark proposed costs included by sellers as a part of their Seller Proposals (12.2.1.4). Independent Cost Estimates serve as a negotiation benchmark and a project scope "red flag" for buyers. Buyers can use the Independent Cost Estimates to assist in negotiating sellers to pricing that is reasonable for the products, services, or results. If the Seller Proposals (12.2.1.4) include pricing offered that is substantially different—either significantly too high or too low—than the Independent Cost Estimates, it is possible that the Procurement Statement of Work (12.1.3.4) was either improperly scoped or the sellers misinterpreted the requirements. In such a case, a buyer would need to amend the Procurement Statement of Work (12.1.3.4) in the Bid Documents (12.1.3.3) and notify the sellers to adjust their proposals accordingly. A buyer may use historical data from prior procurements, conduct Internet or other research, or use a number of third party price benchmarking services or indices to ensure that the Independent Cost Estimates are reasonably accurate.

12.1.3.8 Change Requests

Change Requests, an output (4.3.3.4) resulting from the *Direct and Manage Project Work* (4.3) process of the Project Integration Management Knowledge Area, are formal requests to change any project document, deliverable, or baseline. Change Requests can be used to prevent possible issues, correct identified issues, or for enhancements and can be requested by any stakeholder. Change Requests can be optional, such as for an enhancement, or they may be required, such as to ensure compliance with a legal or regulatory matter that pertains to the project. During the *Plan Procurement Management* process, changes may be required based on either decisions relating to the products, services, or results to be procured or decisions relating to planning the procurement; for example, changes to the Project Management Plan (12.1.1.3), its subsidiary plans such as the Procurement Management Plan (12.1.3.1), or other components may be necessary. Any such Change Requests are processed through the *Perform Integrated Change Control* (4.6) process of the Project Integration Management Knowledge Area.

12.1.3.9 Project Documents Updates

As a result of the project team's work and obtained knowledge in planning the procurement, certain components of the Project Documents (12.1.1.4)—such as the Milestone List (6.2.3.3); Requirements Documentation (5.2.3.1); Requirements Traceability Matrix (5.2.3.2); Risk Register (11.2.3.1); and,

Stakeholder Register (13.1.3.1)—may require revision and updating. The Project Documents Updates acknowledge these necessary updates as well as any updates to the Lessons Learned Register, an output (4.4.3.1) resulting from the *Manage Project Knowledge* (4.4) process of the Project Integration Management Knowledge Area. The Lessons Learned Register (4.4.3.1) is used to record challenges, problems, realized risks, and missed opportunities along with corresponding impact, recommendations, and proposed actions. If a project is using the agile methodology—which will be most likely leveraged as a part of the *Control Procurements* (12.3) process when the selected seller is providing the contracted products, services, or results—agile retrospectives may occur as often as every sprint and will be a key contributor of lessons learned. In the context of the *Plan Procurement Management* process, lessons learned may include many of the *Plan Procurement Management* process tools & techniques and outputs. However, where the Lessons Learned Register (4.4.3.1) is typically thought of as an output used to benefit future projects, any key lessons learned during the *Plan Procurement Management* process should be immediately implemented since the procurement is only being planned at this point and is not being conducted. For example, if the project team determines that a lesson learned involves the Bid Documents (12.1.3.3), that "lesson" should be used to appropriately modify or correct the Bid Documents (12.1.3.3) before proceeding to the *Conduct Procurements* (12.2) process. In addition to the Lessons Learned Register (4.4.3.1) updates, likely updates include:

- Milestone List (6.2.3.3) – The list of milestones describing various procurement activities, such as the issuance of the Bid Documents (12.1.3.3) or occurrence of the Bidder Conferences (12.2.2.3), as well as milestone expectations of the procurement organization regarding seller delivery or performance.

- Requirements Documentation (5.2.3.1) – The substantive and procedural requirements of the project organization, including technical, non-technical, functional, and non-functional requirements.

- Requirements Traceability Matrix (5.2.3.2) – The linkage (traceability) of project requirements from their origin to the deliverables which will fulfill them and, as a result of the linkage, the assessment of the potential impact of any scope changes or deviations.

- Risk Register (11.2.3.1) – Any risks related to the procurement and prospective sellers resulting from, for example, the contract duration, contract type, or project delivery method selected as a part of the Procurement Strategy (12.1.3.2) and the competitive solicitation type—such as an RFP or RFQ—selected for the Bid Documents (12.1.3.3).

- Stakeholder Register (13.1.3.1) – Any additional information relating to stakeholders, particularly any stakeholders related to governmental, regulatory, or compliance entities or related to contractual or legal matters which may affect the Bid Documents (12.1.3.3) or Agreements (12.2.3.2).

12.1.3.10 Organizational Process Assets Updates

Based on the complexity and type of procurement as well as the likelihood of a similar procurement in the future, there may be a range of updates—from insignificant or few to significant or many—to the Organizational Process Assets (12.1.1.6) such as policies, procedures, processes, practices, standards, guidelines, templates, job aids, knowledge bases, and other resources that are used to facilitate the planning of a competitive solicitation and related procurement activities. Organizational Process Assets Updates may include:

- Forms of the Procurement Management Plan (12.1.3.1) and Procurement Strategy (12.1.3.2)
- Prequalified seller list (see Section 12.1.1.6)
- Competitive solicitation templates used for Bid Documents (12.1.3.3)
- Contract templates and types used for Agreements (12.2.3.2)

4 – Legal Considerations of Procurement

In the next process of the Project Procurement Management Knowledge Area, *Conduct Procurements* (12.2), the buyer will be involved in negotiating with sellers and establishing the business relationship between the project organization and the selected seller. The associated procurement agreement, with its terms and conditions, formulates the legal basis of the business relationship. Should the business relationship and all of its corresponding rights and obligations not be reflected appropriately in the procurement agreement, the likelihood of a subsequent dispute between the contracting parties rises. Unfortunately, buyers sometimes focus more attention on price negotiations than on the negotiation of business terms and conditions or contract terms and conditions. This limited focus on terms and conditions is likely due to many buyers being highly skilled in price negotiations and less skilled in terms and conditions negotiations. Thus, before proceeding to the *Conduct Procurements* (12.2) process, it is appropriate that a project manager have at least a cursory understanding of legal considerations relating to procurement. With this understanding, a project manager should be equipped to assess whether a buyer or the legal resource available to the project team has properly prepared and negotiated the terms and conditions contained in the procurement agreement. To that end, this chapter will describe the basic elements of a procurement agreement and explore some of the more critical procurement agreement terms and conditions.

Overview of Contracts

Before conducting a closer examination of a procurement agreement, it is instructive to first define what a contract is in the commercial context. A broad definition of a contract is an agreement formed by two or more parties who promise to perform or refrain from performing some act now or in the future term of the contract. If the contractual promise is not fulfilled, the promising party may be required (as either stated in the contract or as ordered via the outcome of dispute resolution) to pay money damages for failing to perform the promise or, in some cases, be required to perform the promise. For a contract to be considered valid, certain requirements must be met. At its most basic, a contract must include an agreement between the parties, provide for adequate consideration (usually money), be for a legal purpose, and be between parties who have contractual capacity. Parties to a contract must also demonstrate mutual assent to the contract's terms. To demonstrate this assent, the agreement between the parties must include offer and acceptance, with one party offering to enter into a legal agreement and the other party accepting the terms of the offer. A legally recognized offer and an acceptance create what is called a "meeting of the minds" between the parties. Both offer and acceptance must be explicit in a contract.

Consideration is essentially a "bargained exchange," meaning that the parties must exchange something of value. Consideration must be mutual: Both parties must give something of value and receive something of value. If a buyer contracts with a seller for janitorial services, for example, the project organization receives the cleaning services and the seller receives money. If only one party receives value from an arrangement, the arrangement is generally defined as a gift rather than an enforceable contract. Although the exchange of money is typically included under a contract, consideration does not need to include money. It may consist of some right, interest, profit, or benefit that accrues to one party, or alternatively, of some forbearance, loss, or responsibility that is undertaken or incurred by the other party. The market value of the consideration is, for the most part, irrelevant from a legal perspective. The law is concerned with whether the parties desired and assented to the contractual arrangement, not whether the exchange represented a fair market bargain.

The parties entering into a contract must have the legal capacity to do so and the law must recognize them as possessing characteristics that qualify them as competent parties. A party may be an individual, a group of individuals, or even an "artificial person" such as a corporation. Persons who are deemed incompetent, such as from mental illness, lack capacity to enter into contracts. Minors, which in most jurisdictions in the United States refers to persons under the age of 18, may enter into contracts. However, any contract involving a minor is voidable by the minor at the minor's option. When a contract involving a minor goes unfulfilled, it may be affirmed or disaffirmed when the minor reaches maturity or legally becomes an adult. Parties to a contract also must have the legal right to do what the contract promises; for example, one cannot sell what one does not own or does not have the right to sell.

Finally, in order to be valid, a contract must be for a legal purpose and not be contrary to public policy. As an example, an agreement to purchase marijuana in many jurisdictions in the United States is not a legal contract. Because the subject matter of the agreement is illegal, the contract is not enforceable and the parties have no legal remedies for breach.

Once all of these requirements have been met, a valid contract is formed, generally creating enforceable rights and duties between the contracting parties.

Uniform Commercial Code

Contracts in the commercial procurement context in the United States are governed by state contract law. The Uniform Commercial Code (UCC), first published in 1952, is a uniform act created to harmonize the law of sales and other commercial transactions in the United States. The UCC is a product of the National Conference of Commissioners on Uniform State Law and the American Law Institute. The UCC is not itself a law but only a recommendation of model commercial laws to be adopted by states.

Once enacted in a state by the state's legislature, the UCC or some variation thereof becomes law and is codified into the state's code of statutes. When the UCC is adopted by a state, it may be adopted verbatim as written or it may be adopted with specific changes deemed necessary by the state legislature. In one form or another, the UCC has been enacted in all states[15] and has been adopted in the District of Columbia, the Commonwealth of Puerto Rico, Guam, and the United States Virgin Islands. Broadly speaking, the UCC governs the sale of tangible, movable goods, property leases such as business equipment, and financial transactions such as bank deposits and letters of credit. The UCC is divided into articles, each

---

[15] Louisiana has enacted most provisions of the UCC with the exception of Article 2, preferring to maintain its own civil law tradition for governing the sale of goods. This is an important consideration in that a "product" under Project Procurement Management is a "good" for purposes of the UCC. Thus, a procurement contract for products governed by Louisiana law is *not* governed by Article 2 of the UCC.

containing provisions that relate to a specific area of commercial law, with Article 2 covering the sale of goods.[16] The sale of services and real property are not covered by the UCC.

Common Law

Unlike goods, there is no uniform act for services. Instead, services are governed by common law which is a tradition-based but constantly evolving set of judicially-made laws that derives primarily from past court decisions. The *Restatement of Contracts*, created and published by the American Law Institute, summarizes and "restates" common law principles of contract law. Although the restatement does not have the force of law, it is heavily relied upon by legal professionals and practitioners, including judges who often quote the *Restatement of Contracts* in written opinions.

Goods / Services Hybrid

When a contract involves a mix of goods and services, the majority of jurisdictions employ a "predominant factor" test to determine whether such hybrid contracts are transactions of goods, and therefore covered by the UCC, or are transactions of services, and therefore excluded. Under this test, the court determines whether a contract's predominant factor is the provision of a service with the sale of goods incidentally involved or is the sale of goods with the provision of a service incidentally involved. While no single factor is determinative in finding that a hybrid contract is one for goods or services, courts have looked to the predominant objective of the buyer, contractual language, manner of billing, and mobility of goods at the time of contract. For example, procurement agreements that refer to the transaction as a "purchase agreement" and where the price for goods exceeds the price for services are more likely to be controlled by the UCC.

Statute of Frauds

While it is good business practice to reduce all contracts to writing, a contract does not necessarily have to be in writing to be valid. However, oral contracts are vague and frequently do not provide sufficient proof of what terms and conditions were agreed to by the parties to the oral contract, allowing a party to make fraudulent or false claims and forcing the other party to prove the lie. On the other hand, written contracts, which include signatures by authorized representatives of the contracting parties, create a firm record of the agreement and provide greater assurances and evidence of the actual terms and conditions that were agreed to by the parties when the bargain was struck. To prevent injury from fraudulent conduct relating to oral contracts, England enacted the Statute of Frauds in 1677 and required that certain contracts be in writing in order to be enforceable. The statute was later adopted in one form or another by all states in the United States and includes the requirement that any contract for the sale of goods valued at $500 or more[17] or for services that cannot be performed within one year be in writing.

---

[16] Goods are "products" under Project Procurement Management, but the term "goods" will be used in this section for purposes of discussing the UCC.

[17] The portion of the original English statute that applies to goods is currently embodied in UCC 2-201. The most recent revision of UCC 2-201 requires a writing for the price of $500 or more but the amount is state-specific.

The Statute of Frauds does not itself render a contract void. Instead, the statute makes certain contracts "voidable" by one of the contracting parties in the event that the party does not wish to follow through on the agreement.[18] Sometimes, a party to a contract that would otherwise be invalid under the Statute of Frauds will nonetheless be able to enforce it, on the basis of partial performance or what is known as "promissory estoppel." Where partial performance exists, a party who has accepted partial performance by the other party under the contract will typically be barred from asserting the Statute of Frauds in order to avoid meeting its own contractual obligations. Promissory estoppel exists when significant inequities (such as unfairness) would result from releasing a party from the contract who knew or reasonably should have known that those inequities would be created at the time of the original agreement. For example, where the party seeking release knew that the other party would incur significant expense in obtaining materials which cannot be transferred to other work, a court may find that, under the circumstances, the contract should be enforced despite the Statute of Frauds.

Elements of a Procurement Agreement

In the context of a commercial procurement, the definition of a contract narrows to being a binding procurement agreement between a buyer and a seller where the seller must provide the specified products, services, or results in exchange for valuable consideration. In order for the contracting parties—or a court—to be able to enforce a procurement agreement, it must contain reasonably definite terms and conditions that are either expressed in the contract or are capable of being reasonably inferred from it. Most procurement agreements, whether one page or one-hundred pages, follow the same basic format: Beginning with a preamble, recitals, and words of agreement, continuing with the body of the contract, ending with general terms and conditions, and then concluding with the signatures of the contracting parties. The following paragraphs explain the basic elements of a procurement agreement in further detail.

Preamble

The purpose of a preamble is to identify a contract through a title and to identify the contracting parties. Frequently, a preamble to a contract includes the effective date of the agreement. An example of a preamble for a services agreement between a buyer and a seller follows:

MASTER PROFESSIONAL SERVICES AGREEMENT

This Master Professional Services Agreement (the "Agreement") is entered into, to be effective as of February 21, 2019 ("Effective Date"), by and between CFG Enterprises LLC, a limited liability company formed in the State of Florida, with its principle place of business located at 625 17th Avenue Northeast, St. Petersburg, Florida ("Seller") and Guth Ventures LLC, a limited liability company formed in the Commonwealth of Virginia, with its principle place of business located at 814 Second Street, Alexandria, Virginia ("Buyer").

---

[18] A contract that is "void" cannot be enforced. A contract that is "voidable" remains valid unless one of the contracting parties chooses to void the contract.

Recitals

Recitals are statements immediately following the preamble that are used to describe the background and goals of the contract. They are not a required element of a procurement agreement and do not contain any promises or restrictions. The purpose of recitals is to help others quickly comprehend the genesis and context of the contract. Recitals have no contractual force, unless the contract specifically states that they do, because the recitals come before the words of agreement (see the following paragraph) and therefore are not contractual terms and conditions. The following example of recitals describes a procurement agreement resulting from a competitive solicitation and procurement. The example clearly indicates to those who read the recitals—without having to read the entire contract—that the buyer sought to improve quality at a lower cost and selected the seller for those reasons.

RECITALS

WHEREAS, Buyer desired to replace its incumbent seller for domain name registration services (the "Services," as further described herein) in order to improve quality and lower costs;

WHEREAS, Buyer issued a request for proposal (the "RFP") to certain sellers, including Seller, for the purposes of obtaining the Services;

WHEREAS, Seller responded to the RFP with Seller's proposal (the "Proposal");

WHEREAS, Buyer selected the Proposal to the exclusion of all other sellers on the basis of Seller's claims that it would provide the Services at a high quality and for a mutually-agreeable price;

WHEREAS, Seller has experience and expertise in the business of providing the Services;

WHEREAS, Buyer desires to have Seller provide the Services to Buyer; and,

WHEREAS, Seller desires to supply the Services to Buyer on the terms and conditions contained herein.

Words of Agreement

This element serves to demonstrate genuine assent between the contracting parties and that there was a bargained-for exchange of consideration. Words of agreement typically immediately follow the recitals. Generally, unless otherwise stated in a procurement agreement, anything preceding the words of agreement has no contractual force and everything following does. A simple yet fully sufficient example follows:

NOW THEREFORE, in consideration of the mutual promises and covenants contained herein, and for other good and valuable consideration, Buyer and Seller hereby agree as follows.

Body of the Agreement

The body of a procurement agreement contains the heart of the agreement: the rights, responsibilities, liabilities, and obligations of the parties, the subject matter, time of performance, and payment (which forms the basis for the required consideration). The body of the agreement is sometimes referred to as the "business" terms and conditions so as to differentiate them from the purely legal terms and conditions or boilerplate[19] provisions. Frequently, the body of the agreement will either include or incorporate (by reference) a statement of work to describe the subject matter and time of performance. The statement of work is a complete description of the product, services, or results to be provided. Ideally, the contractual statement of work will mirror the Procurement Statement of Work (12.1.3.4). Examples of content contained in the body of the contract include:

- Description of the products, services, or results to be provided (to include unit quantities, which, in the case of services may describe "hours" for cost reimbursable contracts)
- Shipping information including packing instructions, shipping agent, temporary storage / warehousing, delivery locations, and terms of delivery
- Inspection, quality, and acceptance period and criteria, including the project organization's right of Inspection (12.3.2.4) and Audits (12.3.2.5)
- The Milestone List (6.2.3.3) or a similar list of delivery or performance milestones and an associated schedule (in some cases, the contracting parties elect to mutually develop a schedule after the procurement agreement is executed and the approved schedule is then attached as an exhibit)
- In the case of technology products, license or use information such as designated users and designated devices
- Fee structure, amounts, payment holdbacks, payment terms, and schedule
- Key seller staff
- Warranty, support, and maintenance services
- Risk of loss and transfer of title
- The requirement for the seller to provide Work Performance Information (12.3.3.2) or other performance reporting

---

[19] The term "boilerplate" in the context of a procurement agreement means contract language that can be used from contract to contract with little or no change. Boilerplate provisions are often grouped together in a contract—usually near the end—not because there is any commonality between provisions but because there is no other logical place for the provisions to be placed within the contract. The term dates back to the early 1900s, referring to the thick, tough iron plates used in the construction of steam boilers. At that time and into the 1950s, printing plates of standard text intended for widespread reproduction, such as advertisements or syndicated columns, were cast or stamped in steel sheets and distributed to newspapers around the United States. These printing plates resembled the iron plates used on boilers and, thus, became known as "boilerplates." The term has since been applied to generally mean text or graphics that can be used repetitively.

- Service level agreements, service level objectives, or performance measures with or without liquidated damages for non-performance (see Section 12.2.1.2) or incentives for higher levels of performance
- Dispute resolution process (see Chapter 6 – Dispute Resolution)
- Insurance and any bonding requirements
- Change management process to facilitate change requests and Approved Change Requests (12.3.1.5)
- Termination, termination assistance services, and renewals
- Documents incorporated by reference such as the Bid Documents (12.1.3.3) and the Seller Proposals (12.2.1.4)

Conclusion and Signatures

A procurement agreement typically ends with legal terms and conditions (that is, the boilerplate provisions—some of which are described and reviewed in the following section) and concludes with a statement of the parties' intention to create a legally binding agreement. The example below would be followed by signature blocks for the authorized representative of each party, including the printed name, title, and date of signature:

> IN WITNESS THEREOF, the undersigned representatives of Buyer and Seller, intending for their respective parties to be legally bound, have executed this Agreement to be effective as of the Effective Date.

Contract Terms and Conditions

While one procurement agreement compared to another will vary based on the statement of work contained in the body of the contract, there are standard terms and conditions nearly universal to procurement agreements. As previously described, the standard terms and conditions are typically referred to as boilerplate provisions. Despite being commonplace, boilerplate provisions serve key administrative purposes. Typical boilerplate provisions found in procurement agreements are described below, in alphabetical order based on the typical provision name.

Assignment

If a procurement agreement is silent with regard to assignment, a party may assign its rights under the agreement and, as long as a personal skill is not required, may delegate its contractual obligations under the agreement. In most cases this is not a desirable result for a project organization because the organization went through a structured procurement process and a competitive solicitation to select the seller and likely would not want the seller to unilaterally assign the contract to a different seller without notice to or approval from the project organization. To preclude or control assignments, a buyer can include an assignment provision which either prohibits assignment outright or provides a party with the opportunity to consent to the assignment of the other party's rights or obligations under the contract. In order to fully protect a party, it is important for the assignment provision to permit the termination or voiding of the procurement agreement by the non-assigning party if the other party assigns any obligation or right under the procurement agreement without the reasonable notice or express agreement of the non-assigning party.

Confidentiality

A typical confidentiality provision identifies what constitutes confidential information for purposes of the procurement agreement, describes the non-disclosure obligations of the parties relating to any confidential information, stipulates the duration of the obligation, and identifies exceptions that exempt or exclude what would otherwise be considered confidential information from the obligation. The provision must clearly specify what information constitutes confidential information and how the parties are made aware of the confidential nature; for example, by marking confidential material as "confidential." Typical exceptions to an obligation of confidentiality and non-disclosure are where the recipient of the confidential information: (1) is already in receipt of the information prior to the obligation occurring; (2) received the information from a third party that was not under an obligation of confidentiality and non-disclosure; (3) independently developed the information; (4) was able to obtain the information publicly; or, (5) was required by law to disclose the information. In those cases, the obligation of confidentiality and non-disclosure would no longer apply. The procurement agreement should also clearly specify the remedies available in the event of a breach of the confidentiality provision such as liquidated damages or injunctive relief to force a breaching party to comply with the obligation of confidentiality and non-disclosure.

Entire Agreement

Once the parties to a procurement agreement have fully negotiated the statement of work contained in the agreement as well as all of the other terms and conditions, the parties want to rely on the procurement agreement to represent their agreements and understandings. The purpose of an entire agreement provision is for the contracting parties to acknowledge that the procurement agreement is the culmination and entirety of their agreements and understandings and that any other related discussions, negotiations, or understandings not contemplated in the body of the agreement or in any incorporated attachments (such as exhibits or schedules) are superseded by the procurement agreement. An entire agreement provision will also typically include language indicating that the procurement agreement can only be amended in writing as mutually agreed-to and executed by both parties.

Force Majeure

Force majeure literally means "greater force" and a typical force majeure provision excuses a party from liability or performance if some unforeseen event beyond the reasonable control of a party prevents it from performing its obligations under a procurement agreement. Force majeure provisions commonly include natural catastrophes (called "acts of God"), wars, riots, and strikes as unforeseen events. However, under a procurement agreement, a force majeure provision tends to protect the seller (because of the seller's numerous obligations) more than the project organization (because the project organization usually has very limited obligations with the primary obligation being to pay the seller). Therefore, a buyer should seek to narrow the broad application of force majeure by specifying that the force majeure event does not apply if it was caused by the fault or negligence of the delayed party and that any excuse for delay shall last only as long as the event remains beyond the reasonable control of the delayed party. Even if a claim of force majeure may be appropriate in a specific case, the buyer should also ensure that the provision requires the delayed party to use its best efforts to mitigate the delays caused by the force majeure event. Finally, the provision should require that the delayed party notify the other party promptly when a force majeure event occurs and inform the other party of its plans to resume performance.

Governing Law

This provision specifies the body of law of a particular state or jurisdiction in the United States which governs the rights and responsibilities of parties under a contract. Strategically, a buyer would prefer that the governing law of a procurement agreement be the law of the jurisdiction in which the project organization is domiciled because the cost to litigate a contract dispute in another (distant) jurisdiction is inherently higher and because the other jurisdiction may be potentially hostile to a project organization's claim or defense. Within limits, parties may choose which jurisdiction's law will govern matters related to contract formation, interpretation, and enforceability. A governing law provision includes both the substantive law to apply to the contract as well as the procedural law. For example, one jurisdiction's law could govern a contract and another jurisdiction could serve as the place (forum / venue) where the substantive law is applied. For example, contracting parties could agree that Virginia law applies but that Florida will be the forum state. In this example, the Florida courts would apply Virginia law. Mostly, a court will apply whatever governing law was selected by the contracting parties provided that the governing law does not conflict with the public policy of the forum state. However, if the selected governing law is different than the state(s) of domicile for the parties, a court in the forum state generally requires some sort of nexus between the selected governing law, the forum, and the parties.

Indemnification (General)

When one party agrees to indemnify another party, the indemnifying party is agreeing to provide compensation, either directly or by reimbursement, for any loss or damage chargeable to or sustained by the indemnified party as a result of a stated set of circumstances. Broad indemnification provisions can also include an agreement by the indemnifying party to legally defend the indemnified party against any claim asserted by a third party. A buyer usually seeks a *unilateral* general indemnification provision (where only the seller is the indemnifying party) on the basis that the project organization is the only party likely to have a significant claim asserted against it as a result of the procurement agreement and as a result of the seller's performance. On the other hand, the seller is not likely to have a claim asserted against it as a result of the project organization's performance because, arguably, a project organization's only substantial obligation to the seller under a procurement agreement is payment. Most often, a buyer will include an indemnification provision that lists the circumstances resulting in a claim and where indemnification by the seller is required:

(1) any error, omission, or misconduct of seller or its agents; (2) violations of law; (3) death, bodily injury, or property damage; or, (4) breaches of any representations made by the seller under the procurement agreement.

An indemnification provision usually stipulates that the indemnity does not apply to the extent that the claim resulted from the acts or omissions of the project organization. While an indemnity (both general and for proprietary rights) can serve as a substantial risk mitigation tool for buyers, its usefulness can be eroded by a limitation of liability provision and (lack of) insurance. For example, if a limitation of liability provision (which caps a party's financial obligations for damages) is structured such that the obligation of indemnification (which requires a party to be financially liable to the other party) is substantially limited, a project organization may have no real protection because the seller has a limited dollar amount for which it is responsible. Further, even if an indemnification provision is not substantially limited by the limitation of liability provision, a seller may be "judgment proof" if it has limited or no insurance. In other words, if a seller has no insurance or has no substantial assets by which to draw from to pay for any claims resulting from the seller's obligation of indemnification, the obligation is meaningless. Therefore, limitation of liability and insurance provisions are critical to consider in conjunction with an indemnification provision.

Indemnification (Proprietary Rights)

A proprietary rights indemnification provision has the same function as general indemnification except that the protection is specific to proprietary rights such as software or other intellectual property. For example, if a third party claims that a project organization has infringed its proprietary rights by the seller's licensing of certain software to the project organization, the seller will defend the project organization against the claim as a part of the seller's obligation of indemnification. In addition to the general remedy of indemnification, buyers typically add a variety of remedies to proprietary indemnification provisions due to the special nature of the subject matter of the indemnity. These remedies include the seller acquiring the right to use the intellectual property from the third party so that the project organization can continue using the intellectual property, modifying the intellectual property so that it is no longer infringing, or voiding the license between the project organization and seller with the return to the project organization of any paid license fees.

Insurance and Bonds

As explained under the general indemnification provision above and in the discussion of risk-related contract decisions contained within the Risk Register (see Sections 12.1.1.4 and 12.2.1.2), insurance serves to protect project organizations from sellers who have limited or no assets. If there is a breach of a procurement agreement that requires a project organization to seek damages and then receive a legal judgment against the seller, the seller's lack of assets would make the satisfaction of that judgment difficult. Similarly, bonds can be used to ensure that a project organization is protected if a seller defaults in performance (performance bond) or where a seller misappropriates or misuses materials (materials bond).

Limitation of Liability

Limitation of liability provisions are easy to spot in most procurement agreements because of the capitalized text used to ensure that the provision is conspicuous so as to avoid any argument by a contracting party that the limitation was hidden by embodying it among less critical provisions. Other than an indemnification provision, a limitation of liability provision is perhaps the most important risk-shifting provision in a procurement agreement because it shields (limits) or exposes (does not limit) a party to financial liability for damages that arise under the procurement agreement. Properly drafted, the provision can provide protection against contract breaches, negligence, and misconduct by serving as a valuable tool for allocating risk through the limitation of financial exposure. Quite simply, the limit described in a limitation of liability provision constitutes the maximum financial liability for damages recoverable by one party against the other party.

Limitation of liability provisions are usually comprised of four sections that may be found in different order from contract to contract. The first section is referred to as the "exculpation" from the limitation of liability. When a procurement agreement is breached, the recognized remedy for the non-breaching party is the recovery of damages that result directly from the breach. Consequential damages (also sometimes referred to as special or indirect damages) are those damages that do not directly result from a breach but are a consequence of the breach (such as lost profits). Because consequential damages in many cases are not reasonably foreseeable, parties typically agree that no party will be liable for these types of damages. Thus, the exculpation of any liability for consequential damages. The second section of a limitation of liability provision contains an "exclusion" to the exculpation. Under the exclusion, a party *will* be liable for consequential damages where the party caused the damage through their negligence or misconduct. The third section is the actual limitation of liability, which is the core of the provision. This section of the provision states that a party is liable for direct damages up to the stated limitation. The limitation can be specified quantitatively by specifying an exact dollar amount or be described qualitatively such as "fees paid or payable under the Agreement." The fourth section is called an "exception" to the limitation of liability. An exception means that, for the stated exception, there is no limitation of liability and a party's liability relating to the exception will be *unlimited*. Commonly, a party's obligation of indemnification, damages caused by a party's negligence or misconduct, or a breach of a party's obligation of confidentiality are exceptions to the limitation of liability.

Order of Precedence

When a buyer wants to include the Bid Documents (12.1.3.3) associated with the competitive solicitation and the seller's response as a part of the procurement agreement, a question arises as to which document takes precedence over another. To resolve this question, a buyer uses an order of precedence provision to set forth the rank order of the procurement agreement and any incorporated documents in the event that there are conflicts in the language of the individual documents. If there is no order of precedence provision, the courts will typically only consider the general rule of "specific over general" which may not be the result desired by a project organization.

Payment Terms

This provision defines the terms and conditions for a project organization's payments to the seller. It will describe the type of fee structure (such as fixed price or cost reimbursable), the period of time in which the project organization must remit payment to the seller (such as 30-days from the date of the project organization's receipt of the seller's invoice), invoicing procedures, and how credits are handled.

Representations

Representations are statements of past or present fact, made as of a moment in time to induce a party to act. Representations serve a risk-allocating role in that a party which makes a representation is liable for its failure to meet the standard set forth in the representation. Typical representations are that a party has the power and authority to enter into the procurement agreement, is licensed or qualified to do business, and that it will comply with all laws in the performance of the procurement agreement. More substantive representations, usually asked of a seller by a buyer, include that the seller has the skill and knowledge to perform the procurement agreement, that the project organization is relying on the expertise of the seller, and that the procurement agreement will be performed by the seller in accordance with the highest professional standards applicable to the subject matter of the procurement agreement.

Termination for Cause

Even without an express provision in the procurement agreement, a project organization has the right—assuming notice to the seller and a reasonable opportunity for the seller to cure—to terminate a procurement agreement for a material default in performance or other material breach by the seller. However, to be clear as to a project organization's rights, it is wise to include an express termination for cause provision in the procurement agreement. These types of provisions are commonplace but sellers attempt to soften the potential for a harsh result by including a cure period. This allows a seller, when a breach has been committed, to have a specified period of time to cure the breach. When the breach is cured, the project organization no longer has the right of termination related to that breach. Any termination provision, whether for cause or otherwise, should also include what rights and responsibilities are to continue in the event of termination, such as the requirement to maintain the confidentiality of information communicated between the parties.

Termination for Convenience

If a project organization is faced with some uncertainty associated with a procurement, such as the underlying project being cancelled before completion because of changed circumstances, the buyer will likely seek to include a termination for convenience provision in the procurement agreement. This provision gives a project organization the flexibility to unilaterally terminate the procurement agreement at any time without a reason or cause. For a seller, a project organization's right to terminate for convenience represents a risk that the seller will not earn its anticipated revenue and profit. However, if a procurement agreement does not contain a termination for convenience provision, and the project organization terminates the agreement before the seller's performance is complete, the seller would then be entitled to damages equating to the value of the performance plus any profit that the seller would have earned had the procurement agreement not been terminated. Therefore, not surprisingly, most sellers will object to a termination for convenience provision unless it contains certain qualifications that mitigate the financial risk to the seller, such as an extended notification period before the termination is effected. Sellers sometimes require that a termination for convenience provision include not only reimbursement for costs incurred by the seller up to the date of termination, but "unwinding" costs and some sort of liquidated damages that represent a portion of the lost anticipated profit.

Warranties

A warranty is an ongoing promise that a certain fact (or set of facts) will be true. A warranty can be for a set period of time, such as a date certain, or can be indefinite. If the fact of the warranty becomes untrue during the period of the warranty, there is a breach of contract. A warranty is conclusively presumed to be material and the remedy for breach of warranty is a cure or to be made whole (for example, a refund of monies paid). Usually, under a warranty, one party is responsible for the warranty to another party, although certain warranties can be reciprocal. A warranty can be of two types: express (written in the procurement agreement); or, depending on the nature of the transaction, implied (not written in the contract). Express warranties are affirmative promises about the quality and features of the products, services, or results being provided under the associated contract. An example of an express warranty is where a seller stipulates that it has the right to license software to the project organization and that the software does not infringe on any third party's proprietary rights—thus, a warranty of title and non-infringement. If the seller breaches that warranty, an appropriate remedy for the project organization is indemnification (see the proprietary rights indemnification provision previously described).

Under a commercial sale of goods transaction, the UCC creates the implied warranties of merchantability, fitness for particular purpose, and non-infringement. These implied warranties are included as an operation of law in every contract unless expressly disclaimed. In the context of procurement agreements, the UCC applies only to goods; therefore, implied warranties only apply to products in the context of the Project Procurement Management Knowledge Area. In brief, the UCC implied warranties reverse the "buyer beware" rule and chiefly serve to protect a project organization.

The implied warranty of merchantability requires that goods procured by a project organization from a seller conform to ordinary standards of care and that they are of the same average grade, quality, and value as similar goods sold under similar circumstances. For the warranty to apply, the goods must be something that the seller normally sells and the goods must be used by the project organization for the good's ordinary purpose. The policy behind this implied warranty is that sellers are generally better suited than project organizations to determine whether goods conform to their ordinary purpose. Holding the seller liable for goods that are not fit for the ordinary purpose for which the goods are intended shifts the costs of nonperformance from the buyer to the seller. This motivates the seller to ensure the goods' proper performance before placing the goods on the market. For example, if a buyer procures a copier from an office supply company, there is an implied warranty in the procurement agreement that the copier will perform as a project organization would ordinarily expect. If the copier fails to produce copies in a normal office environment, the seller has breached the warranty of merchantability (provided that the seller did not expressly disclaim the implied warranty of merchantability in the procurement agreement). The policy behind limiting the implied warranty of merchantability to the goods' ordinary use is straightforward: A seller may not have sufficient expertise or control over goods to ensure that the goods will perform properly when used for non-ordinary purposes.

Fitness for particular purpose applies if the seller knows or has reason to know that the buyer will be using goods for a particular purpose; if so, the seller impliedly warrants that the goods being sold are suitable for that particular purpose. The rationale behind this warranty is that a buyer typically relies on a seller's skill and expertise to help the project organization find the specific goods that meet that project organization's specific need: It would be patently unfair for a seller to sell goods that the seller knows will not meet the needs of the project organization and then later tell the organization that it is not the seller's fault that the goods did not work for that organization's particular purpose. If the office supply company in the prior example knows that the project organization will be using the copier in a dusty factory environment and the copier subsequently fails to perform, the seller has breached the implied warranty even if the copier was not meant to be used in a factory environment and even if the copier would have performed satisfactorily in an office environment. Also, unlike the implied warranty of merchantability, the implied warranty of fitness for particular purpose does not contain a requirement that the seller be a merchant with respect to the goods sold.

Under an implied warranty of non-infringement, if the seller regularly deals in the goods sold, the seller must hold the buyer harmless against any rightful claim of infringement by a third party. The reasons for this warranty are basic: to deter sellers from selling goods they do not have a right to sell or to profit from goods that infringe upon some third party's intellectual property rights.

Sellers can disclaim both express and implied warranties or limit their scope. To sufficiently disclaim any warranties, the UCC requires that disclaimers be in writing, be conspicuous, and specifically mention the warranty being disclaimed.

5 – 12.2 Conduct Procurements

In simple terms, *Conduct Procurements* is the process of navigating through a procurement and competitive solicitation, negotiating with one or more sellers, and then entering into a procurement agreement with one or more sellers. While the prior process, *Plan Procurement Management* (12.1), is a critically important precursor to a successful procurement, the *Conduct Procurements* process is a part of the Executing Process Group where the execution of all of the planning occurs. Under the *Conduct Procurements* process, the buyer will: (1) issue the Bid Documents (12.1.3.3) through Advertising (12.2.2.2); (2) receive Seller Proposals (12.2.1.4); (3) facilitate the evaluation of the Seller Proposals (12.2.1.4) using the Source Selection Criteria (12.1.3.5); (4) conduct negotiations through Interpersonal and Team Skills (12.2.2.5); and, (5) award Agreements (12.2.3.2) to Selected Sellers (12.2.3.1). If the project requires multiple different procurements, such as where one seller is unable to provide all of the products, services, or results required by the project organization, the *Conduct Procurements* process may be repeated concurrently or sequentially as necessary.

Tables 5-1, 5-2, and 5-3 describe the inputs, tools & techniques, outputs and who is primarily responsible for a particular activity. For each input, tool or technique, and output, the Project Procurement Management Knowledge Area section reference is listed first and, if applicable, the originating reference is listed second within parentheses.

Table 5-1. Conduct Procurements: Inputs

Inputs	Responsibility
12.2.1.1 Project Management Plan (4.2.3.1)	
– Scope Management Plan (5.1.3.1)	– Project Manager
– Requirements Management Plan (5.1.3.2)	– Project Manager
– Communications Management Plan (10.1.3.1)	– Buyer
– Risk Management Plan (11.1.3.1)	– Project Manager
– Procurement Management Plan (12.1.3.1)	– Buyer
– Configuration Management Plan (4.2.3.1)	– Project Manager
– Cost Baseline (7.3.3.1)	– Project Manager
12.2.1.2 Project Documents	
– Lessons Learned Register (4.4.3.1)	– Project Manager
– Project Schedule (6.5.3.2)	– Project Manager
– Requirements Documentation (5.2.3.1)	– Project Manager
– Risk Register (11.2.3.1)	– Buyer
– Stakeholder Register (13.1.3.1)	– Project Manager

Inputs	Responsibility
12.2.1.3 Procurement Documentation – Bid Documents (12.1.3.3) – Procurement Statement of Work (12.1.3.4) – Independent Cost Estimates (12.1.3.7) – Source Selection Criteria (12.1.3.5)	 – Buyer – Buyer – Buyer – Buyer
12.2.1.4 Seller Proposals	Buyer
12.2.1.5 Enterprise Environmental Factors	Buyer
12.2.1.6 Organizational Process Assets	Buyer

Table 5-2. Conduct Procurements: Tools & Techniques

Tools & Techniques	Responsibility
12.2.2.1 Expert Judgment	Project Team
12.2.2.2 Advertising	Buyer
12.2.2.3 Bidder Conferences	Buyer
12.2.2.4 Data Analysis – Proposal Evaluation	 – Seller Selection Committee
12.2.2.5 Interpersonal and Team Skills – Negotiation	 – Seller Negotiation Committee

Table 5-3. Conduct Procurements: Outputs

Outputs	Responsibility
12.2.3.1 Selected Sellers	Seller Selection Committee
12.2.3.2 Agreements	Buyer
12.2.3.3 Change Requests	Project Manager

Outputs	Responsibility
12.2.3.4 Project Management Plan Updates	
– Requirements Management Plan (5.1.3.2)	– Project Manager
– Quality Management Plan (8.1.3.1)	– Project Manager
– Communications Management Plan (10.1.3.1)	– Project Manager
– Risk Management Plan (11.1.3.1)	– Project Manager
– Procurement Management Plan (12.1.3.1)	– Project Manager
– Scope Baseline (5.4.3.1)	– Project Manager
– Schedule Baseline (6.5.3.1)	– Project Manager
– Cost Baseline (7.3.3.1)	– Project Manager
12.2.3.5 Project Documents Updates	
– Lessons Learned Register (4.4.3.1)	– Project Manager
– Requirements Documentation (5.2.3.1)	– Project Manager
– Requirements Traceability Matrix (5.2.3.2)	– Project Manager
– Resource Calendars (9.2.1.2)	– Project Manager
– Risk Register (11.2.3.1)	– Buyer
– Stakeholder Register (13.1.3.1)	– Project Manager
12.2.3.6 Organizational Process Assets Updates	Buyer

12.2.1 Conduct Procurements: Inputs

12.2.1.1 Project Management Plan

As an input to the *Conduct Procurements* process, the Project Management Plan contains certain integrated and consolidated subsidiary plans as described in and updated during the *Plan Procurements* (12.1) process that are integral to the *Conduct Procurements* process, including the Scope Management Plan (5.1.3.1) and the Procurement Management Plan (12.1.3.1). In preparation for conducting the procurement, the Project Management Plan is now expanded to include the: Requirements Management Plan (5.1.3.2); Communications Management Plan (10.1.3.1); Risk Management Plan (11.1.3.1); Configuration Management Plan (4.2.3.1); and, Cost Baseline (7.3.3.1). The Project Management Plan is utilized by the buyer to ensure that the procurement is proceeding on a timely basis and according to plan.

Scope Management Plan (5.1.3.1)

The Scope Management Plan, an output (5.1.3.1) resulting from the *Plan Scope Management* (5.1) process of the Project Scope Management Knowledge Area, contains a description of how a project's scope will be defined, developed, monitored, controlled, and validated. The Scope Management Plan (5.1.3.1) describes how the scope of work being provided by the selected seller will be managed by the project organization and by the seller through the execution phase of the project.

Requirements Management Plan (5.1.3.2)

The Requirements Management Plan is an output (5.1.3.2) resulting from the *Plan Scope Management* (5.1) process of the Project Scope Management Knowledge Area. Whereas the Requirements Documentation component of the Project Documents (12.2.1.2) describes the substantive and procedural requirements of the project organization—including technical, non-technical, functional, and non-functional requirements—the Requirements Management Plan may include:

- How project requirements will be analyzed, documented, and managed
- How Selected Sellers (12.2.3.1) will manage the requirements to be fulfilled under any Agreements (12.2.3.2)
- The requirements prioritization process
- The traceability structure that reflects the requirement attributes captured on the Requirements Traceability Matrix component of the Project Documents (12.1.1.4)

Communications Management Plan (10.1.3.1)

The Communications Management Plan, an output (10.1.3.1) resulting from the *Plan Communications Management* (10.1) process of the Project Communications Management Knowledge Area, describes why, how, when, and by whom information about the project will be communicated. In addition to how project communications will be planned, structured, implemented, and monitored, the Communications Management Plan describes how communications between the buyer and prospective sellers will be conducted. Depending on the operating environment and maturity of the project organization's procurement function, the Communications Management Plan may also include guidelines, templates, and other Organizational Process Assets (12.2.1.6) related to buyer-seller communication, such as:

- Advertising (12.2.2.2) the Bid Documents (12.1.3.3)
- Requesting and receiving intent to bid responses
- Obtaining and responding to seller questions
- Scheduling and conducting Bidder Conferences (12.2.2.3)
- Coordinating the receipt of Seller Proposals (12.2.1.4)
- Notifying disqualified or non-selected sellers
- Requesting and receiving best and final offers
- Notifying selected and finalist sellers
- Announcing the contract award

Risk Management Plan (11.1.3.1)

The Risk Management Plan, an output (11.1.3.1) resulting from the *Plan Risk Management* (11.1) process of the Project Risk Management Knowledge Area: (1) describes the general approach to managing project risks identified within the Risk Register (11.2.3.1; see also Section 12.1.1.4); (2) establishes how those risks will be categorized through a risk breakdown structure; (3) defines the methodology to perform risk management within the project; (4) describes the roles and responsibilities of project team members in managing risk; and, (5) defines when and how often risk management activities will be performed.

Procurement Management Plan (12.1.3.1)

The Procurement Management Plan (12.1.3.1) serves as a decision roadmap for the impending procurement and as a "toolbox" containing all of the necessary materials and resources to facilitate the competitive procurement process. Now, under the *Conduct Procurements* process, the plan is put into action and the buyer executes to the activities described in the Procurement Management Plan.

Configuration Management Plan (4.2.3.1)

The Configuration Management Plan, an output (4.2.3.1) resulting from the *Develop Project Management Plan* (4.2) process of the Project Integration Management Knowledge Area, identifies those project artifacts or deliverables that are configurable, which of those require formal change control, and how to record and report changes to them. In the context of the Project Procurement Management Knowledge Area, a Configuration Management Plan may contain a framework, format, or process by which a seller is required to perform configuration management on any assigned project artifacts as well as the products, services, or results. Any such seller requirements regarding configuration management should be included in the Bid Documents (12.1.3.3) to facilitate the development of Seller Proposals (12.2.1.4) and included in the Source Selection Criteria (12.1.3.5) to assist in proposal evaluations conducted through Data Analysis (12.2.2.4). Agreements (12.2.3.2) should include required configuration management frameworks, formats, or processes.

Cost Baseline (7.3.3.1)

The Cost Baseline, an output (7.3.3.1) resulting from the *Determine Budget* (7.3) process of the Project Cost Management Knowledge Area, includes the project organization's budget for the costs of conducting the procurement process, the cost of the required products, services, or results, and the costs associated with the ongoing management of the selected seller.

12.2.1.2 Project Documents

Project Documents included as inputs for the *Conduct Procurements* process are comprised of documents updated as a part of the *Plan Procurement Management* (12.1) process such as the: Lessons Learned Register (4.4.3.1); Requirements Documentation (5.2.3.1); Risk Register (11.2.3.1); and, Stakeholder Register (13.1.3.1). The Project Schedule, an output (6.5.3.2) resulting from the *Develop Schedule* (6.5) process of the Project Schedule Management Knowledge Area, is an added component to the Project Documents under the *Conduct Procurements* process. The Project Schedule (6.5.3.2) holistically incorporates timetables, schedules, and milestones from various other Project Procurement Management Knowledge Area process inputs and outputs.

Lessons Learned Register (4.4.3.1)

The Lessons Learned Register should be reviewed by the buyer to determine whether any of the prior lessons learned can be applied to improve how the impending procurement is conducted. Many of the lessons learned as a part of the *Plan Procurement Management* (12.1) process—such as through Data Gathering (12.1.2.2), Data Analysis (12.1.2.3), and Meetings (12.1.2.5)—should have already been realized and reflected in the critical inputs to the *Conduct Procurements* process; specifically, the Project Management Plan (12.2.1.1), these Project Documents, and the Procurement Documentation (12.2.1.3). There may, however, be lessons learned that remain and which may improve certain activities of the *Conduct Procurements* process, such as a more effective or efficient means of Advertising (12.2.2.2) the Bid Documents (12.1.3.3), conducting the Bidder Conferences (12.2.2.3), or conducting negotiations as a part of Interpersonal and Team Skills (12.2.2.5).

Project Schedule (6.5.3.2)

The Project Schedule, an output (6.5.3.2) resulting from the *Develop Schedule* (6.5) process of the Project Schedule Management Knowledge Area, contains the dates related to the project activities, procurement phases and activities, and the project organization's desired delivery or performance of the required products, services, or results, including the:

- Procurement phases described in the Procurement Strategy (12.1.3.2)
- Calendar of events contained in the Bid Documents (12.1.3.3)
- Procurement activities and timetable contained in the Procurement Management Plan component of the Project Management Plan (12.2.1.1)
- Milestone List component of these Project Documents
- Schedule contained in the Agreements (12.2.3.2) by which the selected seller must provide the required products, services, or results

Requirements Documentation (5.2.3.1)

Requirements Documentation, updated under Project Documents Updates (12.1.3.9), contains the substantive and procedural requirements of the project organization, including technical, non-technical, functional, and non-functional requirements. The substantive and procedural requirements of the Requirements Documentation which relate to the products, services, or results that the project organization is seeking to procure are communicated to prospective sellers via the Procurement Statement of Work (12.1.3.4) as contained in the Bid Documents (12.1.3.3). Those requirements are then negotiated as a part of Interpersonal and Team Skills (12.2.2.5) with prospective sellers and are ultimately incorporated as seller responsibilities and obligations in the associated procurement agreement when awarded (see Section 12.2.3.2).

Stakeholder Register (13.1.3.1)

Key stakeholders for the *Conduct Procurements* process include the seller selection committee, seller negotiation committee, the contract manager, legal counsel, and those who may assist with:

- Advertising (12.2.2.2) the Bid Documents (12.1.3.3)
- Participating in Bidder Conferences (12.2.2.3)
- Evaluating Seller Proposals (12.2.1.4) through Data Analysis (12.2.2.4) using the Source Selection Criteria (12.1.3.5)
- Conducting negotiations will prospective sellers through Interpersonal and Team Skills (12.2.2.5)
- Awarding Agreements (12.2.3.2) to Selected Sellers (12.2.3.1)

Risk Register (11.2.3.1)

As further described in Sections 12.1.1.4 and 12.1.3.9, the Risk Register contains possible risks, their likelihood and impact, and measures to prevent or mitigate risks. In addition to the risks described in Section 12.1.1.4, the type, likelihood, and impact of seller-related risks can vary widely from seller to seller, depending on many factors such as the:

- Seller's organization
- Products, services, or results being procured
- Contract type
- Amount of spend
- Project delivery method

As a project progresses through the Project Procurement Management Knowledge Area processes, the buyer identifies and develops risk response strategies that are contract-specific. A brief review of common risk prevention and mitigation strategies—contract type, performance and materials bonds, escrow, milestone-based payments and payment holdbacks, insurance, service levels, and termination assistance services—used by buyers to respond to contract-specific risks are described in the following paragraphs.

Contract Type

As further described in Section 12.1.1.6, the most basic method to address contract-specific risk is to match the contract type to the project needs requiring procurement. For example, a buyer can select a firm fixed price contract type to ensure predictability of seller fees and therefore limit cost risks (protection that a time and material contract type, for example, would not provide). For a more complete discussion of contract types and a correlation of contracts to project-specific conditions, see Section 12.1.1.6.

Performance and Materials Bonds

A performance bond is a surety bond issued by an insurance company or a bank to guarantee satisfactory completion of a project by a seller. In the event of default or complete breach of a contract by a seller, the surety may complete the contract or pay damages up to the bond limit. Thus, even if a seller is unwilling or unable to perform the procurement agreement, the project organization is "made whole." Similar to a performance bond, a materials bond is intended to ensure that the seller obtain and provide all of the necessary materials for the satisfactory completion of the project. A materials bond is particularly useful when the project organization has advanced funds to the seller for the purpose of the seller's ordering of materials with lengthy lead-times.

Escrow

Escrow is a legal arrangement where a neutral third party (the "escrow agent") holds an asset and then releases that asset to the designated recipient upon the occurrence of an event or fulfillment of certain conditions as established in a written contract. Therefore, if there is a risk that a seller could become unable to continue its business operations, an escrow arrangement would serve to limit the adverse impact to the project organization resulting from the business interruption. Escrow is most often associated with real estate transactions and software licensing. In the case of software, a licensor places a then-current, unencrypted copy of the software with an escrow agent who only releases the software to the licensee based upon a predetermined event (usually associated with the licensor's unwillingness or inability to provide support for the software).

Milestone-based Payments and Payment Holdbacks

The risk of a seller receiving its price and then subsequently performing shoddily or not at all can be mitigated through the use of a milestone-based payment structure. Rather than withholding payment until the contract has been performed (under a fixed price contract) or paying a time and material rate for work performed, a buyer can create a payment structure so that payments are only due when certain milestones have been achieved by the seller. This is a mutually beneficial risk mitigation strategy in that the structure matches payments to progress, with a seller receiving payment in alignment with the project organization receiving value. Milestone-based payments are well suited for procurement agreements that include a seller's delivery or performance under the agile methodology.

Assuming that the procurement agreement is structured such that payments will be made on a periodic basis (for example, milestone-based), a buyer can further mitigate risk by specifying that a percentage of the periodic payment due to the seller be retained by the project organization as a "holdback." The retained amount or holdback is then paid when the next milestone is achieved or until the procurement agreement has been fully and sufficiently performed. Payment holdbacks are very common in the construction industry and in large software development projects.

Insurance

In all cases, a buyer should require that a seller obtain insurance in amounts sufficient to cover the obligations and liabilities incurred by the seller under the contract. Should there be some sort of breach of contract, damage, or liability caused by the seller and the seller has no insurance or insufficient insurance, the project organization may find itself financially liable. Further, where a seller has no assets or few assets, the project organization may be unable to collect damages.[20]

To ensure that a seller has the correct types and amounts of coverage, buyers frequently request— on an annual basis for the duration of a contract—a "certificate of insurance" or "COI" from the seller. A COI is generally issued by or on behalf of the insurance carrier. A COI does not confer any actual rights upon the certificate holder that have not already been provided in the actual insurance policy. A COI merely provides evidence that certain insurance policies are in place on the date the COI is issued, and that those policies have the limits and policy periods as shown on the COI.

As further described in the following paragraphs, there are certain seller-provided coverages commonly requested by buyers and specified in procurement agreements: (1) commercial liability insurance and excess liability insurance; (2) workers' compensation and employers' liability; (3) professional liability; and, (4) more recently, cyber and privacy liability. Figure 5-1 describes typical coverage amounts and approximate costs for seller-provided insurance.

Commercial general liability insurance (also referred to as "CGL" insurance) covers claims made against the project organization as a result of the contract performance by the seller and will pay for the defense the seller has an obligation to provide to the project organization under the seller's duty of indemnification. CGL insurance coverage provides protection against bodily injury and property damage claims arising from the operations of the seller and applies to its contractual liability (which covers torts). A CGL insurance policy normally limits all loss payments to two aggregate limits, one for products and services and completed operations, and one for all other losses. **Excess liability** insurance provides additional protection when the seller exceeds insurance limits on underlying insurance policies. Generally, excess liability insurance is more affordable coverage than having higher insurance policy limits. However, excess liability insurance does not extend coverage on a professional liability insurance policy. Excess liability insurance is sometimes referred to as "umbrella insurance," but there is a difference between the two: Excess liability goes into effect only when the underlying policies are totally exhausted, while umbrella insurance covers claims in excess of limits and can also fill coverage gaps in underlying policies. Therefore, an umbrella policy can become the primary policy for certain claims.

Workers' compensation insurance is necessary (and state mandated) if the seller has a certain number of employees. **Employers' liability** insurance, which is not mandatory, is a practical necessity. Workers' compensation insurance protects employees by paying an employee's medical bills for work-related injuries and illnesses and employers' liability insurance protects the employer by paying the employer if the injured or sickened employee sues the employer. The two forms of insurance are usually included in the same policy.

---

[20] Sellers with no insurance or assets are referred to as "judgment proof," meaning that the project organization may obtain a judgment against the seller but will likely never be able to collect on the judgment.

Professional liability insurance provides coverage for actual or alleged errors, omissions, negligence, breach of duty, misleading statements, and similar claims resulting from the performance—or non-performance—of certain services. Most policies cover both the defense costs (such as attorneys' fees and court costs) and settlements or judgments. Intentional wrongdoing is typically not covered. Professional liability insurance is required by law in some areas for certain kinds of professional practices (especially medical and legal) but is also frequently required by a project organization when the organization is a beneficiary of the advice or service provided by the seller. While traditionally for professionals such as physicians and attorneys, professional liability insurance can be specifically procured for technology-related services. This type of professional liability insurance is referred to as "technology errors and omissions insurance" or "technology professional liability insurance."

Cyber and privacy liability insurance provides coverage for a project organization that procures technology products or services which may expose the organization's confidential information to unauthorized access or use. As project organizations seek to take advantage of third party provided technologies, such as software as a service, their confidential information is subject to the increased risk of unauthorized access and disclosure—and is subject to privacy laws and regulations.

To protect the interests of project organizations and to ensure compliance with privacy laws and regulations, procurement agreements between sellers of technology products or services and project organizations more frequently impose a duty of care on the seller to safeguard a project organization's confidential information. The duty of a seller generally includes an obligation of the seller to not disclose any confidential information, to use the seller's best efforts to identify and prevent the unauthorized access or disclosure of the confidential information, and to advise the project organization if the seller believes or knows that there has been unauthorized access or disclosure of the confidential information.

Cyber and privacy liability insurance (sometimes also referred to as "network liability" insurance) covers a seller's liability if the project organization's confidential information is accessed or used in a manner not permitted by the procurement agreement—such as a data breach. This insurance covers a variety of expenses associated with data breaches, including costs associated with notifying impacted individuals, legal defense, fines and penalties, credit monitoring, and loss resulting from identity theft of the impacted individuals. In addition, the insurance commonly covers liability arising from business interruption and denial of access, data loss or destruction, computer fraud, and cyber extortion.

	Minimum Coverage Amount	Type of Coverage	When Required	Estimated Annual Cost
Commercial General Liability (and Excess Liability)	$1,000,000 per occurrence, $2,000,000 in aggregate	Property damage, injury, death	Should always be required	Approx. $500
Workers' Compensation and Employers' Liability	Statutory limits; $500,000 per accident	Employee claims	Seller employee count meets state statutory requirement for coverage	Varies based on payroll
Professional Liability	$1,000,000 per occurrence, in aggregate	Errors and omissions	Recommended when intellectual property is provided by seller	Approx. $2,000
Cyber and Privacy Liability	$1,000,000 per occurrence, in aggregate	Technology-related claims	Seller has access to project organization's data	Varies; basic coverage approx. $10,000

Figure 5-1. Seller-Provided Insurance Coverage Examples

Service Levels

A service level is a measurable, reportable standard of service performance that: (1) quantitatively defines the performance expectation of the project organization and the corresponding performance target of the seller; (2) sets the minimum threshold of acceptable service performance; (3) describes exceptions to the performance target (which excuse non-performance); and, (4) describes remedies for non-performance such as liquidated damages (sometimes called service or performance credits). Service levels are also sometimes referred to as performance measures, performance metrics, service standards, or key performance indicators. Service levels most often address the availability, quality, or speed of a service that a seller provides. With some thought, service levels can be developed for any type of service that a seller can provide, from services provided by a seller's staff to services provided by a seller's system.

A service level can take the form of a service level "objective" or a service level "agreement," with the difference being that a service level objective is merely an objective whereas a service level agreement typically includes the payment of liquidated damages (commonly but mistakenly referred to as "penalties") by the seller to the project organization for not achieving service levels. Less frequently, a service level includes the payment of rewards (as an incentive) by a project organization when the seller exceeds service levels.

Service levels are commonly used in procurement agreements to set performance expectations for a seller and to avoid interpretive differences of performance by providing clear standards and measurements. While some service levels can be complex due to the nature of the services being provided by a seller, the concept of service levels are simple: If a seller does not perform to the standard of service paid for by the project organization, the project organization should only be responsible to pay for the level of performance actually received. Stated differently, if the seller does not perform, then the project organization receives the "value of the difference" (as liquidated damages) between the level of service paid for and the level of service actually received. That "value of the difference" is not intended to punish the seller; rather, it is to ensure that the project organization does not pay for what it did not receive.

For example, if a project organization pays a seller $1,000 every month to provide a software subscription service that will be available to the project organization ninety-five percent of the time and the seller is only able to make the service available eighty percent of the time, the project organization should receive a service credit from the seller that represents the lost value of the fifteen percent unavailability. In the procurement agreement with the seller, the service level will clearly and quantitatively define the parameters of when the service is to be provided, how the seller's performance will be calculated, and, if the seller does not achieve the required level of performance, how the liquidated damages will be calculated. As described in the following list, an effective service level will be specific, measurable, accountable, reportable, and time-bound:

- **Specific** – The most critical attribute of a service level is its degree of specificity. A service level must be clear yet concise and remove as much interpretation as possible. Defined terms should be used and used consistently. Explanations or examples are critical. Each component of a service level should stand on its own and not be combined with other components.
- **Measurable** – A service level might be well drafted, but if the data associated with that service level cannot be captured and then measured, the service level is worthless. It is critical that a seller have the ability to capture the data necessary to measure the service level. If so, the seller and the project organization must then have the ability to accurately measure performance, optimally through the use of a quantitative, mathematical formula using the captured data.
- **Accountable** – Accountability is best established through liquidated damages. A service level should have some element of liquidated damages such that the project organization receives a credit representing the cost or lost value resulting from a seller's subpar performance.
- **Reportable** – This attribute is linked to the Measurable attribute in that any data which measures the service level must be reported by the seller and reported in such a way that the project organization can understand the data. Ideally, the project organization should specify

how a service level is reported and the frequency of the reporting. In some cases, a project organization needs to provide some or all of the data necessary for a seller to create a service level report, but the seller should be ultimately responsible for creating or, at the very least, validating the report.

- **Time-Bound** – A service level must specify some duration of time in order for the service level to be monitored and measured. The period of measurement should have some relevance to the service being provided. For example, if a seller is being measured on timeliness of submitting deliverables over a three-year contract, a monthly measurement period is likely more relevant to delivery or performance versus an annual measurement period.

In addition to the foregoing attributes and as explained further in the following list, a well-drafted service level is best described through the components of definitions, service level standard, calculation, service credit, and example calculation:

- **Definitions** – This component defines the key terms of the service level. Definitions provide clarity, allow a term to be used multiple times without redefinition, and provide consistency of use and understanding.
- **Service Level Standard** – The service level standard states a clear, measurable expectation of service and is quantitative (rather than qualitative).
- **Calculation** – This component includes a formula that the seller and project organization can use to determine the actual performance of the service level as compared to the service level standard. The seller uses the calculation to measure and report performance and the project organization uses the calculation to verify what the seller reports is accurate. So that the calculation is clear to both the seller and the project organization, the formula must be mathematical in nature, use defined terms, and be unambiguous.
- **Service Credit** – This component describes when a service credit (in the form of liquidated damages) is due and the amount of the service credit. A service credit can take a variety of forms; for example, it may be one fixed amount, multiple fixed amounts, or a variable amount.
- **Example Calculation** – The inclusion of an example calculation does two things: (1) an example illustrates how the service level and its attributes or components work in totality; and, (2) perhaps most important, the example calculation helps the drafter of the service level to determine if the service level actually functions correctly. It is not uncommon for the drafter of a service level to uncover flaws or mistakes in the service level by testing it through one or more examples. An example calculation should use detailed assumptions and use a step-by-step approach to describe the assumptions, the calculation, and how and if a service credit is determined.

The following "Availability Service Level" is an example taken from a software as a service agreement which includes the foregoing attributes and components.

Availability Service Level.

1) Definitions.

   (a) "Actual Uptime" shall mean the total minutes in the reporting month that the Services were actually available to Authorized Users for normal use.

   (b) "Maintenance Window" shall mean the total minutes in the reporting month represented by the following day(s) and time(s) during which Service Provider shall maintain the Services: [Day(s) and Time(s)].

   (c) "Scheduled Downtime" shall mean the total minutes in the reporting month represented by the Maintenance Window.

   (d) "Scheduled Uptime" shall mean the total minutes in the reporting month less the total minutes represented by the Scheduled Downtime.

2) Service Level Standard. Services will be available to Authorized Users for normal use 100% of the Scheduled Uptime.

3) Calculation. (Actual Uptime / Scheduled Uptime) * 100 = Percentage Uptime (as calculated by rounding to the second decimal point).

4) Performance Credit.

   (a) Where Percentage Uptime is greater than 99.98%, no Performance Credit will be due to Subscriber.

   (b) Where Percentage Uptime is equal to or less than 99.98%, Subscriber shall be due a Performance Credit in the amount of 10% of the Services Fees (as calculated on a monthly basis for the reporting month) for each full 1% reduction in Percentage Uptime.

5) Example Calculation.

   (a) Assuming reporting month is February 2012 (41,760 minutes).

   (b) Assuming a Maintenance Window of Sundays from Midnight to 4:00 a.m. Eastern Standard Time (equals Scheduled Downtime of 960 minutes).

   (c) Scheduled Uptime equals 40,800 minutes (total minutes of 41,760 in February 2012 less 960 minutes of Scheduled Downtime).

   (d) Assuming Actual Uptime of 40,000 minutes. A Percentage Uptime is calculated as follows: (40,000 / 40,800) *100 = 98.04%.

   (e) The threshold of 99.98% less the Percentage Uptime of 98.04% = 1.94%.

   (f) The difference is greater than a 1% reduction but is less than a 2% reduction; therefore, Subscriber is due 10% of the Services Fees as a Performance Credit.

While the prior example includes liquidated damages in the form of a performance credit, such damages for missed service levels sometimes have a limited beneficial effect for a project organization. The liquidated damages may even have a negative effect on a project organization in terms of seller pricing: Even where sellers are generally capable of achieving a service level, sellers commonly increase prices to mitigate any possible liquidated damages. An alternative model that can drive the desired effect of seller accountability without any corresponding increase in price are service levels with seller-oriented escalations instead of liquidated damages. Escalation paths, unlike liquidated damages as a mere financial transaction, tend to ensure visibility of seller non-performance to increasing levels of buyer and seller management. Under this model, each management level of a seller must answer to the next level of the seller's management where the seller did not achieve a service level. The effects on a seller's human and organizational behavior with this type of service level model can have a significant and far-reaching impact, with resulting tangible benefits for the buyer.

The escalation model also forces "partnership-in-practice" behavior. As much as buyers hope to believe that sellers are their business partners, a seller is, and will always be, a seller. Service levels with liquidated damages tend to be contractually oriented buyer-seller procurement relationships, where the impact of an unachieved service level is in the form of a clinical financial transaction. As a result, the liquidated damages model does little to bring a buyer and seller closer together in terms of the business relationship. On the other hand, service levels with organizational peer-to-peer escalations tend to drive deeper relationships, with the seller being more inclined to understand the adverse business implications to the buyer of unachieved service levels. The primary objective of the service level with escalations model is to ensure the seller understands that its relationship with the buyer centers on achieving required service levels. The construct of this model should focus on and encompass:

- Detailed peer-to-peer escalation procedures, to include escalation "triggers" and timeframes for escalation to the next level when resolution is not achieved
- A predetermined set of actions to occur when performance measurement points are below minimum service level targets (the escalation trigger)
- Clear identification of escalation levels (peers, by name and title), responsibilities, and accountability
- The methodology for a joint problem resolution process
- Post-mortem procedures defined for root cause analyses
- Goals for long-term improvement, focused both on process and relationship
- Acting on the intent of the contract, rather than solely on the written content
- An operating principle of fairness, not exploitation of any contract inefficiencies

Termination Assistance Services

Many sellers benefit when their business relationship with a project organization becomes such that the seller is entrenched within the project organization's business. The degree of entrenchment is commonly referred to by buyers and sellers as "stickiness." While some "stickiness" is desired in that both parties should have some reasonable degree of commitment to each other, there is the risk that deep or broad entrenchment will inhibit a buyer's ability to transition to successor sellers if necessary (for example, a seller may become complacent if it is deeply entrenched in the project organization's business operations). If a buyer perceives that the prospective business relationship will have a tendency toward entrenchment, the buyer can mitigate that risk by including contractual language requiring the seller to provide termination assistance services. These services work to make the transition from an incumbent seller to a successor seller more orderly and, more importantly, without business disruption. Termination assistance services typically include an incumbent seller performing the following activities:

- Developing a plan for the orderly transition of the terminated or expired contract to the successor seller
- Providing reasonable training to project organization staff and / or the successor seller
- If any licenses exist, granting the project organization the right to continue using certain seller resources until the transition to the successor seller is complete
- Using commercially reasonable efforts to assist the project organization (at the organization's cost and expense) in obtaining any necessary rights to legally and physically access and use any third party technologies or services used by the incumbent seller

The mere existence of termination assistance services language in a procurement agreement mitigates performance risk in that the seller is aware that the leverage resulting from an entrenched relationship (which benefits the seller) is diluted. Thus, a seller has an incentive to perform under the procurement agreement and is keenly aware that the project organization has the ability to terminate the agreement and move unhindered to a successor seller should the incumbent seller not satisfactorily meet its contracted obligations.

12.2.1.3 Procurement Documentation

Procurement Documentation is essentially a package of various procurement-related documents that serves multiple different purposes, including providing the: (1) prospective sellers, through Advertising (12.2.2.2), with the information necessary via the Procurement Statement of Work (12.1.3.4) and Bid Documents (12.1.3.3) to develop their proposals; (2) project organization's seller selection committee with Independent Cost Estimates (12.1.3.7) and Source Selection Criteria (12.1.3.5) to appropriately and effectively evaluate Seller Proposals (12.2.1.4); and, (3) materials and basis for the development and negotiation of the Agreements (12.2.3.2) with Selected Sellers (12.2.3.1).

The Bid Documents (12.1.3.3) are the vehicle by which the project needs, in the form of a competitive solicitation, are communicated to prospective sellers. The Procurement Statement of Work (12.1.3.4) is integral to the Bid Documents (12.1.3.3) in that it describes the project need and required products, services, or results. Additionally, once a seller is selected by the project organization, the Procurement Statement of Work (12.1.3.4) serves an important purpose in that it—or some portion thereof—becomes a part of any Agreements (12.3.1.3) between the project organization and the selected seller.

12.2.1.4 Seller Proposals

Seller Proposals are those proposals prepared by sellers in response to the Bid Documents (12.1.3.3) issued by the buyer through Advertising (12.2.2.2). Once received, the seller selection committee will apply the Source Selection Criteria (12.1.3.5) to the Seller Proposals using proposal evaluation techniques as a part of Data Analysis (12.2.2.4). However, prior to a seller selection committee receiving the Seller Proposals for its evaluation, it is a common procurement practice for the buyer to first review the responsiveness and qualification of sellers to provide the required products, services, or results. By doing so, the buyer facilitates the project organization's identification of potential financial, operational, and reputational risks and the project organization's decision to: (1) eliminate those risks by not selecting the seller; (2) seek to mitigate those risks during procurement negotiations with a seller conducted as a part of Interpersonal and Team Skills (12.2.2.5); or, (3) seek to transfer those risks via Agreements (12.2.3.2) with the selected seller.

The initial evaluation by a buyer should first determine whether a seller's proposal is responsive or non-responsive. A proposal may be deemed non-responsive if mandatory requirements are not met, any of the required information is not provided, or the submitted price is found to be out of range of the criteria stated in the Bid Documents (12.1.3.3). If any proposal is found to be non-responsive during the initial evaluation, the corresponding seller should be eliminated from further consideration. The basis for elimination should be documented and used when providing feedback to the eliminated sellers. If found to be responsive, the buyer then proceeds to evaluate the qualification of the seller.

For purposes of determining the qualification of a seller, the review should assess whether a seller has the integrity and reliability that will assure good faith performance and that the seller is financially sound. This review, which determines the *eligibility* of a seller to be awarded a contract, is separate and distinct from assessing the operational capability of a seller, which occurs during and as a part of the proposal evaluation (see Section 12.2.2.4). To aid in the qualification review, a buyer may include requests for information in the Bid Documents (12.1.3.3) that inform and facilitate the review; for example:

- Financial statements
- Current or past civil or criminal judgments, sanctions, fines, or violations
- Revocation, suspension, disbarment, or sanction related to any business, professional permits, or licenses
- Investigations, indictments, or convictions

- Conflicts of interest
- Termination of prior contracts due to performance

Where a review of the information reveals civil or criminal issues, a conflict of interest, or inadequate prior performance, the buyer may elect to conduct an additional review to determine whether the seller has taken appropriate corrective action or the circumstances were beyond the seller's control. In determining financial soundness, the buyer will examine the financial information provided by a seller and, if needed, independently obtain information to validate that the seller has the solvency, liquidity, profitability, and financial capacity necessary to deliver or perform under the procurement agreement.

Along with information provided by a seller, a buyer can independently use various Internet-based resources to assist in the qualification review. These resources can be fee-based or free. In the United States, there are numerous databases at the federal and state level that provide information relating to a seller as a business entity and its finances (particularly if the seller is publicly traded). The information is even more detailed—including contract and seller performance information—if the seller has contracted with federal or state agencies. Upon the buyer's review of all of the seller-provided or self-obtained information, the buyer determines whether a seller is qualified and, if not, can then elect to disqualify the seller from the competitive procurement process. The seller selection committee would then evaluate the proposals of remaining responsive and qualified sellers using Data Analysis (see Section 12.2.2.4).

12.2.1.5 Enterprise Environmental Factors

Under the *Plan Procurement Management* (12.1) process, the Enterprise Environmental Factors that were beyond the full control of the project team could nevertheless be more easily controlled through mitigation or avoidance because the inputs, tools & techniques, and outputs were associated with a Planning Process Group; meaning that the project team was conducting procurement planning activities that were primarily internal to the project organization. Now, under the *Conduct Procurements* process, certain inputs, tools & techniques and outputs—such as the Bid Documents (12.1.3.3), Seller Proposals (12.2.1.4), and Bidder Conferences (12.2.2.3)—can originate externally, terminate externally, or involve external parties. Consequently, *Conduct Procurements* process activities are at a greater risk of being constrained or negatively influenced by Enterprise Environmental Factors. Factors that merit a buyer's consideration, some of which are continued from Enterprise Environmental Factors (12.1.1.5) under the *Plan Procurement Management* (12.1) process, include:

- Current economic conditions
- Marketplace conditions that affect the price, availability, or lead-times for the required products, services, or results
- Legal or regulatory requirements impacting the procurement, such as the requirement to use local sellers or a certain type or category of sellers
- Inability to source qualified sellers

- Bid Documents (12.1.3.3) or a Procurement Statement of Work (12.1.3.4) that do not accurately describe the procurement need
- Non-responsive or unqualified sellers
- Seller Proposals (12.2.1.4) that do not adequately fulfill the procurement needs
- Seller pricing that is inconsistent with Independent Cost Estimates (12.1.3.7)
- Seller selection or seller negotiation committee member lack of expertise
- Project organization attributes, such as size, financial strength, potential revenue to sellers resulting from the procurement, which impact negotiation leverage for both business and contract terms and conditions
- Geographic factors including local, national, or international constraints and requirements
- Strengths and weaknesses of the procurement function within the project organization
- Current or prior agreements in place with incumbent sellers which may impact the ability to procure the required products, services, or results
- Systems used by the project organization such as solicitation management, document management, and contract management

12.2.1.6 Organizational Process Assets

While the Organizational Process Assets Updates (12.1.3.10) from the *Plan Procurement Management* (12.1) process—Project Documents (12.2.1.2) and Procurement Documentation (12.2.1.3)—contain important Organizational Process Assets such as the prequalified seller list, competitive solicitation template used for Bid Documents (12.1.3.3), and contract template used for the Agreements (12.2.3.2), the buyer should consider any additional assets to the extent that they facilitate conducting the procurement.

Past experiences with prospective sellers are Organizational Process Assets that also shape how a competitive procurement will be conducted. For example, the lessons learned from a prior procurement may indicate that including detailed seller demonstrations or a proof-of-concept would be a prudent approach for the current procurement and should be a part of the Source Selection Criteria (12.1.3.5) contained in the Procurement Documentation (12.2.1.3).

Prior agreements—meaning an existing procurement agreement between the project organization and a seller—are an element of Organizational Process Assets that can influence the *Conduct Procurements* process. If a project organization has a prior agreement with a seller that is capable of providing the required products, services, or results, the project organization may elect to forgo a competitive solicitation and amend the procurement agreement or enter into a new procurement agreement with that seller. If the project organization so elects, the competitive procurement activity of issuing Bid Documents (12.1.3.3) to multiple prospective sellers can be bypassed and the *Conduct Procurements* process activities would then be oriented specifically to modifying the prior agreement or entering into a new procurement agreement with the incumbent seller. In this case, any tools & techniques or outputs within the *Conduct Procurements* process that implicate a competitive solicitation—such as a Bidder Conferences (12.2.2.3)—are bypassed. Instead, the buyer and incumbent seller are focused on developing a Procurement Statement of Work (12.1.3.4), conducting procurement negotiations as a part of Interpersonal and Team Skills (12.2.2.5), and drafting and finalizing the Agreements (12.2.3.2).

12.2.2 Conduct Procurements: Tools & Techniques

12.2.2.1 Expert Judgment

Expert Judgment in the *Conduct Procurements* process is specifically focused on the seller selection committee, which evaluates the Seller Proposals (12.2.1.4), and the seller negotiation committee, which negotiates price and business terms and conditions with prospective sellers and assists the buyer in his or her negotiation of the Agreements (12.2.3.2). It is very common for seller selection committee members to represent multiple organizational units and disciplines including research, design, manufacturing, sales, accounting, finance, and legal. The cross-functional nature of the committee provides the technical, functional, and financial expertise needed to properly evaluate seller proposals. In procurement negotiations, a seller negotiation committee may have little to no negotiation expertise, and, if so, the buyer must have substantial negotiation expertise and judgment to ensure that the procurement results are fair and reasonable.

12.2.2.2 Advertising

Advertising is the process of making the Bid Documents (12.1.3.3) available to prospective sellers. This may include: (1) emailing the Bid Documents (12.1.3.3) to sellers on the project organization's prequalified seller list (see Sections 12.1.1.6 and 12.2.1.6) and to other prospective sellers resulting from market research conducted during Data Gathering (12.1.2.2); (2) making the Bid Documents (12.1.3.3) available on Internet websites; and, (3) including notices in various publications. Some procurements which involve government funding may require that the competitive solicitation be advertised so that certain types of sellers, such as minority business enterprises and woman business enterprises, are afforded ample opportunity to participate.

Ideally, to source the largest pool of qualified sellers, the buyer will make the Bid Documents (12.1.3.3) available through a variety of different types of Advertising. It is desirable to have at least three to five prospective sellers receive the competitive solicitation in the form of the Bid Documents (12.1.3.3). Three is considered the lower end of the range since a buyer needs to have at least two sellers to ensure some degree of competitive leverage and including at least three sellers serves as a contingency should one seller drop out of or be disqualified from the competitive procurement process. Any number below three sellers may also raise ethical questions as to whether the procurement is truly competitive or if it is merely a guise of going through a procurement for the sake of policy with the hidden intention being to award the procurement agreement to a predetermined seller.

Prior to the advent of email, a competitive solicitation was mailed to sellers who would then mail or physically deliver their proposals in return. Subsequently, with the proliferation of email, buyers typically email or electronically "post" competitive solicitations, yet sellers—unless otherwise mandated by the buyer—sometimes mail or physically deliver their proposals. The primary reason that sellers elect to send proposals in a hard-copy format has more to do with the amount of collateral or advertising materials—which are best suited to a printed form—sent along with a proposal than anything else. Frequently, these materials are marketing focused and have little relevance to a buyer in evaluating the proposal. Even in their electronic form, these materials typically add so much volume to the overall proposal that the responses routinely exceed typical email receipt storage limits of project organization email systems and are therefore blocked from being received. Buyers often require that sellers provide their responses in an electronic format not to exceed a certain data size. This requirement inherently forces sellers to eliminate unnecessary marketing materials and whittle proposals down such that sellers focus on the substantive content—which allows buyers and the seller selection committee to more easily and efficiently evaluate proposals. Proposals in electronic formats have other benefits inherent to such a format, such as eliminating the need to predetermine how many hardcopies are required from sellers and then having to request additional copies if the predetermined amount is incorrect. Thus, email has become the preferred vehicle of issuing Bid Documents (12.1.3.3) and associated communications as well as receiving proposals.

To determine whether sellers are interested in responding to a competitive solicitation, a buyer can issue what is called an "intent to bid"[21] (ITB) request to prospective sellers. An ITB request simply requests that prospective sellers respond to the buyer as to whether a seller is or is not interested in responding to a competitive solicitation. If a buyer included a leading or important seller as a recipient to an ITB request and that seller fails to respond or indicates that it will no-bid the competitive solicitation, the buyer can make contact with the seller to resolve any issues or to entice the seller to respond. An ITB request can be used as a precursor to releasing the Bid Documents (12.1.3.3) or it can be used at the same time the Bid Documents (12.1.3.3) are released. As a precursor to a competitive solicitation, the purpose of an ITB request is to provide advance notice to a seller of an impending procurement and to determine if a seller is even interested in receiving the competitive solicitation. If a seller is not interested, a buyer can replace that seller with another seller prior to the issuance of the competitive solicitation. If the buyer had merely issued the competitive solicitation to sellers instead of including an ITB request and then discovered that a seller was not interested, the buyer may be required to hastily find a replacement seller. Depending on the timing, the replacement seller may then have a competitive disadvantage because it has less time to develop and provide a proposal than the other sellers that already received the competitive solicitation. Another reason for using an ITB request is to correct recipient errors. For example, a buyer may be using an incorrect email address that is "kicked-back" by the receiving email system. It is more effective and convenient for a buyer to discover this at the point of an ITB request versus when the Bid Documents (12.1.3.3) are issued.

Another purpose of an ITB request is when Bid Documents (12.1.3.3) contain confidential information of the project organization. In such a case, a buyer will likely require sellers to enter into a non-disclosure agreement with the project organization prior to the sellers receiving the Bid Documents (12.1.3.3). Thus, an ITB request provides the vehicle to issue notice of the competitive solicitation, its

---

[21] An "intent to bid" is different than an "invitation to bid," which is a type of competitive solicitation (see Section 12.1.3.3).

confidential nature, and the non-disclosure agreement. ITB requests can be as simple as an email requiring a return email response or as complex as a form that must be signed by a seller-authorized official and returned to the buyer. A simple email example that requires a non-disclosure agreement follows. This example refers to "company" generically as an efficiency measure so that it can be sent to all of the sellers without having to tailor the email to each specific seller. An additional efficiency measure is to email all of the sellers at the same time using the same email by having the buyer send the email to himself or herself with all of the seller recipients being "blind copied." Thus, all of the sellers receive the same email but are not aware of the other sellers.

> Your company has been selected by [project organization] to respond to a Request for Proposal (RFP) for a financial system software solution. If your company desires to receive the RFP, within three (3) business days of receipt of this email, you must reply to this email indicating your company's intent to bid and email the attached Non-Disclosure Agreement, signed by an authorized company official, to [Name] at [Email Address]. Your company will be disqualified if its intent to bid and the executed Non-Disclosure Agreement are not received within the required timeframe.

When the competitive solicitation is sent to sellers following an ITB request, a similarly simple email can be used with the competitive solicitation as an attachment. The following email example also notifies sellers that any unauthorized communications may result in the disqualification of a seller. The reason for this notice is to ensure that sellers do not, or do not attempt to, obtain an unfair advantage by receiving privileged information or by influencing the project organization in some way.

> Thank you for your company's interest in responding to [project organization's] Request for Proposal (RFP) for a financial system software solution. The attached RFP describes the requirements of [project organization], a timetable for RFP activities, and instructions on how to respond to the RFP. Please follow the communications protocol as described in the RFP as unauthorized communications with [project organization] may result in the immediate disqualification of your company. If your company elects to no-bid the RFP, please destroy the RFP.

Where a buyer believes that there is an adequate number of sellers and ample competition, when a non-disclosure agreement is not required prior to releasing the competitive solicitation, or when a buyer is less concerned about recipient email address errors, an ITB request issued at the same time the competitive solicitation is released is sufficient. In that case, the purpose of the ITB request is to merely determine and track which sellers will be responding to the competitive solicitation. The following email example can be used to communicate the ITB request and competitive solicitation to prospective sellers:

> Your company has been selected by [project organization] to respond to a Request for Proposal (RFP) for a financial system software solution. The attached RFP describes the requirements of [project organization], a timetable for RFP activities, and instructions on how to respond to the RFP. If your company desires to respond to the RFP, within three (3) business days of receipt

of this email, you must reply to this email indicating your company's intent to bid. Your company will be disqualified if its intent to bid is not received within the required timeframe. Please follow the communications protocol as described in the RFP as unauthorized communications with [project organization] may result in the immediate disqualification of your company. If your company elects to no-bid the RFP, please destroy the RFP.

For more complex procurements, buyers commonly permit the submission of written questions by sellers regarding the content of the Bid Documents (12.1.3.3). It is very possible that a buyer may not have explained an instruction or requirement sufficiently or in such a way that a seller can understand. This lack of clarity, if resolved, may assist all of the sellers in formulating more complete proposals. Thus, after a time period during which written questions are gathered, the buyer provides the responses to all sellers either prior to, or at, Bidder Conferences (12.2.2.3).

Frequently, a seller tracking list is used by the buyer to facilitate monitoring the issuance of the competitive solicitation and the receipt of proposals. Table 5-4 provides an example of typical data elements contained in a seller tracking list. Each of the fields described in the example seller tracking list is tracked specific to a seller. It may seem unnecessary and redundant, for example, to specify the date that a competitive solicitation is issued on a seller-by-seller basis since the competitive solicitation is released to all sellers at the same time. While that is generally true, it is not uncommon for sellers that did not initially receive the competitive solicitation to request it after the "official" release date; for example, as a result of the news of a major procurement spreading rapidly within the relevant industry. It is the right of a buyer to refuse to issue a previously released competitive solicitation to another seller not initially invited to participate in the competitive procurement but there are many legitimate reasons, including the buyer having overlooked a very capable seller, to issue the competitive solicitation to a new seller. As a consequence, certain dates on the seller tracking list must be tracked individually by seller rather than on a seller-wide basis. However, when a new seller requests the competitive solicitation after the initial issuance and the buyer agrees to provide the competitive solicitation, it is uncommon for a buyer to allow the seller more time to prepare a proposal and to submit the proposal later than other sellers. One reason that a buyer does not permit this is that staggering dates for proposal submission and receiving proposals on different dates could adversely impact and complicate the schedule for the seller selection committee to evaluate proposals. Another reason is that the other sellers are diligently preparing their proposals and have not been provided any concessions by the project organization such as being permitted to provide a "late" submission. In that type of situation, typically, the buyer requires the new seller to provide a proposal by the original proposal submission due date or the buyer extends the proposal submission due date for all sellers.

Table 5-4. Seller Tracking List Data Elements

Data Element	Description
Seller Entity Name	The legal name of the seller's entity, which will also be input to the procurement agreement (if the seller is selected)
Seller Website	Allows the buyer to easily reference the seller's website at a later time, if necessary
Seller Contact Name and Title	Name of the seller's representative who is authorized to respond on behalf of the seller relating to any matter associated with the seller's proposal
Seller Contact Address, Phone, and Email	The email address of the seller's contact is the most important to obtain as that is where the competitive solicitation will be sent (if not posted)
Date Intent to Bid Request and Competitive Solicitation Issued	This date may vary by seller
Intent to Bid Request Response Received?	If the seller responds that it intends to submit a proposal, the date of that response is recorded. Alternatively, if a seller declines to respond, the buyer would record the reason, if known. If the seller fails to respond, the buyer may optionally contact the seller to confirm that it does not intend to respond (and why).
Date Written Questions Due	This date may vary by seller
Written Questions Received?	Whether the seller provided written questions regarding any clarifications to the competitive solicitation
Date / Time of Pre-Proposal Bidder Conference	The date / time will be the same across all sellers
Attended Pre-Proposal Bidder Conference?	Whether the seller attended the pre-proposal bidder conference or not
Proposal Submission Due Date	This date may vary by seller. If the seller fails to provide a proposal by the due date, the buyer may elect to contact the seller to determine the status of the proposal.
Proposal Submission Receipt Date	The date the seller's proposal is received by the buyer

Data Element	Description
Responsive and Qualified?	Whether the seller responded to the competitive solicitation in a complete manner and is qualified to provide the products, services, or results or not. The buyer may elect to record the reasons that a seller was not responsive or qualified.
Disqualification Notification Date	The date that the seller was notified that it was disqualified as a result of the buyer's responsiveness and qualification review
Date / Time of Post-Proposal Bidder Conference	As these conferences are independent and confidential to individual sellers, the date / time will vary by seller (if invited to a conference). The seller selection committee may elect to not invite a seller to a post-proposal bidder conference for any reason, including that the seller's proposal is so complete that no clarification is required or because the seller's proposal is so deficient that the seller is unlikely to be selected.
Selection / Non-Selection Notification	Whether the seller is selected to proceed to negotiations or not. If not, the buyer may elect to summarize the reason for non-selection.
Selection Status Notification Date	The date that the seller is notified of its selection or non-selection
Best and Final Offer Submission Due Date	This date may vary by seller. If the seller fails to provide a best and final offer by the due date, the buyer may elect to contact the seller to determine the status of the offer.
Best and Final Offer Submission Receipt Date	The date the seller's best and final offer is received by the buyer
Finalist Selection / Non-Selection Notification	Whether the seller is selected to proceed as a finalist to negotiations or not. If not, the buyer may elect to summarize the reason for non-selection.
Finalist Selection Status Notification Date	The date that the seller is notified of its selection or non-selection
Date / Time of Finalist Procurement Negotiations Conference	The date / time of concluding negotiations with the finalist seller
Comments / Notes	Any relevant comments or notes

12.2.2.3 Bidder Conferences

Bidder Conferences are intended to clarify the contents of the Bid Documents (12.1.3.3) so that all sellers are theoretically on the same level in terms of their basic understanding of the procurement and the competitive solicitation. Such Bidder Conferences are commonly called "pre-proposal" or "pre-response" Bidders Conferences, with all participating sellers invited to collectively attend the conference. Bidder Conferences may also be conducted after Seller Proposals (12.2.1.4) are received by a buyer and after the seller selection committee has had an opportunity to conduct a review of the proposals, with the purpose of the conference being for each seller to clarify its proposal. Such Bidder Conferences are commonly called "post-proposal" or "post-response" Bidders Conferences, with each responding seller invited independently to present its proposal to the seller selection committee. The determination of whether Bidder Conferences are needed is made by a buyer in consultation with the project manager and is largely based on the complexity of the procurement. This determination should be made during the *Plan Procurement Management* (12.1) process and be included as a part of the Procurement Management Plan (12.1.3.1).

All sellers are invited to the pre-proposal bidder conference, where the buyer: (1) presents the theme and highlights of the procurement and the Bid Documents (12.1.3.3); (2) reviews the project organization's responses to any written questions previously submitted by sellers; (3) asks for and responds to any verbal questions; and, (4) then reviews the competitive procurement schedule. The seller selection committee may or may not be in attendance. One disadvantage to the seller selection committee attending is that the committee members are no longer anonymous to the sellers: The anonymity of the committee members helps to ensure that the sellers cannot identify the committee members and therefore cannot inappropriately influence them. A theoretical benefit of pre-proposal Bidder Conferences is that the sellers become acutely aware that there are other competing sellers and, consequently, the sellers become more competitive in their proposals. A buyer may stipulate in the Bid Documents (12.1.3.3) that the Bidder Conferences are mandatory or optional. A lack of attendance at this conference by a seller may be indicative of a lack of interest to continue in the competitive procurement and the buyer may consider contacting the non-attending seller to determine the reason for the seller's failure to attend.

It is important for the buyer to control Bidder Conferences and to eliminate any seller confusion as to date, time, location, and other logistics. Too frequently, sellers bring many more representatives than needed as a show of force and to impress. Further, some sellers have the unfortunate habit of showing up significantly early which is more apt to be intentional rather than circumstance—the seller is most likely hoping to have an opportunity to speak with the buyer or get the "lay of the land" of the project organization so as to advantage the seller somehow. Therefore, it is necessary for a buyer to provide not only notice of Bidder Conferences but to provide guidelines as well. The following email is an example of such notice and guidelines for pre-proposal Bidder Conferences:

> The purpose of this email is to schedule a pre-proposal bidder conference for [project organization's] Request for Proposal (RFP). At the conference, [project organization] will briefly describe the main points and theme of the RFP, review the competitive procurement schedule, review responses to

written questions previously submitted by sellers, and respond to verbal questions of attending sellers. Your company is strongly encouraged to submit written questions no later than three days prior to the conference.

Your company's representatives should be at [project organization's] facility no earlier and no later than five minutes before the scheduled conference time. If your company is unable to attend the conference in person, a telephone conference can be arranged. Please reply to this email if attending at [project organization's] facility is not possible.

Please bring no more than three company representatives. The individual who is proposed to be the point-of-contact for your company's RFP response must be present at the conference.

If you have any questions, please reply to this email well in advance of the conference.

Unlike pre-proposal Bidder Conferences, which are conducted before proposal submission and with all prospective sellers in collective attendance, post-proposal Bidder Conferences are conducted independently and confidentially with each individual seller. In some cases, the buyer or a seller selection committee may do a cursory elimination of sellers or "short list" sellers such that only those sellers that truly have an opportunity to be awarded a contract are invited to post-proposal Bidder Conferences. During the post-proposal Bidder Conferences, the sellers present the details of their proposals to the seller selection committee and respond to any questions of the seller selection committee. When developing the Procurement Management Plan (12.1.3.1), if the buyer determines that post-proposal Bidder Conferences may be required, the buyer will likely schedule all the individual post-proposal Bidder Conferences in contiguous blocks so as to conduct the conferences in a short expanse of time. Therefore, it is crucial that each seller completes its presentation on time so that the next seller can begin. As with pre-proposal Bidder Conferences, it is necessary for a buyer to provide both notice and guidelines relating to post-proposal Bidder Conferences. An example follows:

The purpose of this email is to schedule a post-proposal bidder conference for your company to present its proposal submitted in response to [project organization's] Request for Proposal (RFP). The desired date and time is: [date and time]. The seller selection committee may ask questions throughout the presentation, so no separate question and answer time will be required.

Your company's representatives should be at [project organization's] facility no earlier and no later than five minutes before the scheduled conference time. In some cases, conferences are conducted back-to-back with other sellers. To be courteous to the next seller, the conference must be concluded five minutes before the scheduled end time to allow time for disconnecting of any audio-visual equipment. The seller selection committee will politely but firmly end a presentation in progress to keep to schedule.

Please bring no more than three company representatives. The individual who is proposed to be the account relationship manager for [project organization] must be present at the presentation.

It is possible that not all seller selection committee members will be in attendance. The absence of a committee member should not be interpreted by your company as a lack of interest in its proposal.

A conference room projection and audio system will be provided and will be the only audio-visual equipment permitted. Wireless Internet access will also be provided.

If you have any questions, please reply to this email well in advance of the conference.

In more complex procurements, post-proposal Bidder Conferences may include demonstrations by sellers of their proposed solution. Demonstrations are an excellent way for a seller selection committee to evaluate sellers, but the demonstrations must be conducted in a structured, thoughtful way in order to extract the information needed by committee members to conduct their evaluations. The buyer must, with each seller, plan the logistics required for each demonstration. Planning includes not only the technological aspects of the demonstration, but the administrative activities such as developing the agenda. Having an agenda is particularly important to ensure that sellers do not deviate too far from the objectives of the demonstration and the needs of the seller selection committee. Without parameters for the demonstration, the sellers may be reviewing an element of their proposal that has only an incidental relationship to the procurement requirements. The agenda should permit time after a demonstration is concluded for the seller selection committee to conduct a separate debrief (without the seller present) and to provide feedback to the buyer. Similar to confidential information possibly contained in the competitive solicitation, if there is a possibility that any confidential information of the project organization will be revealed during the demonstration, the buyer must ensure that an appropriate non-disclosure agreement is in place with the seller. As with any bidder conference, the buyer should specify the limit on the number of seller representatives who can be present at the demonstration.

12.2.2.4 Data Analysis

In preparation of evaluating Seller Proposals (12.2.1.4), if a buyer has not already distributed the Source Selection Criteria (12.1.3.5) to the seller selection committee during the *Plan Procurement Management* (12.1) process, the buyer should do so at a point early enough in the *Conduct Procurements* process so that the seller selection committee can familiarize themselves with the criterion prior to their evaluation. Where there is a desire, organizational requirement, or regulatory requirement for a seller selection committee to focus solely on the substantive elements of seller proposals, the buyer should specify in the Bid Documents (12.1.3.3) for sellers to provide a separate financial proposal and the buyer should only include criterion in the Source Selection Criteria (12.1.3.5) that are related to technical, non-technical, functional, and non-functional requirements. The buyer, or some other designated stakeholder or stakeholders, would separately evaluate seller financial proposals. The rationale for this type of segregated evaluation structure—particularly for an RFP competitive solicitation format where price is generally not the deciding factor—is that, typically, a seller selection committee does not have the expertise to evaluate the financial elements of a seller's proposal, that the financial elements may positively or negatively bias an evaluator's decisions, and that the proposed financial elements represent a non-negotiated price which very well may be negotiated by the buyer or the seller negotiation committee to a dramatically lower price. Where the seller selection committee will be evaluating substantive elements that include seller pricing, the buyer should also provide any Independent Cost Estimates (12.1.3.7) to the seller selection committee so that the evaluators can assess whether a seller is within the competitive range from a pricing perspective.

It is not uncommon for seller selection committee members to be inexperienced in competitive procurements and to have never formally evaluated sellers as a part of a competitive solicitation. Thus, to promote efficiency, a buyer should explain to the committee members their roles in evaluating proposals, familiarize the seller selection committee with the Source Selection Criteria (12.2.1.3) and the corresponding response evaluation method *in advance of* receiving proposals, and describe how the criteria is to be used and applied. Depending on the procurement, seller selection committee members may have varying sections of proposals to review and rate versus rating all proposal sections. For example, a buyer may evaluate qualifications such as financials and customer references, subject matter expert committee members may evaluate the technical sections of the proposals, and other committee members may evaluate the financial elements or pricing sections.

Once proposals are received and the sellers have been determined by a buyer to be responsive and qualified (see Section 12.2.1.4), the buyer will make the proposals available to the seller selection committee so that committee members can conduct their individual evaluations using their Expert Judgment (12.2.2.1). The buyer should instruct the committee members to review all proposals, take notes, prepare questions for committee discussion, and only then individually score the proposals. When the proposals have been evaluated and scored by individual committee members, the entire seller selection committee should meet to discuss the proposals and their individual evaluations. The objective of this meeting is to arrive at a final scoring and the selection of at least two finalist sellers (so as to ensure continued competitive leverage). The buyer serves as the facilitator of the meeting and aggregates all of the individual evaluations. In the meeting, the buyer should briefly review the Source Selection Criteria (12.2.1.3) and the major points of each seller's proposal so that there is a unified understanding of the criterion and seller proposals.

The next stage for the seller selection committee is for each committee member to discuss his or her ratings and the basis for the ratings. During committee discussions, committee members may change their initial rating as they see fit. The seller selection committee should strive to reach a consensus through an appropriate method, such as a consensus score, a total of all of the scores given by individual committee members, or an average of the individual scores. If additional information or clarification is needed from a seller that is critical to the evaluation process, the seller selection committee should complete all other evaluations and ratings. Upon adjourning the committee, the buyer should contact the seller and relay any information back to the seller selection committee, which will again meet to consider the requested information and factor such information into the evaluation process.

It is important that the seller selection committee maintain confidentiality during the process of evaluation. No committee member can communicate preliminary conclusions or results of what was proposed by a seller or that a given seller will or will not be selected. All internal workings of the seller selection committee must be kept confidential until the committee has completed its work and all sellers have been officially notified of selection or non-selection.

12.2.2.5 Interpersonal and Team Skills

Interpersonal and team skills in the context of the *Conduct Procurements* process are focused on negotiations with the goal being to obtain the best overall result—meaning price, business terms and conditions, and contract terms and conditions—for the project organization while at the same time ensuring a fair and reasonable profit for the Selected Sellers (12.2.3.1). The culmination of the negotiation are Agreements (12.2.3.2) executed by the contracting parties. A negotiation should be led by the most experienced negotiator, who should not only have sophisticated and extensive negotiation knowledge, skills, and abilities but also have the project organization's authority to make binding commitments. Ample time should be allowed for negotiations as a rushed negotiation will severely diminish the negotiation leverage of the project organization and will only serve to advantage the seller.

Too often, parties to a procurement conducted in the absence of a structured procurement methodology tend to rush to the negotiation stage, leaping past other considerations critically important to the transaction. Those who make that mistake find themselves having to resort to negotiation trickery and being forced to engage in intense, high-pressure negotiations. These frenzied negotiations directly translate into what is referred to in the procurement profession as "leaving money on the table." Further, procurements negotiated in haste more often than not result in later contract disputes that require unnecessary time, effort, and expense to unwind and correct. The most common root cause in rushing to the negotiations phase of a procurement is unsophisticated parties attempting to conduct the procurement in the vacuum of a structured procurement methodology. This root cause is eliminated by the logical processes of a structured procurement methodology, such as the Project Procurement Management Knowledge Area, which calls for the use of a competitive procurement process.

A competitive procurement, by its very nature, involves sellers aggressively attempting to differentiate themselves, mostly on capability and price, from other sellers in order to win a project organization's business. Many view a competitive procurement as the activities of identifying viable sellers, selecting the most qualified seller, and then negotiating a procurement agreement with the selected seller. Unfortunately, once a seller is selected and the parties begin to negotiate, the buyer has lost the valuable and significant negotiation leverage of sellers having to compete with one another. At the point of selection, the selected seller correctly assumes that the other sellers have been eliminated by the buyer and possibly notified of their non-selection. In other words, the seller's competition has been eliminated by the buyer. If the seller's sales representatives are shrewd, they will drag out the negotiations, seeking to create a length of time from the point of their selection. In doing so, the seller causes the buyer to make a time investment in that seller and it makes reverting back to a previously non-selected seller that much more difficult. In that situation, the buyer has a vested interest in bringing the procurement to a close and is forced to use other forms of leverage, such as positional power, timing, and outright manipulation to "negotiate" with the seller to achieve any desired concessions. If the seller is opportunistic, the buyer will leave a large sum of money and concessions on the table. This type of competitive procurement is referred to as the selection / negotiation model.

Another more productive competitive procurement model is known as "pre-negotiations." Under this model, pre-negotiations occur during the period of time between the receipt of seller proposals and the contract award—there are no subsequent negotiations of any real substance once the contract has been awarded. Rather than a buyer selecting a seller and then negotiating with the seller under the selection / negotiation model, a better strategy is for the buyer to create a "short list" of sellers and then select two or more finalist sellers to pre-negotiate with before making a contract award. Creating a short list simply entails eliminating non-viable sellers and creating a list of sellers that closely approximate the capabilities and pricing required by the project organization. Sellers that are on the short list are requested by the buyer to provide "best and final offers" (also known as "BAFOs"). If the BAFOs are not competitive enough, the buyer can guide the sellers (without revealing confidential information of the other finalist sellers) to a more competitive proposal. Another option is for a buyer to combine the best attributes of all proposals, including any concessions desired by the project organization, and communicate the desired transaction to the finalist sellers: The remaining sellers must strive to meet the exact transaction at the stated price or drop out of bidding. The request for BAFOs can be repeated—and thus the competition among the sellers prolonged—until the buyer achieves the desired results. With each BAFO iteration, as the offers become more aggressive, sellers may non-select themselves from further bidding and narrow the seller list. Only when the buyer achieves the desired results—in all aspects including terms and conditions—does the buyer award the procurement agreement and announce the finalist seller.

12.2.3 Conduct Procurements: Outputs

12.2.3.1 Selected Sellers

Selected Sellers are those sellers that have met the requirements, including price, stated in the Bid Documents (12.1.3.3) and that have been selected by the seller selection committee for contract award. In most procurements, there will be only one selected seller. As described under Interpersonal and Team Skills (12.2.2.5), all aspects of the procurement will have been negotiated with each selected seller, including the terms and conditions. At this point, all that remains is the formality of final approvals and execution of the Agreements (12.2.3.2) with each selected seller.

In addition to notifying the selected seller, a buyer should also immediately notify the other sellers that participated in the competitive procurement of their non-selection. Most often, the notice of non-selection is sent via email by the buyer to the seller, but those sellers that have or had a valued business relationship with the project organization should also be notified by the buyer via telephone as a courtesy. In either case, it should be made clear to the non-selected seller that the basis for non-selection will be communicated *after* the contract award has been formally announced. Rather than distracting the buyer and the project team at the time when arrangements with the selected seller are being finalized, the best policy is to notify sellers of non-selection, cease communication until post-award, and only then describe to non-selected sellers the basis for non-selection. An example of an email notifying a seller of non-selection is provided below. The reason for the reminder of the communication protocol within the competitive solicitation (in this example, an RFP), which prohibits the seller from making contact with anyone other than the buyer, is so that the seller does not try to contact the seller selection committee or to escalate the non-selection within the project organization's hierarchy in an effort to influence the procurement decision.

> [Project organization] appreciates the efforts of your company in responding to the Request for Proposal (RFP). After careful evaluation, [project organization] has chosen to proceed in its procurement with another seller. Unfortunately, to ensure that [project organization] does not disrupt project momentum and distract the progress of the seller selection committee, [project organization] is unable to provide specific non-selection details at this time, but will contact you to discuss those details following final contract award. Please note that the communication protocol described in the RFP is still in force. Thank you again for your participation in [project organization's] procurement process.

12.2.3.2 Agreements

Agreements represent the contractual relationship between the project organization and Selected Sellers (12.2.3.1), and contain each contracting party's rights, responsibilities, liabilities, and obligations as well as many or all of the boilerplate provisions described in Chapter 4 – Legal Considerations of Procurement. The Agreements can be as simple as a purchase order or as complex as a multi-exhibit procurement agreement, but Agreements will generally contain the elements as described in Chapter 4 – Legal Considerations of Procurement such as the: (1) Procurement Statement of Work (12.1.3.4); (2) Milestone List (6.2.3.3) or similar schedule of seller delivery or performance; (3) requirement for the seller to provide Work Performance Information (12.3.3.2) or other performance reporting; and, (4) project organization's right of Inspection (12.3.2.4) and Audits (12.3.2.5). In certain instances, such as to ensure that a project organization's needs as originally communicated as a part of the competitive solicitation are fulfilled, the project organization may elect to incorporate the Bid Documents (12.1.3.3) and the Seller Proposals (12.2.1.4) into the Agreements.

It is important to create a distinction between a *formal* contract such as a procurement agreement and a *formalized* intent or understanding between two or more parties. A letter of intent or memorandum of understanding are tools sometimes used to outline the terms of an intended future final agreement and to indicate that the parties will seek to negotiate in good faith to an agreed-upon outcome (that is, the future procurement agreement). While these tools may contain legally binding language requiring the parties to negotiate in good faith, they do not legally bind the parties to carry out the obligations of the future procurement agreement. Frequently, upon entering into a letter of intent or a memorandum of understanding, project organizations immediately experience difficulties negotiating favorable terms and conditions in their final procurement agreement with a seller. These difficulties are directly attributable to a loss of negotiation leverage: Once a seller has been selected and the business relationship is formalized via a letter of intent or memorandum of understanding, the project organization has lost much or all competitive bargaining power it once had with that seller. Ideally, as previously described, a project organization should include a contract template in a competitive solicitation and insist that the procurement agreement be fully negotiated prior to selecting the seller—and avoid rushing into a letter of intent or memorandum of understanding.

12.2.3.3 Change Requests

During the *Conduct Procurements* process, changes may be required to the Project Management Plan (12.2.1.1), Procurement Management Plan component of the Project Management Plan (12.2.1.1), the Project Schedule component of the Project Documents (12.2.1.2), or as a part of the Project Documents Updates (12.2.3.5). Any such Change Requests are processed through the *Perform Integrated Change Control* (4.6) process of the Project Integration Management Knowledge Area.

12.2.3.4 Project Management Plan Updates

As documented via Change Requests (12.2.3.3), certain integrated and consolidated subsidiary plans and baselines of the Project Management Plan (12.2.1.1)—such as the Requirements Management Plan (5.1.3.2); Quality Management Plan (8.1.3.1); Communications Management Plan (10.1.3.1); Risk Management Plan (11.1.3.1); Procurement Management Plan (12.1.3.1); Scope Baseline (5.4.3.1); and, Cost Baseline (7.3.3.1)— may require revision and updating based on changes to project requirements, quality standards, communication needs, risk management approach, procurement activities, timetable, project scope, or cost. The Project Management Plan Updates include any updates to the Schedule Baseline, an output (6.5.3.1) resulting from the *Develop Schedule* (6.5) process of the Project Schedule Management Knowledge Area. The Schedule Baseline (6.5.3.1) may need to be revised to reflect any changes in the seller's schedule, period of delivery or performance, milestones, or deadlines contained in the Procurement Statement of Work (12.1.3.4). In addition to the Schedule Baseline (6.5.3.1) updates, likely updates include:

- Requirements Management Plan (5.1.3.2) – Changes identified by Selected Sellers (12.2.3.1) relating to project requirements or their prioritization.

- Quality Management Plan (8.1.3.1) – Alternative standards, codes, or solutions identified by Selected Sellers (12.2.3.1) to achieve the quality objectives of the project.

- Communications Management Plan (10.1.3.1) – Revisions to the buyer-seller communication approach, method, and content used by the project organization that are necessary to meet the unique circumstances and needs of Selected Sellers (12.2.3.1).

- Risk Management Plan (11.1.3.1) – Newly identified risks related to Selected Sellers (12.2.3.1) and associated Agreements (12.2.3.2), incorporated into the Risk Register (11.2.3.1), that require adjustments to the project organization's approach to managing project risks.

- Procurement Management Plan (12.1.3.1) – Enhancements or updates based on the results of negotiations conducted as a part of Interpersonal and Team Skills (12.2.2.5), such as the contract templates used for the Agreements (12.2.3.2), project metrics, service level requirements, and seller and contract management procedures. Enhancements can also be included within the Lessons Learned Register component of the Project Documents Updates (12.2.3.5).

- Scope Baseline (5.4.3.1) – Changes to the project WBS, the products, services, or results to be provided by the Selected Sellers (12.2.3.1), and associated acceptance criteria as defined by the Procurement Statement of Work (12.1.3.4).

- Cost Baseline (7.3.3.1) – Changes in the seller's prices to the project organization for the contracted products, services, or results—such as labor and material prices—based on fluctuations or other external economic environment factors. In the case of a firm fixed price contract type (see Section 12.1.1.6), the seller is at risk for absorbing any price impacts and there should be no changes in the seller's price charged to the project organization unless there are Change Requests (12.2.3.3).

12.2.3.5 Project Documents Updates

As a result of the project team's work and obtained knowledge in conducting the procurement or as a result of Change Requests (12.2.3.3), certain components of the Project Documents (12.2.1.2)—such as the Lessons Learned Register (4.4.3.1); Requirements Documentation (5.2.3.1); Requirements Traceability Matrix (5.2.3.2); Risk Register (11.2.3.1); and, Stakeholder Register (13.1.3.1)—may require revision and updating. The Project Documents Updates include any updates to the Resource Calendars component of the Project Documents (9.2.1.2), an input to the *Estimate Activity Resources* (9.2) process of the Project Resource Management Knowledge Area. Resource Calendars (9.2.1.2) specify the quantity, availability, capabilities, and skills of identified project resources. Under the *Conduct Procurements* process, the Resource Calendar (9.2.1.2) for a project may need to be revised to reflect the availability of sellers or the availability of any contracted resources, such as contingent workers, that result from the procurement. In addition to the Resource Calendar (9.2.1.2) updates, likely updates include:

- Lessons Learned Register (4.4.3.1) – Any lessons learned while conducting the procurement, such as the competitive solicitation, and during interactions with sellers. When a project organization buys certain products, services, or results infrequently from sellers that sell the required products, services, or results on an ongoing basis, it is very common for there to be a lack of clarity or specificity in the Bid Documents (12.1.3.3). Meetings (12.1.2.5) with prospective sellers and Bidder Conferences (12.2.2.3) are an excellent opportunity to learn from sellers and to capture lessons learned to improve future procurements. During the *Conduct Procurements* process, the buyer should seek out opportunities to routinely update the Lessons Learned Register.

- Requirements Documentation (5.2.3.1) – Based on interactions with sellers and any changes made to the Procurement Statement of Work (12.1.3.4) as described in Agreements (12.2.3.2) with the Selected Sellers (12.2.3.1), revisions to the substantive and procedural requirements of the project organization, including technical, non-technical, functional, and non-functional requirements.

- Requirements Traceability Matrix (5.2.3.2) – The linkage (traceability) of project requirements to the capabilities of Selected Sellers (12.2.3.1) to the products, service, or results to be provided under the Agreements (12.2.3.2).
- Risk Register (11.2.3.1) – Any risks related to the Agreements (12.2.3.2) entered into with Selected Sellers (12.2.3.1) or risks with the Selected Sellers (12.2.3.1) themselves. The contract template and contract payment type (see Section 12.1.1.6), the contract term, the project delivery method described in the Procurement Strategy (12.1.3.2), and other terms and conditions may represent certain risks absorbed by either the project organization or the Selected Sellers (12.2.3.1) which must be assessed and mitigated or accepted. Additionally, if a buyer conducted a qualification of the sellers (see Section 12.2.1.4), the buyer may have knowledge of any risks relating to the financial soundness, reliability, capacity, and capability of the Selected Sellers (12.2.3.1). Any such seller risks should also be included in the Risk Register updates.
- Stakeholder Register (13.1.3.1) – Any additional information relating to stakeholders that result from Agreements (12.2.3.2) made with Selected Sellers (12.2.3.1).

12.2.3.6 Organizational Process Assets Updates

While the *Plan Procurement Management* (12.1) process may result in some number of Organizational Process Assets Updates (12.1.3.10), the conclusion of the *Conduct Procurements* process—which is the execution process of issuing a competitive solicitation, obtaining responses from prospective sellers, selecting a seller, and awarding a procurement agreement—will likely result in substantial Organizational Process Assets Updates. Additional updates may be necessitated by Project Management Plan Updates (12.2.3.4) and Project Documents Updates (12.2.3.5). Organizational Process Assets Updates may include:

- Forms of the Procurement Management Plan (12.1.3.1) and Procurement Strategy (12.1.3.2)
- Procurement policy and related procedures and guidelines
- Stakeholder role definitions (see Section 12.1.1.4) and stakeholder training for evaluating Seller Proposals (12.2.1.4) using Data Analysis (12.2.2.4) and for negotiating with Selected Sellers (12.2.3.1) using Interpersonal and Team Skills (12.2.2.5)
- Templates and formats for buyer-seller communications such as Meetings (12.1.2.5), Advertising (12.2.2.2), and Bidder Conferences (12.2.2.3)
- Prequalified seller list (see Section 12.1.1.6)
- Seller tracking list for tracking of competitive solicitations (see Section 12.2.2.2)
- Statement of work format for the Procurement Statement of Work (12.1.3.4)
- Competitive solicitation templates for Bid Documents (12.1.3.3)
- Competitive solicitation finishing checklist used to prepare the Bid Documents (12.1.3.3) for issuance (see Section 12.1.3.3)
- Methods of Advertising (12.2.2.2)

- Seller qualification criteria (see Section 12.2.1.4)
- Seller proposal evaluation matrix templates for developing the Source Selection Criteria (12.1.3.5) based on the Source Selection Analysis (12.1.2.4) in preparation for evaluating Seller Proposals (12.2.1.4) using Data Analysis (12.2.2.4)
- Seller risk mitigation strategies, including insurance and bonding (see Section 12.2.1.2)
- Contract templates and types used for Agreements (12.2.3.2)
- Service level catalog (used to collect example service levels for future procurements)
- Negotiation tactics in preparation for negotiating with Selected Sellers (12.2.3.1) using Interpersonal and Team Skills (12.2.2.5)
- Knowledge base of experiences with sellers

6 – Dispute Resolution

It is a role of a buyer in the prior process, *Conduct Procurements* (12.2), to predict issues or conflicts that may arise under a procurement agreement and to institute preventative measures to avoid possible disputes. These measures include researching and selecting responsive and qualified sellers, conducting deliberate and thorough proposal evaluations, appropriately mitigating possible risks and transferring actual risks, and negotiating a procurement agreement that is clear and free of ambiguity. In many cases, the contracting parties do an admirable job of identifying roles, responsibilities, and obligations within a procurement agreement—but then do *not* address what should occur if a dispute arises and what remedial actions or remedies, such as liquidated damages, may be triggered. Thus, instead of having an easily implementable remedy that satisfies the aggrieved party when a dispute arises, the parties further compound their dispute by quarreling over possible remedies. Some avoid the description of remedies in a contract, because it means admitting that something may go wrong with the relationship in the future. This "head in the sand" approach practically ensures future failure because, even in the best of buyer-seller relationships, some sort of issue will undoubtedly occur, such as an unmet expectation. The quickest solution that allows the contracting parties to move past a dispute and get the business relationship moving forward again is implementable remedies. Thus, it is absolutely necessary for buyers to consider breaches, define events of breach and default, and pre-determine appropriate remedies. In many organizations, the role of the buyer ends with the *Conduct Procurements* (12.2) process, and a project team member with contract management responsibilities (the "contract manager") takes over with the next process, *Control Procurements* (12.3). Because of this hand-off, the buyer is additionally responsible for constructing and negotiating procurement agreements in such a way that, if a dispute does arise, the agreement enables the contract manager to come to a speedy and fair resolution. If that is not achieved, a dispute can escalate to the point that more formal methods are required for resolution, ultimately resulting in wasted time and unnecessary expense for both the project organization and the seller—no matter who the "winner" ends up being. Thus, before proceeding to the *Control Procurements* (12.3) process and examining contract management, it is appropriate to first review the elements of a contract dispute and how such disputes can be resolved.

Breaches

The most likely cause for a dispute to arise under a procurement agreement is a breach of the agreement. If one of the parties to a procurement agreement fails to carry out its obligations under the agreement, that party may be in breach of contract. The main types of breach of contract, each of which is explained further in the following paragraphs, are minor, material, and anticipatory.

Where a breach has occurred, the non-breaching party must act in a timely and affirmative manner. When a non-breaching party has knowingly accepted defective performance or non-performance from the breaching party on multiple occasions and has failed to seek a remedy for the breaches, the non-breaching party may not be entitled to subsequent relief. This pattern of conduct is referred to as "waiver," and, thus, the non-breaching party has essentially waived its future right to seek remedies. To avoid waiver, the non-breaching party must immediately, upon a breach, provide notice to the breaching party and demand performance, seek a remedy, or permit the breach without seeking a remedy. The act of a non-breaching party providing notice but permitting the breach without seeking a remedy is called "forbearance" and avoids waiver by preserving (through the notice) the non-breaching party's right to seek a remedy for a future breach. As further explained in the later section on remedies, the non-breaching party has the duty to mitigate—by reasonable means—the effect of a breach.

Minor Breach

A minor breach, also called a simple, partial, immaterial, or technical breach, occurs when the breaching party renders performance that deviates slightly from complete performance such that the breaching party has still substantially performed the procurement agreement. Under a minor breach, the non-breaching party can seek damages associated with the breach but is *not* entitled to an order for specific performance (specific performance is reviewed further in this chapter) of the breaching party's obligations.

Material Breach

A material breach occurs when the breaching party's performance is so inferior or deficient that the essence of the procurement agreement is substantially impaired or destroyed. Under a material breach, the non-breaching party can enforce or rescind the agreement. If the non-breaching party chooses to enforce the procurement agreement, that party can seek an order for specific performance of the breaching party's obligations or seek damages associated with the breach. Alternatively, the non-breaching party can choose to rescind the procurement agreement in order to be discharged from performing the agreement and seek restitution of any compensation already paid under the agreement to the breaching party.

Anticipatory Breach

An anticipatory breach occurs when the breaching party unequivocally indicates that it will not perform the procurement agreement when performance is due (called "repudiation") or when a situation arises in which future non-performance is inevitable. The mere assertion that a party is encountering difficulties in preparing to perform, is dissatisfied with the procurement agreement, or is otherwise uncertain whether performance will be rendered when due is insufficient to constitute repudiation. Upon repudiation, the non-breaching party can demand that the breaching party perform. This demand does not impact the non-breaching party's right to claim damages—the non-breaching party may pursue any remedy for breach of contract, even though the breaching party has been notified that the non-breaching party will await performance. Additionally, under an anticipatory breach, the non-breaching party does not have to perform its obligations and cannot be liable for not doing so. Therefore, an anticipatory breach is often used by the *non-breaching* party as a defense to a lawsuit for failure of payment or failure to perform a procurement agreement.

Monetary Remedies

Monetary remedies are also referred to as "money damages" or "damages." As the name implies, when a party breaches a procurement agreement, the non-breaching party may be entitled to money damages. In order to be entitled to money damages, the non-breaching party must prove that there was breach, there was a loss due to the breach, and that the nature of the loss would lead to compensation. The broad types of money damages, each of which are explained later in this section, are nominal, compensatory, and liquidated damages. Punitive damages—which are designed to punish the wrongdoer and deter similar conduct in the future—are generally not recoverable in breach of contract actions unless the breaching party's actions give rise to a separate tort claim. The rationale behind punitive damages not being available under contract is because the purpose of remedies, including equitable remedies described in the following section, is to restore the non-breaching party to the economic position occupied at the time the procurement agreement was entered into or to prevent the breaching party from being unjustly enriched—and nothing more. Further, it is the role of courts, not private parties, to mete out punishment and, therefore, punitive damages under a contract are viewed as being against public policy.

In most situations, when a breach of contract occurs, the non-breaching party has a duty to take whatever action is *reasonable* to mitigate the damages caused by the breach. "Reasonable" implies that there is no undue risk or expense placed on the non-breaching party in order to mitigate the damages. If the non-breaching party fails to reasonably mitigate damages, the remedies available to the non-breaching party are either not recoverable or will be diminished.

Nominal Damages

There are situations where a party breaches a procurement agreement and there is a "technical" injury but the non-breaching party sustains no real loss or damages. In these situations, a court may award what are called nominal damages—which consist of a small cash amount—to the non-breaching party. Cases involving nominal damages are usually brought on principle and are often sought to obtain a legal record of which party was at fault.

Compensatory Damages

At their most basic, compensatory damages are intended to make the non-breaching party whole. Within the broad category of compensatory damages, there are three major theories of recovery that flow *directly from a breach*: expectation damages, reliance damages, and restitution. There are also damages that flow *indirectly from a breach*: consequential damages and incidental damages (which are damages associated with the non-breaching party's costs of avoiding further loss stemming from a breach).

The expectation that parties have in entering into a procurement agreement is to achieve what is called the "benefit of the bargain." When one party materially breaches a procurement agreement, the non-breaching party does not achieve its expectation from the agreement and suffers the loss of the bargained-for benefit. The intent of compensatory damages is to compensate the non-breaching party for the loss directly resulting from the breach and to place the non-breaching party in the same position as if the procurement agreement had been fully performed (called "expectation damages").

When it is not possible or not practicable for a court to award expectation damages, a court may award damages designed to restore a non-breaching party to the economic position it occupied at the time the procurement agreement was entered into (called "reliance damages") or designed to prevent the breaching party from being unjustly enriched (called "restitution"). Reliance damages usually equal the amount a non-breaching party expended in performing or in preparing to perform a procurement agreement. Restitution usually equals the value to a breaching party of the non-breaching party's performance; the value being the amount the breaching party would actually have to pay to acquire the non-breaching party's performance (and not the subjective value to the breaching party).

Damages which do not flow directly and immediately from a breach but instead flow from the results of the breach are recoverable as consequential damages. To be liable for these types of damages, a breaching party must know or have reason to know (meaning that the damage was reasonably foreseeable at the time the breach occurred) that the breach will cause special damages to the non-breaching party.

Incidental damages compensate a non-breaching party for reasonable costs that it incurs after a breach in an effort to avoid further loss. The amount of the damages must correlate to commercially reasonable charges that result from the non-breaching party's efforts to salvage the procurement agreement, retrieve or protect products delivered under the procurement agreement, or otherwise mitigate damages.

Liquidated Damages

Rather than contracting parties quarrelling (usually in court) over what the amount of damages should be in the case of a breach, the parties can specify, at the time of contract execution, the damages associated with a future breach as a fixed amount or as a formula within the procurement agreement. In the event that a party does breach the procurement agreement, that party simply pays the amount of damages specified in the agreement to the non-breaching party. This creates efficiency in dispute resolution and helps to avoid costs resulting from a protracted contract dispute. For liquidated damages to be enforceable, actual damages must be difficult or impracticable to determine and the liquidated amount must be reasonable considering the circumstances of the breach—that is, the damages must be a genuine pre-estimate of the loss that may be suffered by a party. Where the amount of liquidated damages appears to be excessive as compared to the loss resulting from the breach or bears no reasonable relationship to the value of performance, the damages will appear to be more of a penalty than compensatory (therefore punitive in substance) and courts will not enforce the damages. Frequently, when referring to liquidated damages, contracting parties will stipulate in the procurement agreement that the damages amount is to be paid "…as liquidated damages, and not as a penalty." However, such language is not determinative and a court will look at the substance of the damages amount to ascertain whether the amount is compensatory or a penalty. Conversely, a court will uphold liquidated damages even if it means that the non-breaching party receives less than the actual loss resulting from the breach. The rationale is that the contract provision describing the liquidated damages constitutes an agreement between the parties—if the contracting parties agreed to a liquidated amount less than the loss that may occur, a court will not reform the contract provision.

Equitable Remedies

In addition to the various types of monetary remedies, there are several equitable (meaning non-monetary) remedies available: specific performance, injunction, rescission, and reformation. Equitable remedies are discretionary in nature, meaning that they are not available as a matter of right and courts can choose, in their discretion, whether to grant an equitable remedy or not. Equitable remedies are typically granted by a court only if money damages are insufficient or impracticable to make the non-breaching party whole and the equitable remedy will not cause undue hardship on the breaching party or be especially difficult to supervise or enforce.

Specific Performance

When a party fails to perform some act promised under a procurement agreement, the non-breaching party may seek an order from the court that requires the breaching party to perform the act. This court order to perform is called specific performance. This type of equitable remedy is used by courts when no other remedy (such as money damages) will adequately compensate the non-breaching party. If an award of money damages will put the non-breaching party in the position it would have been had the procurement agreement been fully performed, then the court will award money damages instead of ordering specific performance. It is uncommon for money damages to not be a sufficient remedy; therefore, specific performance is usually only ordered when the subject of the contract is unique, such as for real estate or a work of art. Further, a court will only order specific performance where it would be just and equitable to do so. Thus, where the party seeking the order has acted unfairly or unconscionably, a court will not grant the order and will instead award money damages.

Injunction

An injunction is like specific performance except that the breaching party is ordered to perform a *negative* obligation. There are two broad categories of injunctions: prohibitory and mandatory. A prohibitory injunction is an order that something *must not* be done. A mandatory injunction is an order that something *must* be done; for example, to demolish a structure that was erected in breach of contract. Like specific performance, a court exercises its discretion to order an injunction according to the same principles as with specific performance. To obtain an injunction, a non-breaching party must show that it will suffer irreparable injury if the injunction is not issued.

An injunction is a remedy that is commonly found in procurement agreements specific to the obligation of confidentiality. If a party breaches its obligation of confidentiality and discloses confidential information belonging to the non-breaching party, the value of the confidential information would be difficult to assess in order to calculate money damages and it is reasonable that the breaching party be ordered to cease disclosure of the confidential information. To ensure that courts understand the intent of the contracting parties, contract provisions stipulating the appropriateness of an injunction is nearly universally included in procurement agreements. An example of such a contract provision follows:

> The parties acknowledge that the breach of a party's obligation of confidentiality may give rise to irreparable injury to the non-breaching party, which damage may be inadequately compensable in the form of monetary damages. Accordingly, the non-breaching party may seek and obtain injunctive relief against the breach or threatened breach of the obligation of confidentiality, in addition to any other legal remedies which may be available, to include, at the sole election of the non-breaching party, the immediate termination, without penalty to the non-breaching party, of this contract in whole or in part.

Rescission

The remedy of rescission allows a court to essentially dissolve a procurement agreement. The result is as if the agreement never existed. Thus, rescission discharges all contracting parties from the obligations of the procurement agreement and restores the parties to the positions they held before the formation of the agreement. Rescission may be granted by a court where there is fraudulent representation, mutual mistake, lack of legal capacity, an impossibility not contemplated by the parties to perform a procurement agreement, or duress and undue influence. Mere inadequacy of consideration, however, is not a sufficient reason to justify rescission. When the consideration is so inadequate that it shocks the conscience of the court or is so closely connected with suspicious circumstances or misrepresentations as to provide substantial evidence of fraud, inadequacy of consideration can furnish a basis for relief. A party seeking rescission must do so promptly after the basis for the rescission occurs; otherwise, a court is not likely to grant rescission unless excuse or justification for the delay is shown.

Reformation

Where a procurement agreement, through fraud or mutual mistake, does not express the intention of the parties, a party can request a court to reform the agreement. Under the remedy of reformation, a court has the discretion to re-write a contract such that it reflects the true intent of the parties. Under this remedy, a court has only the right to impose what the contracting parties had already agreed upon but did not accurately express in their contract; a court cannot impose a contract on parties who do not agree to the terms of the reformed contract. Because a court must place itself between and in the minds of the parties that had been free to contract among themselves, reformation is an extremely uncommon remedy and courts will only exercise the remedy when there is clear and convincing evidence of the original intent of the parties.

Dispute Resolution Methods

When a dispute between contracting parties does occur, there are a range of methods that facilitate the resolution of the dispute. These methods range from the informal to what is known as alternative dispute resolution (ADR) to litigation. There are many obvious advantages to informal dispute resolution and ADR including reduced costs, faster resolutions, less emotional stress, the ability to construct solutions that are outside of the courts' authority and, in some cases, the opportunity to preserve business relationships that might otherwise be destroyed by litigation. Forms of ADR—mediation, non-binding arbitration, and binding arbitration—are frequently specified in procurement agreements. An agreement may limit the contracting parties to ADR as the only and final means of dispute resolution (binding arbitration) or require that the parties attempt to resolve their dispute through ADR (mediation and / or non-binding arbitration) before proceeding to litigation. Even if a procurement agreement does not require that the parties seek resolution through ADR, parties frequently agree to ADR when a dispute does arise. Sometimes, courts order contracting parties to attempt resolution through ADR before proceeding to trial. Ultimately, the goal of a buyer and a project organization is to ensure that disputes are resolved at the lowest level possible and are not escalated.

Negotiation

As a dispute resolution method, direct negotiation between representatives of the contracting parties who are responsible for the day-to-day administration and management of the procurement agreement involves the exchange of offers and counteroffers and a discussion of the strengths and weaknesses of each party's position. This method of dispute resolution is the most efficient and least disruptive, but is most effective only if both parties have an incentive to reach an agreed resolution. When a buyer becomes aware of a contract dispute for which no remedy is contractually triggered, the buyer should facilitate a discussion between the contracting parties and seek to prevent any emotional rush by either party to escalate the dispute to a higher form of dispute resolution. Rather, the parties should work diligently to seek a reasonable and agreeable solution and, only if the parties "agree to disagree," should the dispute be escalated.

Informal Mediation

Informal mediation is similar to negotiation, except that it is usually specified in the procurement agreement and is intended to be invoked when negotiations between lower level representatives of the contracting parties fail to reach a resolution. The following contract language describes the process of informal mediation:

> In the event of any dispute or disagreement between the parties with respect to the interpretation of any provision of this Agreement, or with respect to the performance of either party hereunder, the respective project managers will meet for the purpose of resolving the dispute. If the parties are unable to resolve the dispute within five (5) working days, or as otherwise agreed, either project manager will have the right to submit the dispute to their respective party's vice president level management who will meet as often as the parties deem reasonably necessary in order to gather and furnish to each other all essential, non-privileged information that the parties believe germane to resolution of the matter at issue. During the course of these non-judicial dispute resolution proceedings, documents used to resolve the dispute shall be limited to essential, non-privileged information. All requests for documents by a party shall be made in good faith and be reasonable in light of the economics and time efficiencies intended by the dispute resolution proceedings. No formal proceedings for the judicial resolution of any dispute may be commenced until sixty (60)

calendar days following initiation of negotiations under this section or for such shorter period as the parties may mutually agree to in writing. Either party may then seek whatever remedy is available in law or in equity. The provisions of this section will not apply to any dispute relating to the parties' obligations of non-disclosure and confidentiality.

Mediation

When contracting parties have been unable to initiate a productive dialogue to resolve their dispute or where the parties have been in resolution discussions and have reached a seemingly insurmountable impasse, mediation may be the next logical step in attempting to resolve the dispute. While informal dispute resolution is the preferable method to resolve a dispute, mediation is often the preferred formal method of settling disputes between parties who will, either by necessity or desire, have a continuing business relationship. Because of the flexible nature of mediation, the parties are able to spend more time focusing on the specifics of their dispute and how to resolve the conflict as opposed to having to focus on following the rules and regulations of more formal dispute resolution methods. In pursuing mediation, the parties agree on an acceptable, impartial, and neutral third party mediator. The objective of the mediator is to assist the parties in voluntarily reaching an acceptable (but not necessarily fair) resolution of the dispute. A mediator, like a facilitator, makes primarily procedural suggestions regarding how parties can achieve resolution. Occasionally, a mediator may suggest some substantive options as a means of encouraging the parties to expand the range of possible resolutions under consideration. A mediator often works with the parties individually in caucuses to explore acceptable resolution options or to develop proposals that might move the parties closer to resolution. Mediators may differ in their degree of control while assisting disputing parties. Some mediators set the stage for bargaining, make minimal procedural suggestions, and intervene in the negotiations only to avoid or overcome a deadlock. Other mediators are much more involved in forging the details of a resolution. Other than to achieve resolution, a mediator has no vested interest in the outcome of a particular dispute nor does the mediator have the goal or responsibility to ensure that the outcome is fair: The ultimate goal of a mediator is to facilitate the disputing parties to an agreeable result regardless of fairness or equity. If one party has more leverage or negotiation power than the other party and that other party yields to come to an agreement of resolution, the mediator will still view that as a successful outcome.

Arbitration

Arbitration involves presenting a dispute to an impartial or neutral individual (arbitrator) or a panel (arbitration panel) for issuance of an advisory or non-binding decision (non-binding arbitration) or a final and binding decision (binding arbitration). The disputing parties have input into the selection process of the arbitrator or the arbitration panel, allowing the parties to select an individual or panel with some expertise and knowledge of the subject matter of the dispute. Generally, the individuals or panels chosen are those known to be impartial, objective, fair, and who have the ability to evaluate and make judgments about data or facts. Arbitration differs from mediation in that an arbitrator reaches an independent conclusion, whereas a mediator attempts to facilitate a negotiated settlement between the parties. Unlike litigation, arbitrators do not have to follow established legal precedents in reaching their decisions and are not required to explain the reasons behind their decisions. Under non-binding arbitration, the decision is more of an advisement in that the parties do not have to abide by the decision. After hearing all sides, the arbitrator renders a decision that carries the limited force of an opinion. The decision may or may not include a suggested award of damages. Non-binding arbitration is commonly used by disputing parties to "test the waters of litigation" and to get a sense of the strength of their position. If the arbitration decision is not mutually agreeable, the parties are free to engage in other forms of ADR or to enter into litigation to resolve the dispute. If the parties do agree on the arbitration decision, an agreement is executed between the parties stating that the resolution is mutually acceptable and that the parties agree to abide by the decision. In binding arbitration, all parties agree to abide by the arbitrator's decision before the process begins. Once rendered, the arbitrator's decision carries the same legal weight as the ruling of a court.

Litigation

Litigation is the judicial resolution of a contract dispute, where the contracting parties argue the merits of their case before the court. Usually, contracting parties with a dispute view litigation as a last resort based on cost, time, and unwanted publicity. While ADR is usually faster and less expensive, court dockets are much quicker to hear a case than in decades past and legal fees are not as high as they once were due to competitive pressures. Unlike binding arbitration, if a party is not pleased with the results, appeals can be made. However, appeals further delay and extend the timeline to a final resolution. Lawyers are competitors by the nature of what they do and, once litigation begins, they strive to win using every tactic legally and ethically available. Unfortunately, an occasional by-product of zealous legal representation is cost and ill will. Further, the contracting parties, likely business people in their everyday lives, often transfer their normal productive and constructive drives into the adversary context of litigation. Thus, litigation results in significant expense to buyers and sellers, reinforces and increases adversity between the contracting parties, and distracts buyers and sellers from productive activities.

7 – 12.3 Control Procurements

The third and final process of the Project Procurement Management Knowledge Area, *Control Procurements*, signifies the end of the Executing Process Group and the beginning of the Monitoring and Controlling Process Group. This Process Group consists of activities which track, review, and regulate the progress and performance of the project. Monitoring includes collecting of performance data, reporting performance information, identifying where changes are required, and initiating those changes. Controlling compares actual performance to planned performance, analyzing trends to identify potential process improvements, assessing alternatives, and recommending any necessary corrective actions. In the context of the *Control Procurements* process, monitoring and controlling represent the post-procurement activities of contract management and administration. For the *Plan Procurement Management* (12.1) and *Conduct Procurements* (12.2) processes, the buyer served in a lead role. That lead role is now transitioned from the buyer[22] to a contract manager, who takes on responsibility for the *Control Procurements* process. The National Contract Management Association defines contract management as "the process of managing contracts, deliverables, deadlines, and contract terms and conditions while ensuring customer satisfaction." To that end, the contract manager and Selected Sellers (12.2.3.1) must each manage and administer the Agreements (12.3.1.3) to ensure that the contracting parties meet their contractual obligations and that their respective rights are protected. The *Control Procurements* process is not merely the performance of a procurement agreement—it is the proactive process of overseeing performance to ensure that the value created through the procurement process is realized and maintained. In layperson's terms, and quite aptly, *Control Procurements* is the "getting what you paid for" process of the Project Procurement Management Knowledge Area. Broadly, that means:

- Actively managing the project organization-seller relationship
- Monitoring and managing seller performance through a formal governance framework
- Resolving any disputes that may arise at the lowest possible levels
- Performing contract administration activities
- Controlling and managing changes, including the documentation of any decisions that affect the procurement agreement or business relationship
- Formally closing out the procurement agreement

In order to successfully manage and administer the Agreements (12.3.1.3) with the Selected Sellers (12.2.3.1), the contract manager must have knowledge of both the project organization's and seller's

---

[22] The *PMBOK Guide* continues to use the term "buyer" for the *Control Procurements* process, but the reader should recognize that it is very likely that the buyer will be replaced by a contract manager—a different person with different skills—when transitioning from the *Conduct Procurements* (12.2) process to the *Control Procurements* process. In contrast to the *PMBOK Guide*, the term "contract manager" is used herein to emphasize the different roles.

business being conducted under the procurement agreement and knowledge of the procurement agreement itself. This requires a turn-over of the procurement agreement and seller relationship from the buyer to the contract manager, where the buyer fully apprises the contract manager of the parties' roles and responsibilities under the procurement agreement and makes available all relevant documentation to the contract manager. While the *Control Procurements* process combines management and administrative activities into one process, there is often an organizational delineation between the management activities of the contract manager and the administrative activities—such as the payment of seller invoices—performed by other teams or individuals within the project organization. Even though the contract manager may not personally perform all aspects of the *Control Procurements* process, the contract manager is the focal point for the individuals that support him or her and the contract manager must ensure that everything contractually required of the project organization or the seller is accomplished. Administrative activities may include:

- Collecting performance data and reporting performance information
- Obtaining ancillary seller deliverables such as certificates of insurance
- Maintaining a contract file, including detailed records of contract and financial performance
- Tracking change requests and approvals
- Drafting administrative contract amendments such as extensions
- Assisting with or conducting audits and inspections
- Documenting receipt of products, services, or results
- Facilitating approval of received products, services, or results
- Making timely payment of accurate seller invoices

Mirroring a team-based approach to managing and administering a procurement agreement, the *Control Procurements* process is dependent upon the application of processes contained in other Knowledge Areas to aid in managing the contracted business relationship:

- Work Performance Data, an output (4.3.3.2) from the *Direct and Manage Project Work* (4.3) process of the Project Integration Management Knowledge Area, to validate a seller's performance in accordance with the Project Schedule component of the Project Documents (12.2.1.2)
- Approved Change Requests, an output (4.6.3.1) from the *Perform Integrated Change Control* (4.6) process of the Project Integration Management Knowledge Area, to ensure that changes proceed through a structured and deliberate change control procedure
- Verified Deliverables, an output (8.3.3.2) from the *Control Quality* (8.3) process of the Project Quality Management Knowledge Area, to execute quality control measures to validate seller performance

- Work Performance Information, an output (10.3.3.1) from the *Control Communications* (10.3) process of the Project Communications Management Knowledge Area, to monitor a seller's performance and compliance with the procurement agreement
- Project Documents Updates (11.6.3.2) as a result of updates to the Risk Register component of the Project Documents, an output from the *Implement Risk Responses* (11.6) process of the Project Risk Management Knowledge Area, to identify risks that arise in the course of contract performance and to develop risk mitigation strategies

A key point for buyers to consider for the future success of a contract manager is that the foundation for the *Control Procurements* process is laid in the *Plan Procurement Management* (12.1) and *Conduct Procurements* (12.2) processes. To enable the *Control Procurements* process, the terms of the procurement agreement should include elements that provide for efficiency of contract management: (1) service level objectives with financial incentives / disincentives (in the form of liquidated damages); (2) metrics and measurements for performance reporting; (3) timetables; (4) pricing mechanisms; (5) defined change control procedure; (6) predetermined remedies for various types of breaches; and, (7) other necessary mechanisms that facilitate the performance of the agreement. If a procurement agreement was poorly constructed by the buyer, the *Control Procurements* process will be a difficult process for both contracting parties and contract disputes are more likely to result. Additionally, as alluded to under the discussion of the various contract types (see Section 12.1.1.6), the contract type used for a procurement agreement directly affects the degree of project organization effort required to monitor and manage the agreement and the business relationship. For example, under a firm fixed price procurement agreement, a contract manager will not be overly concerned with tracking seller cost overruns since any additional costs beyond the firm fixed price must be absorbed by the seller.

The most critical activity performed under the *Control Procurements* process is the monitoring and management of seller performance. A contract manager must monitor whether the products, services, or results are being provided according to the agreed-upon specifications and at the agreed-upon price. Monitoring includes: (1) reviewing Work Performance Data (12.3.1.6) collected by the project organization internally and submitted by a seller; (2) conducting performance reviews as a part of Data Analysis (12.3.2.3) to assess seller progress against contracted commitments described in the procurement agreement; and, (3) conducting an Inspection (12.3.2.4) and Audits (12.3.2.5) to verify seller compliance with products, services, or results specifications. In practice, defective performance or non-performance of a performance agreement by the seller is often blamed on the agreement; that the seller did not understand the procurement agreement or that the contract manager and seller disagree on a particular interpretation of the agreement. To prevent that type of misunderstanding, the contract manager should conduct a post-award, pre-performance meeting with the selected seller. The purpose of the meeting is so that both parties are clear as to matters relating to the monitoring and management of future performance, including details on how monitoring will be performed and how the contracting parties will communicate with each other regarding contract performance. Management differs from monitoring in that the management of seller performance involves taking necessary actions stemming from monitoring activities, including remedial measures, implementation of any breach remedies, and dispute resolution.

In managing a contract, the contract manager should not only monitor the seller's performance but ensure that the project organization is meeting its contractual obligations as well. While those obligations may be far less than those of the seller, there is one critical project organization obligation that the seller is keenly concerned with: payment. Thus, the *Control Procurements* process activities include a management component that involves the financial transactions between the contracting parties: (1) issuance of purchase orders; (2) receipt of satisfactory products, services, or results; (3) receipt of invoices; and, (4) payment of accurate invoices. The *Control Procurements* process activities also include a financial management component that involves monitoring of payments to the seller.

Despite the best of planning, contract changes are inevitable and, in many cases, appropriate. However, contract changes invariably have an impact on schedule and / or cost (depending on contract type) and may therefore introduce unanticipated risk to the overall project. Where contract changes introduce the most risk is when the contracting parties bypass a formal change control procedure and changes are made based on informal, undocumented agreements. To ensure that changes comply with the procurement agreement, that no unauthorized changes occur, and to mitigate risks such as schedule and cost impacts, the contract manager must implement and follow an effective change control procedure. Most procurement agreements specify that a change control procedure will be followed and provide some description of the procedure; however, a contract manager must ensure that an adequate procedure is documented and then communicate the details of the procedure to the seller.

Tables 7-1, 7-2, and 7-3 describe the inputs, tools & techniques, outputs and who is primarily responsible for a particular activity. For each input, tool or technique, and output, the Project Procurement Management Knowledge Area section reference is listed first and, if applicable, the originating reference is listed second within parentheses.

Table 7-1. Control Procurements: Inputs

Inputs	Responsibility
12.3.1.1 Project Management Plan (4.2.3.1)	
– Requirements Management Plan (5.1.3.2)	– Project Manager
– Risk Management Plan (11.1.3.1)	– Project Manager
– Procurement Management Plan (12.1.3.1)	– Contract Manager
– Change Management Plan (4.2.3.1)	– Project Manager
– Schedule Baseline (6.5.3.1)	– Project Manager

Inputs	Responsibility
12.3.1.2 Project Documents	
– Assumption Log (4.1.3.2)	– Contract Manager
– Lessons Learned Register (4.4.3.1)	– Contract Manager
– Milestone List (6.2.3.3)	– Contract Manager
– Quality Reports (8.2.3.1)	– Contract Manager
– Requirements Documentation (5.2.3.1)	– Project Manager
– Requirements Traceability Matrix (5.2.3.2)	– Project Manager
– Risk Register (11.2.3.1)	– Contract Manager
– Stakeholder Register (13.1.3.1)	– Project Manager
12.3.1.3 Agreements	Contract Manager
12.3.1.4 Procurement Documentation	Contract Manager
12.3.1.5 Approved Change Requests	Contract Manager
12.3.1.6 Work Performance Data	Contract Manager
12.3.1.7 Enterprise Environmental Factors	Contract Manager
12.3.1.8 Organizational Process Assets	Contract Manager

Table 7-2. Control Procurements: Tools & Techniques

Tools & Techniques	Responsibility
12.3.2.1 Expert Judgment	Project Team
12.3.2.2 Claims Administration	Contract Manager
12.3.2.3 Data Analysis	
– Performance Reviews	– Contract Manager
– Earned Value Analysis	– Contract Manager
– Trend Analysis	– Contract Manager
12.3.2.4 Inspection	Contract Manager or designee
12.3.2.5 Audits	Contract Manager or independent party

Table 7-3. Control Procurements: Outputs

Outputs	Responsibility
12.3.3.1 Closed Procurements	Contract Manager
12.3.3.2 Work Performance Information	Contract Manager
12.3.3.3 Procurement Documentation Updates	Contract Manager
12.3.3.4 Change Requests	Contract Manager
12.3.3.5 Project Management Plan Updates – Risk Management Plan (11.1.3.1) – Procurement Management Plan (12.1.3.1) – Schedule Baseline (6.5.3.1) – Cost Baseline (7.3.3.1)	 – Contract Manager – Contract Manager – Contract Manager – Contract Manager
12.3.3.6 Project Documents Updates – Lessons Learned Register (4.4.3.1) – Resource Requirements (9.2.3.1) – Requirements Traceability Matrix (5.2.3.2) – Risk Register (11.2.3.1) – Stakeholder Register (13.1.3.1)	 – Contract Manager – Contract Manager – Contract Manager – Contract Manager – Contract Manager
12.3.3.7 Organizational Process Assets Updates	Contract Manager

12.3.1 Control Procurements: Inputs

12.3.1.1 Project Management Plan

As an input to the *Control Procurements* process, the Project Management Plan contains certain integrated and consolidated subsidiary plans and baselines as described in and updated during the *Conduct Procurements* (12.2) process that are integral to the *Control Procurements* process, including the: Requirements Management Plan (5.1.3.2); Risk Management Plan (11.1.3.1); Procurement Management Plan (12.1.3.1); and, Schedule Baseline (6.5.3.1). In preparation for controlling the procurement, the Project Management Plan is now expanded to include the Change Management Plan (4.2.3.1). The Project Management Plan is utilized by the contract manager to ensure that the seller is providing the required products, services, or results in the manner and in the timeframe required by the project organization.

Requirements Management Plan (5.1.3.2)

The Requirements Management Plan, an output (5.1.3.2) resulting from the *Plan Scope Management* (5.1) process of the Project Scope Management Knowledge Area, describes how the seller requirements will be analyzed, documented, and managed. At this point in the Project Procurement Management Knowledge Area, the requirements are mostly set unless otherwise changed as agreed-upon by the project manager and the seller.

Risk Management Plan (11.1.3.1)

The Risk Management Plan, an output (11.1.3.1) resulting from the *Plan Risk Management* (11.1) process of the Project Risk Management Knowledge Area, describes seller-based risks identified within the Risk Register (11.2.3.1) and how risk management activities will be structured and performed.

Procurement Management Plan (12.1.3.1)

The Procurement Management Plan (12.1.3.1) contains the activities to be performed by the contract manager in order to effectively monitor and manage the procurement agreement and the seller relationship. The results of these activities should be formally documented to evidence active contract management and for retention purposes. Typical activities for a contract manager to consider for his or her component of the Procurement Management Plan may include:

- Initiate contract and onboard seller
- Conduct seller orientation training
- Obtain initial certificate of insurance and / or bonding documents
- Review and approve any subcontractors (if permitted)
- Build contract file with procurement agreement and related documentation such as any warranties
- Obtain attestation of information security and data and privacy controls (such as a SOC 2 Type II report)
- Obtain attestation of seller's testing of its business continuity and disaster recovery plan
- Document changes such as amendments to the procurement agreement
- Document seller performance such as deliverables received, deadlines met, quality standards attained, and service levels achieved
- Validate and timely pay accurate seller invoices upon receipt of accepted products, services, or results
- Track spend-to-contract to ensure budget adherence
- Document and resolve any non-compliance, including any missed service levels or deadlines, and document any corrective actions taken or service credits provided
- Identify any risks associated with the seller relationship and develop a mitigation plan
- Conduct, as appropriate, end user surveys
- Conduct regularly scheduled seller account reviews
- Initiate contract close-out and offboard seller
- Ensure receipt of any assets (including project organization data) or, as applicable, destruction of assets

- Obtain transition assistance, if required, from the incumbent seller
- Reconcile any final invoices
- Formally terminate contract unless naturally expired
- Close-out contract file and follow appropriate retention procedures

Change Management Plan (4.2.3.1)

The Change Management Plan, an output (4.2.3.1) resulting from the *Develop Project Management Plan* (4.2) process of the Project Integration Management Knowledge Area, contains procedures on how requested changes will be processed, authorized, and incorporated. While Change Requests (12.1.3.8, 12.2.3.3) under the *Plan Procurement Management* (12.1) and *Conduct Procurements* (12.2) processes are documented, reviewed, and processed in accordance with the Change Management Plan, it is common that requested changes go through a much more rigorous, formalized process once Agreements (12.3.1.3) are entered into with Selected Sellers (12.2.3.1) due to the contractual nature of the business relationship. Based on the scope and complexity of the Agreements (12.3.1.3), the Change Management Plan may include a committee—typically referred to as a change control board—that has the responsibility to review, approve, defer, or reject change requests in accordance with the Change Management Plan. The Change Management Plan describes the roles and responsibilities of the contract manager and the change control board, the extent of their authority, and how the contract change control system (see Section 12.3.1.7) will be implemented. Changes requested by the contract manager or seller may involve any aspect of the contractual relationship but most frequently involve the: (1) scope as described in the Agreements (12.3.1.3) and the Scope Baseline component of the Project Management Plan (12.3.1.1); (2) seller's schedule contained in the Procurement Statement of Work (12.1.3.4) described in the Agreements (12.3.1.3), the Project Schedule component of the Project Documents (12.2.1.2), and the Schedule Baseline component of the Project Management Plan (12.3.1.1); or, (3) seller fees described in the Agreements (12.3.1.3) and the Cost Baseline component of the Project Management Plan (12.3.1.1). Requested changes that are agreed-upon by all parties then become Approved Change Requests (12.3.1.5). The Change Management Plan also includes procedures for when the contract manager and seller cannot agree upon a change or otherwise contest a change request. In such a case, the contested change is referred to as a "claim" and is then addressed under Claims Administration (12.3.2.2).

Schedule Baseline (6.5.3.1)

The Schedule Baseline, an output (6.5.3.1) resulting from the *Develop Schedule* (6.5) process of the Project Schedule Management Knowledge Area, reflects any changes in the seller's schedule, period of delivery or performance, milestones, or deadlines contained in the Procurement Statement of Work (12.1.3.4) described in the Agreements (12.3.1.3). The originator of any cause for delay—either the project organization or the seller—and the reason for the delay should be recorded to facilitate the determination of any contract payment changes or to assist with possible dispute resolution.

12.3.1.2 Project Documents

Project Documents included as inputs for the *Control Procurements* process are comprised of documents updated as a part of the *Plan Procurement Management* (12.1) and *Conduct Procurements* (12.2) processes such as the: Lessons Learned Register (4.4.3.1); Milestone List (6.2.3.3); Requirements Documentation (5.2.3.1); Requirements Traceability Matrix (5.2.3.2); Risk Register (11.2.3.1); and, Stakeholder Register (13.1.3.1). The Assumption Log, an output (4.1.3.2) resulting from the *Develop Project Charter* (4.1) process of the Project Integration Management Knowledge Area, is an added component to the Project Documents under the *Control Procurements* process. The Assumption Log (4.1.3.2) is used to record any assumptions and constraints identified during the project. Another added component is the Quality Reports, an output (8.2.3.1) resulting from the *Manage Quality* (8.2) process of the Project Quality Management Knowledge Area. Quality Reports (8.2.3.1) identify compliance-to-quality, highlight quality issues, summarize findings, and make recommendations for improvements and corrective actions.

Assumption Log (4.1.3.2)

As a competitive procurement progresses, the buyer and the project team make certain assumptions related to the project organization, the sellers, and the external environment. An assumption is a key piece of information which has not or cannot be verified but nevertheless influences project-related decisions and the Project Procurement Management Knowledge Area inputs, tools & techniques, and outputs. Such assumptions are recorded on the Assumption Log for review throughout the project. Based on Expert Judgment (12.1.2.1, 12.2.2.1, 12.3.2.1) under the Project Procurement Management Knowledge Area, assumptions are generally believed to be valid—until determined to be invalid—even without basis or evidence. The Assumption Log is useful in managing a project as it enhances the ability to foresee potential risks and issues that may impact the project. When assumptions become known or verified as valid or invalid, those assumptions may become inputs to the Risk Register component of the Project Documents. A project team should review the Assumption Log on a regular basis and undertake activities to validate assumptions. At a minimum, an Assumption Log should include:

- The date an assumption was logged
- An assumption category, such as budget or schedule
- Name and description of the assumption
- Status of the assumption, such as validated or invalidated
- The likelihood of the assumption and the impact to the project if the assumption is invalidated
- An action plan if the assumption is likely to be invalidated and the impact is significant

The *Plan Procurement Management* (12.1) and *Conduct Procurement* (12.2) processes, with their intended result being a contract award to a seller, have a far shorter duration (typically measured in months) and have far less complexity than the *Control Procurements* process, which is the ongoing management of the seller's delivery or performance of the products, services, or results (typically measured in years). Thus, the ramifications of assumptions in an Assumption Log may have a disproportionate effect on a contract manager as compared to a buyer. As an example, a project team may assume that prospective sellers have the ability to utilize offshore resources resulting in a lower cost basis and an expedited delivery or performance of the products, services, or results enabled by a "follow-the-sun" workflow model. Based on that assumption, the project team develops the Independent Cost Estimates (12.1.3.7) and the Project Schedule component of the Project Documents (12.2.1.2). Even with Expert Judgement (12.1.2.1, 12.2.2.1), the project team may not be able to validate or invalidate the assumption until all prospective seller proposals are received. From the perspective of the *Conduct Procurements* (12.2) process, if the Independent Cost Estimates (12.1.3.7) were merely used to benchmark the pricing of seller proposals, the impact of the risk related to the offshore resource assumption would be low. However, from the *Control Procurements* process perspective, if the offshore resource assumption were to be invalidated on the basis that no sellers offered it as a part of their proposals, the contract manager could be more significantly impacted. If the Independent Cost Estimates (12.1.3.7) where used as input to the project budget, the contract manager may have to seek approval from the project sponsor to utilize a significant portion of the project budget's management reserve, perhaps raising executive concern with the project's progress and leaving an insufficient management reserve for other unidentified risks. Further, as a result of the invalidation of the offshore resource assumption, the project schedule could be significantly impacted, requiring the contract manager to initiate substantial change requests to extend the project schedule due to the delay in obtaining the required products, services, or results. Considering the foregoing example, it is a critical step for a contract manager to carefully review and update the Assumption Log and, if necessary, revise the Risk Register component of these Project Documents. Ideally, if a contract manager is identified before the initiation of the *Plan Procurement Management* (12.1) process activities, the contract manager should review and have input to the Assumption Log before the *Control Procurements* process commences.

Lessons Learned Register (4.4.3.1)

The Lessons Learned Register should be reviewed by the contract manager to determine whether any of the prior lessons learned can be applied to improve the management of the procurement agreement, ensure the satisfactory delivery or performance of the contracted products, services, or results, and achieve the benefits expected from the buyer-seller relationship. In addition to reviewing the Lessons Learned Register, the contract manager should coordinate with the buyer to obtain the buyer's perspective on any recommendations for managing the buyer-seller relationship that may not be recorded in the Lessons Learned Register.

Milestone List (6.2.3.3)

The Milestone List, which may also be incorporated in the Agreements (12.3.1.3) or an exhibit attached thereto, describes all of the delivery or performance milestones that the seller must fulfill. The Milestone List is used by a contract manager to monitor and manage the performance of a seller in terms of achieving the expected project schedule but is also used by the contract manager to manage the performance and obligations of the project organization, such as when the project team must review or accept contract deliverables.

Quality Reports (8.2.3.1)

A contract manager utilizes the information contained in Quality Reports—which can be graphical, numerical, or qualitative—to identify whether seller processes and procedures or the contracted products, services, or results are in compliance or out of compliance with project quality expectations and those contractual quality requirements contained in the Agreements (12.3.1.3). Quality Reports are comprised of: (1) quality management issues escalated by the project team; (2) recommendations to improve quality; (3) recommendations for corrective actions to remedy quality deficiencies; and, (4) the summary of findings from the *Control Quality* (8.3) process, the purpose of which is to monitor and record the results of quality management activities used to assess compliance. The contract manager can then undertake or cause the seller to undertake: (1) preventative actions to seller processes or procedures to reduce the probability of non-compliance; or, (2) corrective actions to detect or remedy non-compliance before the products, services, or results are delivered to the project team. Based on any identified preventative or corrective actions, the contract manager may need to adjust how tools & techniques are applied to contract management activities, such as conducting an Inspection (12.3.2.4) on all or only a sample of the products, services, or results.

Requirements Documentation (5.2.3.1)

Requirements Documentation includes the substantive and procedural requirements (see Sections 12.1.1.4 and 12.2.1.2) that the seller is required to satisfactorily fulfill under the Agreements (12.3.1.3). The contract manager will utilize Work Performance Data (12.3.1.6), findings from Data Analysis (12.3.2.3), results of any Inspection (12.3.2.4) for substantive requirements, results of any Audits (12.3.2.5) for procedural requirements, and any other observations—all of which are compared to the Quality Reports component of the Project Documents—to assess whether the seller has satisfactorily performed or if corrective action is needed.

Requirements Traceability Matrix (5.2.3.2)

The Requirements Traceability Matrix, which links project requirements from their origin to the deliverables which will fulfill them, facilitates the determination of whether seller-requested change requests are warranted or whether the contract manager should contest any such change requests under Claims Administration (12.3.2.2).

Risk Register (11.2.3.1)

As further described in Sections 12.1.1.4 and 12.2.1.2, the Risk Register contains possible risks, their likelihood and impact, and measures to prevent or mitigate risks. The contract manager may also identify additional risks not yet contained in the Risk Register that resulted from his or her review of any invalidated assumptions contained in the Assumption Log component of the Project Documents. Risks that the contract manager should consider in managing the procurement agreement and the seller include:

- Seller-specific risks such as those relating to financial soundness, reliability, capacity, and capability—particularly if those risks may impact the seller's ongoing ability to provide the products, services, or results
- The selected contract template and contract payment type (see Section 12.1.1.6) of the Agreements (12.3.1.3)
- The term of the Agreements (12.3.1.3)
- The fees described in the Agreements (12.3.1.3)
- The project delivery method described in the Procurement Strategy (12.1.3.2)
- Any risks that the seller was unwilling to absorb under the Agreements (12.3.1.3) and that are not yet accepted or for which there is not yet a mitigation plan

Stakeholder Register (13.1.3.1)

With the Agreements (12.3.1.3) having been executed with the selected seller, the Stakeholder Register now includes information about identified stakeholders who have a specific stake or interest in the *Control Procurements* process such as the seller's staff, which may include the seller's executives, project manager, contract manager, project staff, and contingent workers.

12.3.1.3 Agreements

The procurement agreement (further described in Section 12.2.3.2) executed between the project organization and the selected seller is the most critical input to the *Control Procurements* process on the basis that the procurement agreement contains all of the roles, responsibilities, undertakings, obligations, and rights of the contracting parties. The contract managers of the contracting parties will continually refer to the procurement agreement throughout the *Control Procurements* process as a reference to ensure that each party is meeting its contracted obligations. The procurement agreement also serves as a baseline to Approved Change Requests (12.3.1.5).

12.3.1.4 Procurement Documentation

Even though the Bid Documents (12.1.3.3) and Procurement Statement of Work (12.1.3.4) are outputs from the *Plan Procurement Management* (12.1) process and serve the primary purpose of communicating a procurement and the competitive solicitation (such as an RFP) to prospective sellers, they represent important inputs to the *Control Procurements* process. Along with the Agreements (12.3.1.3), which may incorporate the Bid Documents (12.1.3.3) and Procurement Statement of Work (12.1.3.4), Procurement Documentation is an important reference for the contract manager in that it contains critical information pertaining to the project requirements, statement of work, project delivery, and schedule. In cases where the Procurement Documentation is specifically incorporated into the procurement agreement, the Procurement Documentation is more than mere input; rather, it contains contractual requirements that the seller is obligated to meet. In either case, the contract manager will monitor and manage the procurement agreement and measure the seller according to the Procurement Documentation as well as other *Control Procurements* process inputs.

12.3.1.5 Approved Change Requests

Approved Change Requests, an output (4.6.3.1) resulting from the *Perform Integrated Change Control* (4.6) process of the Project Integration Management Knowledge Area, are those Change Requests (12.1.3.8, 12.2.3.3) which have been processed according to the Change Management Plan component of the Project Management Plan (12.3.1.1) and were approved by, as the case may be, the project manager, change control board, or contract manager. Requested changes—originating from the project organization or the seller—provide for flexibility in managing and administering the contractual relationship, allowing contracting parties to modify the products, services, or results, pricing, schedule, contract terms and conditions, or any other aspect of the relationship to suit their changed needs. Approved Change Requests may impact multiple stakeholders, including other sellers, and should be communicated accordingly by the contract manager. Changes likely to be requested or required under the *Control Procurements* process include:

- Changed business needs or priorities of the project organization
- Inadequacies or errors in the procurement or in associated materials which necessitate changes to the Procurement Statement of Work (12.1.3.4)
- Changes required in the contracted products, services, or results
- Changes to various components of the Project Management Plan (12.3.1.1) such as the Requirements Management Plan (5.1.3.2) and Schedule Baseline (6.5.3.1)
- Correction or enhancement of terms and conditions contained in the Agreements (12.3.1.3)
- Legislation, regulations, rules, or standards affecting the subject matter of the procurement that have changed or have been subsequently enacted
- Other initiatives or projects which in some way affect the project

12.3.1.6 Work Performance Data

Work Performance Data, an output (4.3.3.2) from the *Direct and Manage Project Work* (4.3) process of the Project Integration Management Knowledge Area, includes raw observations and measurements identified and resulting from activities being performed to carry out the project work. Specifically, in the context of the Project Procurement Management Knowledge Area, Work Performance Data is comprised of data obtained and developed by a project organization relating to a seller's performance under a procurement agreement, including elements of quality, timeliness, and cost. As an example, a project organization may track products delivered by a seller, whether the quality criteria for the acceptance of those products have been met or not, what products the seller has submitted an invoice for, and what costs have been committed and incurred. Work Performance Data may be both provided by a seller and developed by the project organization. For example, a seller may provide raw data to the project organization which supports the measurement and achievement of a software as a service availability service level. For that same service level, the project organization may collect its own raw observations and measurements so as to validate what has been provided by the seller.

12.3.1.7 Enterprise Environmental Factors

While certain Enterprise Environment Factors originate internally, such as systems used by the project organization, many of the Enterprise Environmental Factors under the *Control Procurements* process are likely to originate externally, terminate externally, or involve external parties such as the seller. Consequently, *Control Procurements* process activities are at a greater risk of being constrained or negatively influenced by Enterprise Environmental Factors. Factors that merit a contract manager's consideration, some of which are continued from Enterprise Environmental Factors (12.1.1.5) under the *Plan Procurement Management* (12.1) process and Enterprise Environmental Factors (12.2.1.5) under the *Conduct Procurements* (12.2) process, include:

- Current economic conditions
- Marketplace conditions that affect the price, availability, or lead-times for the contracted products, services, or results
- The Agreements (12.3.1.3) or Procurement Statement of Work (12.1.3.4) that do not accurately describe project requirements
- A sub- or non-performing seller—including seller staff—either due to the fault of the seller or due to other external factors
- Geographic factors including local, national, or international constraints and requirements
- Strengths and weaknesses of the contract management function within the project organization
- Current or prior agreements in place with incumbent sellers which may affect or impact the ability of the selected seller to provide the required products, services, or results
- The project organization's code of ethics related to sellers such as conflicts of interest and prohibitions on seller-provided gifts to project organization staff (see Chapter 8 – Ethical Considerations)
- Systems (as further described in the following paragraphs) used by the project organization to manage contracts such as contract change control, payment, and records management

In general, contract managers pay a great deal of attention to managing change. Allowing the scope of a procurement or the overall project to change following the execution of Agreements (12.3.1.3) usually means added costs, greater risks, and a longer duration. Not surprisingly, many projects fail due to poor change control management. One of the key Enterprise Environmental Factors that assist contract managers in their responsibilities is a contract change control system which manages change by requiring that requested changes follow a structured and deliberate change control procedure which allows such changes to be assessed in terms of cost, risk, and schedule. Administratively, a contract change control system provides for requesting, reviewing, approving, tracking, and documenting of changes to ensure that:

- Unauthorized or unintended changes are prevented and avoided
- Action on requested changes occurs deliberately and prudently, but without undue delay and without interfering disproportionately with project progress
- The cost, schedule, and technical impacts of requested changes are developed and evaluated by all affected parties
- The collected evaluations of requested changes are considered in the approval or rejection of such changes
- Requested changes are evaluated, reviewed, and dispositioned at the proper level of authority
- All affected parties are informed of change requests and their dispositions
- Baseline documentation, such as the procurement agreement, is controlled and updated as appropriate to reflect Approved Change Requests (12.3.1.5)

Since sellers are focused on obtaining timely payment for the provided products, services, or results, it is important for a project organization to have a capable payment system. Payment systems are either a manual or an automated means to process payments to a seller. These systems can be extremely simple or robust, with the common denominator being that an invoice submitted by a seller must be approved by someone who has verified that the invoice is correct and that the products, services, or results were received and satisfactory. In more robust, feature-rich payment systems, a requisition is electronically generated to permit an approved expense to occur, a purchase order is subsequently generated and provided to the seller, and then payment is made when the invoice is received and reconciled against the purchase order following verification that the products, services, or results have been satisfactorily delivered or performed. Any payments made by a project organization must be in accordance with the contract terms, with the intent that payments are made on time; unless there is a pre-payment discount, early payments do not benefit the contract manager and late payments may constitute a breach of contract as well as negatively affecting the relationship between the contracting parties. Frequently, project organizations have a specific individual or department responsible for the accounts payable function, which relieves a contract manager of that responsibility.

A records management system is used by a project manager and contract manager to manage all of the documentation, correspondence, and other records produced by or in support of a procurement agreement. Although appearing chronologically late in the Project Procurement Management Knowledge Area, a contract manager should seek to have a records management system available—as a consolidated automated system, a combination of disparate automated systems, or as a manual process—at the onset of a procurement and as a part of the *Plan Procurement Management* (12.1) process. Ideally, a records management system would be an automated and integrated system that provides a contract manager with electronic access to content that is needed to conduct *Control Procurements* process activities. A records management system also serves as a repository of historical information that supports the recording of Work Performance Data (12.3.1.6), Work Performance Information (12.3.3.2), Procurement Documentation Updates (12.3.3.3), Project Documents Updates (12.3.3.6), and Organizational Process Assets Updates (12.3.3.7). Additionally, in support of the *Control Procurements* process, a records management system would include a record of activities, correspondence, reports, and payments between the project organization and the seller, such as:

- Business case associated with the procurement
- Competitive solicitation
- Seller's proposal to the competitive solicitation
- Procurement agreement including any attachments, schedules, exhibits, and amendments
- Change request log, describing approved and unapproved change requests
- Contract correspondence log, including emails, telephone calls, and meeting agendas and minutes
- Onboarding and any training of the seller
- Documentation of subcontractor approvals and any changes in subcontractors
- Seller certificates of insurance and evidence of bonds (such as performance bonds)
- Documentation of any required seller licensing, certifications, or background checks
- Payment history and payment records, including documentation supporting verification and approval of invoices and payments, other expenditures, total spend against contracted amount, and any balances or amounts due
- Receipt, inspection, audit, and acceptance or approval records relating to the products, services, or results
- Reporting relating to seller performance, such as service levels, and records relating to the receipt of any associated liquidated damages (such as service credits)
- Documentation of any deficiencies, remedial actions, disputes, and negotiated settlements
- Warranties and guarantees
- Installation, user, technical, and maintenance manuals and records
- Reports or data provided by the seller
- Results of any seller account reviews or project organization site visits of seller's facility
- Copies of seller-provided documentation, such as disaster recovery or business continuity plans, incident response plans, and attestations and validations of internal controls (for example, relating to information security and data privacy)
- Documentation relating to procurement agreement expiration or termination
- Documentation of contract close-out activities

- Evidence of the receipt or destruction of any items or information required to be returned or destroyed by the seller, such as confidential information

12.3.1.8 Organizational Process Assets

Organizational Process Assets Updates (12.2.3.6) from the *Conduct Procurements* (12.2) process and other Organizational Process Assets specific to the *Control Procurements* process that will assist the contract manager in managing and administering the Agreements (12.3.1.3) may include:

- Contract management policy and related procedures and guidelines
- Seller onboarding and offboarding checklist
- Seller orientation materials
- Contract monitoring tool
- Change control procedure
- Claims administration procedure
- Receiving and seller payment procedures
- Templates and formats such as end user surveys, contract amendments, and contract terminations
- Seller account review guidelines
- Corrective action and dispute resolution procedures
- Record retention policy and procedures

12.3.2 Control Procurements: Tools & Techniques

12.3.2.1 Expert Judgment

Expert Judgment required to manage and administer the Agreements (12.3.1.3) as well as to ensure the satisfactory delivery or performance of the contracted products, services, or results may require a wide variety of specialized knowledge or training such as:

- Project management
- Iterative and adaptive delivery methodology and related expertise such as agile, scrum, Kanban, and lean
- Contract management
- Vendor management
- Supply management
- Enterprise risk management
- Enterprise resiliency (business continuity and disaster recovery)
- Information technology
- Organizational change management

- Process improvement
- Legal expertise
- Compliance
- Ethics
- Security and privacy
- Benefits realization

12.3.2.2 Claims Administration

Claims can originate from the contract manager or the seller and involve changes that are: (1) contested changes; (2) potential constructive changes where the contract manager and the seller cannot reach an agreement on compensation for the change; or, (3) a disagreement between the contract manager and the seller that a change has occurred.   Claims frequently result from a disagreement between the contract manager and the seller over the interpretation of the Requirements Documentation component of the Project Documents (12.3.1.2) or the Procurement Statement of Work (12.1.3.4) contained in the Agreements (12.3.1.3).   That type of interpretive disagreement is why project organizations sometimes incorporate the Bid Documents (12.1.3.3) and Seller Proposals (12.2.1.4) into the Agreements (12.3.1.3): It is difficult for a seller to make an argument over interpretation when the Agreements (12.3.1.3) require delivery or performance consistent with both the Bid Documents (12.1.3.3) and Seller Proposals (12.2.1.4). Claims Administration involves documenting, processing, adjudicating, and communicating the results of adjudication.   When claims cannot be successfully resolved between the contracting parties, they become disputes and finally appeals.   For contract relationships with a lengthy term or that involve complex delivery or performance, the contracting parties should establish a Claims Administration procedure similar in formality to a contract change control system (see Section 12.3.1.7) in order to facilitate the timely adjudication of any claims.   If the contracting parties cannot agree on whether a claim is appropriate or cannot agree on a remedy to a claim, the parties may elect to resort to one of the dispute resolution methods described in Chapter 6 – Dispute Resolution.   As described in that chapter, negotiation is the preferred method of resolution since it is the most effective and cost-efficient method.

12.3.2.3 Data Analysis

Data Analysis represents techniques that are used by a contract manager to monitor the seller's delivery or performance under the Agreements (12.3.1.3) and to determine whether the seller is providing the products, services, or results in accordance with the contracted requirements, schedule, and budget—which may have been amended by any Approved Change Requests (12.3.1.5).   Techniques for Data Analysis include performance reviews, earned value analysis (EVA), and trend analysis.   Where there is a deficiency in performance, the contract manager utilizes the results of the Data Analysis to assist in improving the seller's performance, as a basis to support a claim (see Section 12.3.2.2), or to initiate a subsequent dispute.   Data

Analysis also serves as historical documentation to indicate whether a seller should be included on the prequalified seller list (see Section 12.1.1.6) for future procurements.

Performance reviews are methodical and evaluative in structure, based on Work Performance Data (12.3.1.6), any results from an Inspection (12.3.2.4), any Audits (12.3.2.5), and a contract manager's personal observations. A contract manager compiles all of the source data and information and then develops a comparison of seller delivery or performance to the contracted requirements, quality standards, level of resources, schedule, and budget as described in the Agreements (12.3.1.3). Performance reviews are not ad hoc and are conducted on a regularly scheduled basis using a format that has typically been shared with the seller in advance. The contract managers of the contracting parties then collectively discuss the results of the performance review and develop preventative or corrective actions to resolve any performance deficiencies.

EVA, one of the Data Analysis tools & techniques (7.4.2.2) for the *Control Costs* (7.4) process of the Project Cost Management Knowledge Area, compares schedule and cost variances to schedule and cost performance targets to determine the degree of variance from the targets. EVA combines the Scope Baseline, Cost Baseline, and Schedule Baseline components of the Project Management Plan (12.3.1.1) into a "performance measurement baseline" and uses that combined baseline to compare against three key dimensions: (1) planned value, which represents the authorized budget for work to be performed on a project activity during a specific time period; (2) earned value, which represents the authorized budget for work performed on a project activity during a specific time period; and, (3) actual cost, which represents the cost incurred for work performed on a project activity during a specific time period.

Trend analysis, one of the Data Analysis tools & techniques (4.5.2.2) for the *Control Scope* (4.5) process of the Project Integration Management Knowledge Area, is used to forecast future performance based on past results. A contract manager can utilize a trend analysis to forecast potential schedule slippages and cost performance deterioration.

Where there is a disagreement between the contract managers of the contracting parties as to the seller's delivery or performance, the result may be a claim (see Section 12.3.2.2) or rise to the level of a dispute which may require the parties to resort to one of the dispute resolution methods described in Chapter 6 – Dispute Resolution.

12.3.2.4 Inspection

An Inspection is a structured and formal review conducted by a contractor manager or a designated third party to determine whether a seller's performance is satisfactory. Based on the complexity of the products, services, or results and based on the needs of the contract manager, an Inspection may range from a simple review to an intensive examination of the seller's performance; for example, an Inspection may involve the mere review of written work product, a physical examination of provided products, services, or results, or a site visit of a seller's facility in another country. For complex procurements, the information resulting from Data Analysis (12.3.2.3), Work Performance Data (12.3.1.6), Work Performance Information (12.3.3.2), or a contract manager's personal observation of a seller's performance may be insufficient to gauge actual performance. In some cases, a contract manager may not have sufficient knowledge of the product, services, or deliverables to adequately evaluate performance and may require other expertise to assist in the Inspection. To address those cases, the contract manager should ensure that the Agreements (12.3.1.3) include a contract provision that permits an Inspection to be conducted—with the full cooperation and support of the seller—by the contract manager, other parties of the project organization, or a third party.

12.3.2.5 Audits

Audits, one of the tools & techniques (8.2.2.5) for the *Manage Quality* (8.2) process of the Project Quality Management Knowledge Area, are structured and formal reviews conducted by independent parties—such as internal or external auditors—to determine if project activities comply with project organization policies, processes, and procedures. A comprehensive audit may result in observations that identify any nonconformities and deficiencies and may identify any leading practices that could serve to improve or benefit the seller's performance of the Agreements (12.3.1.3). Audit observations are reviewed by the contract managers of the contracting parties, resulting in possible preventative actions, corrective actions, Approved Change Requests (12.3.1.5), or claims that require adjudication under Claims Administration (12.3.2.2). A project organization's right to audit and the seller's obligation to comply and cooperate with audit requests should be described in a specific contract provision that is included in the Agreements (12.3.1.3). A robust audit provision would:

- Require the seller to retain full and detailed business records for the contract term and a specified period after contract expiration or termination
- Describe the business records that must be retained such as financial records, daily logs, diaries, estimates, reports, and memoranda
- Afford access by the contract manager or his or her designee to the business records
- Require the seller to implement changes that would resolve any nonconformities and deficiencies observed by the audit

12.3.3 Control Procurements: Outputs

12.3.3.1 Closed Procurements

At some point, whether by natural expiration, complete fulfillment of the contracting parties' obligations, early termination by a contracting party, or as a result of a dispute, the Agreements (12.3.1.3) between the project organization and the seller will come to an end. Closed Procurements is the project activity of evaluating what needs to take place when a procurement agreement is coming to an end or has ended and then properly closing out the procurement. Procurement agreements almost universally specify a duration, a specific termination date, or a specific event such as a final delivery upon which the contract expires. Mostly, procurements are "closed" when all of the obligations and undertakings contained in the associated procurement agreement have been satisfied; for example, the products, services, or results have been provided by a seller and accepted by the contract manager. In the case of normal termination (meaning no breaches or early termination), Closed Procurements includes the verification of whether the products, services, or results were provided in accordance with the requirements of the procurement agreement and whether the same were acceptable to the contract manager. Regardless of how a procurement agreement is completed or terminated, the contract manager must formally signify and document the close-out of the agreement. The procedure by which this occurs is typically described in the Procurement Management Plan component of the Project Management Plan (12.3.1.1) or specified in the Agreements (12.3.1.3). This procedure should clearly and comprehensively describe the responsibilities, obligations, liabilities (including costs or amounts due), and any notice requirements of the contracting parties upon expiration or termination. Notice may involve a simple letter to "the file" or a formal written notice from a contract manager to the seller that the contract has been completed or terminated. Additionally, the contract manager may provide written notice to the seller as to whether the provided products, services, or results have been accepted or rejected.

Negotiations between the contract manager and the seller may be required to finally resolve or settle any remaining issues, amounts due, claims, or disputes. If the products, services, or results are deficient or non-conforming, based on the terms and conditions of the procurement agreement, the seller may be required to correct the deficiencies or non-conformities (at the cost of seller) or provide some sort of credit to the project organization in order to obtain the contract manager's final acceptance. When a procurement agreement naturally expires—and assuming that a project organization has adequately managed the procurement agreement, for example, through the use of the *Control Procurements* process tools & techniques—negotiations will likely be minimal or non-existent because the contract manager and the seller would have resolved or settled any operational or financial matters as they occurred. However, if the contract manager failed to adequately manage the procurement agreement, the negotiations may be more extensive. Where the close-out of a procurement agreement is due to an early termination or a contract breach, the contracting parties may have material or highly adversarial disagreements that require extensive negotiations. Where the project organization and the seller cannot resolve their disagreements through negotiations, the contracting parties may resort to resolving their disagreements via one of the dispute resolution methods described in Chapter 6 – Dispute Resolution.

Whether a procurement agreement ends pre-maturely or when intended, future unresolved claims may arise from the procurement that could be subject to dispute and litigation. To be prepared for this possibility and for archival purposes, all documentation related to Closed Procurements should be retained in a records management system (see Section 12.3.1.7). Record retention related to contract finalization and close-out is addressed by the *Close Project or Phase* (4.7) process of the Project Integration Management Knowledge Area.

12.3.3.2 Work Performance Information

Work Performance Information, an input (4.5.1.3) to the *Monitor and Control Project Work* (4.5) process of the Project Integration Management Knowledge Area, collectively includes the observations and findings of

Data Analysis (12.3.2.3), any Inspection (12.3.2.4), and any Audits (12.3.2.5) as well as the transformation of Work Performance Data (12.3.1.6) into intelligible and actionable information. This collection of information—the Work Performance Information—is compared against components of the Project Management Plan (12.3.1.1), components of the Project Documents (12.3.1.2), and other project variables to measure project and seller performance, identify current or potential issues and risks with the seller, ensure seller performance and compliance with the Agreements (12.3.1.3), and serve as a record for any disputes. Work Performance Information is used by a contract manager in the day-to-day management of the seller and Agreements (12.3.1.3) to ensure that any problems are timely and satisfactorily addressed. Various formats, such as performance reports, balanced scorecards, and dashboards can be utilized as appropriate so as to best present the substance of the Work Performance Information.

12.3.3.3 Procurement Documentation Updates

Procurement Documentation Updates in the context of the *Control Procurements* process is not related to, and should not be confused with, the components utilized in the *Plan Procurement Management* (12.1) and the *Conduct Procurements* (12.2) processes to communicate the project needs and to select sellers, such as the Bid Documents (12.1.3.3) and the Source Selection Criteria (12.1.3.5). Rather, at this point, Procurement Documentation Updates have a historical retention purpose and are comprised of all of the information related to the procurement and subsequent contract management of the Agreements (12.3.1.3); for example, Approved Change Requests (12.3.1.5), Work Performance Data (12.3.1.6), Data Analysis (12.3.2.3), Inspection (12.3.2.4), Audits (12.3.2.5), and Work Performance Information (12.3.3.2). The foregoing contain data and information such as invoices, payment records, contract changes, inspection results, audit results, and warranties and guarantees surviving the Agreements (12.3.1.3). Procurement Documentation is collected, indexed or cataloged, filed, and retained. Frequently, Procurement Documentation is in the form of an index and information summaries that "point" to where information is stored—electronically in a records management system (see Section 12.3.1.7) or otherwise—and how that information can be accessed or retrieved. In addition to serving as a record, Procurement Documentation can inform future competitive procurements and the maintenance of a prequalified seller list (see Section 12.1.1.6).

12.3.3.4 Change Requests

During the *Control Procurements* process, changes may be required to the Project Management Plan (12.3.1.1) and its subsidiary plans and baselines or the Project Documents (12.3.1.2). Any such changes are processed through the *Perform Integrated Change Control* (4.6) process of the Project Integration Management Knowledge Area. Unresolved or contested Change Requests are addressed by Claims Administration (12.3.2.2).

12.3.3.5 Project Management Plan Updates

As documented via Change Requests (12.3.3.4), certain integrated and consolidated subsidiary plans and baselines of the Project Management Plan (12.3.1.1)—such as the Risk Management Plan (11.1.3.1); Procurement Management Plan (12.1.3.1); Schedule Baseline (6.5.3.1); and, Cost Baseline (7.3.3.1)—may require revision and updating based on adjustments to the risk management approach, the identification of improvements to contract management activities, schedule revisions, and changes in costs:

- Risk Management Plan (11.1.3.1) – Risks related to Selected Sellers (12.2.3.1) and associated Agreements (12.3.1.3), incorporated into the Risk Register (11.2.3.1), that occurred during delivery or performance of the contract and which may require adjustments to the project organization's approach to managing future project risks.

- Procurement Management Plan (12.1.3.1) – Enhancements or updates to the project activities which enable the effective management of seller relationships and the monitoring of procurement agreements. Enhancements can also be included within the Lessons Learned Register (4.4.3.1) component of the Project Documents Updates (12.2.3.5).

- Schedule Baseline (6.5.3.1) – Revisions due to significant schedule changes which impacted schedule performance as well as any cascading impacts of delays caused by the Selected Sellers (12.2.3.1) which may impact the delivery or performance of any other sellers.

- Cost Baseline (7.3.3.1) – Changes in the seller's prices to the project organization for the contracted products, services, or results—such as labor and material prices—based on fluctuations or other external economic environment factors. In the case of a firm fixed price contract type (see Section 12.1.1.6), the seller is at risk for absorbing any price impacts and there should be no changes in the seller's price charged to the project organization unless there were Approved Change Requests (12.3.1.5). However, any changes in costs—whether or not they are absorbed by the seller—will inform future procurements and may result in improvements to the development of Independent Cost Estimates (12.1.3.7).

12.3.3.6 Project Documents Updates

As a part of the *Control Procurements* process activities and the contract manager's active management of the seller's delivery or performance, certain components of the Project Documents (12.3.1.2)—such as the Lessons Learned Register (4.4.3.1); Resource Requirements (9.2.3.1); Requirements Traceability Matrix (5.2.3.2); Risk Register (11.2.3.1); and, Stakeholder Register (13.1.3.1)—may require revision and updating:

- Lessons Learned Register (4.4.3.1) – Any lessons learned while managing the seller relationship and maintaining the scope, schedule, and cost of the contracted products, services, or results. Where the results of Data Analysis (12.3.2.3), any Inspection (12.3.2.4), or any Audits (12.3.2.5) indicate variances, the Lessons Learned Register should be updated to reflect the effectiveness of any preventative or corrective actions and their effectiveness in mitigating the variances. Additionally, any preventative actions to avoid claims or disputes that were addressed by Claims Administration (12.3.2.2) should be recorded to inform future procurements. During the *Control Procurements* process—which is likely to result in significant lessons learned due to the dynamic buyer-seller relationship—the contract manager should seek out opportunities to routinely update the Lessons Learned Register.

- Resource Requirements (9.2.3.1) – Changes to the types or quantities of resources (such as people, equipment, or materials) required for the *Control Procurements* process activities performed by the contract manager or required by the seller to satisfactorily provide the contracted products, services, or results within the required scope, cost, and schedule.
- Requirements Traceability Matrix (5.2.3.2) – Information on completed project requirements.
- Risk Register (11.2.3.1) – Any risks related to the Agreements (12.3.1.3) entered into with Selected Sellers (12.2.3.1) or risks with the Selected Sellers (12.2.3.1) themselves arising during the delivery or performance of the products, services, or results. The contract template and contract payment type (see Section 12.1.1.6), the contract term, the project delivery method described in the Procurement Strategy (12.1.3.2), and other contract terms and conditions may represent certain risks pertaining to either the project organization or the Selected Sellers (12.2.3.1) which must be assessed and mitigated or accepted. Any such seller risks should also be included in the Risk Register updates.
- Stakeholder Register (13.1.3.1) – Any changes in Selected Sellers (12.2.3.1) or the staff of Selected Sellers (12.2.3.1) such as contingent workers.

12.3.3.7 Organizational Process Assets Updates

The conclusion of the *Control Procurements* process—which is the monitoring and controlling process of managing a seller's performance and obtaining the contracted products, services, or results—will likely result in substantial Organizational Process Assets Updates. Additional updates may be necessitated by Project Management Plan Updates (12.3.3.5) and Project Documents Updates (12.3.3.6). Organizational Process Assets Updates which benefit the buyer-seller relationship or inform future procurements may include:

- Results of the contract monitoring tool (including seller performance evaluation), which, depending on the seller's performance, may impact the seller's ability to be included on prequalified seller lists or participate in future procurements
- Receiving and seller payment records
- Results of seller account reviews
- Preventative and corrective actions undertaken by the contract manager or the seller
- Results of resolving any claims or disputes
- Inclusion of the Lessons Learned Register component of the Project Documents Updates (12.3.3.6) and inclusion of the results of the project as compared to expectations in a lessons learned repository to inform and improve future procurements
- Contract file for record retention purposes

8 – Ethical Considerations

Ethics is a branch of philosophy that examines moral ideals and goals, motives of choice, and patterns of "good" and "bad" conduct. Ethics is derived from the Greek *ethikos*, meaning "character." Issues of personal character, and the search for the best patterns for living, were at the core of Greek ethical philosophy. In the context of ethics, *normative* ethics (also known as moral theory) is the study of what makes actions right and wrong. The focus of this chapter is *applied* ethics, which seeks to apply ethical theory to real-life situations. While applied ethics attempts to define what is "good" and "bad" conduct, ethics is interwoven through all types and parts of societies throughout the world and is therefore highly subjective. The lens through which ethics are viewed or evaluated is also subjective based on the perspective. Theologians study ethics in light of religious teachings. Psychologists seek to understand how people's ethical values influence their thinking and actions. Sociologists attempt to identify and explain ethical norms and practices. Professional and trade associations try to identify principles and standards of ethical conduct by which their members can avoid ethical misdeeds. Businesses (and local, state, and federal government) shape their concepts of ethics into codes of conduct for their employees. As a consequence, an individual's decision to act or not act in a certain way is filtered through multiple different perspectives of ethical beliefs and ethical standards.

Professional ethics and business ethics, as forms of applied ethics, are an attempt to create a model code of ethics by which individuals of a certain profession or employees of an organization can operate by. Government entities and most larger organizations have codes of ethics for their employees as do most professional and trade associations for their members. Professional and trade association codes of ethics are usually written by and for members of the profession through a central organization (such as the PMI). However, even the best codes of ethics cannot guarantee ethical conduct—they merely express the ideals and values of their respective organizations and professions. The decision to act ethically or unethically is a personal one and up to the individual.

This chapter will explore applied ethics in the context of procurement, from the broadest perspective of ethics through to the narrowest: (1) the law of agency; (2) professional ethics; (3) business ethics; and, (4) personal ethics. First, however, this chapter describes ethical risks that may arise in procurements, including their warning signs and prevention.

Procurement-Related Ethical Risks

At its most rudimentary level, the role of a buyer is to spend the money of a project organization to procure needed products, services, or results and the role of a contract manager is to ensure that value is received for the money spent. However, quite simply, a buyer and a contract manager must spend and manage the project organization's money only in the way in which it is meant to be spent and managed. Conflicting with that basic tenet are competing business pressures (faster turnaround times, better quality results, lower prices) and personal pressures (debt, unexpected expenses, financial losses) that a buyer or contract manager may face. Those pressures can increase the potential for procurement-related ethical risks and result in breaches of ethical conduct, including two of the most common breaches: conflicts of interest and fraud.

Conflicts of Interest

A conflict of interest arises when an employee has or appears to have a competing interest, either professional or personal, that could or does make it difficult for that employee to properly discharge his or her duties and responsibilities or that could or does lead to a disregard of duties or responsibilities owed to the employer. A conflict of interest in the context of procurement arises when someone having influence over a procurement or a contract—such as a buyer or a contract manager—could or does use his or her position for personal gain or for the gain of any third party. A conflict between the professional or personal interests of a buyer or contract manager and the interests of the project organization can arise directly or indirectly and can be actual or apparent. The fact that a conflict of interest may exist, even if an employee or a third party does not inappropriately benefit from it, can create an appearance of impropriety which can undermine confidence that the buyer or contract manager can properly perform his or her duties and responsibilities. Examples of an actual or apparent conflict of interest include a buyer or contract manager who:

- Is managing a competitive procurement or contract that includes a prospective seller partially owned by a family member of the employee
- Owns stock of a seller participating in a competitive procurement
- Purchases stock of a selected seller prior to an award announcement
- Has received an offer of employment from an incumbent seller
- Has secondary employment
- Personally purchased an item from a prospective seller at a special, discounted price
- Accepts a gift from an incumbent seller
- Attends a lunch paid for by a seller's representative during the timeframe of a competitive procurement

The most frequent occurrence of an actual or apparent conflict of interest results from a buyer's or contract manager's relationship with a seller where the seller provides gifts such as meals and entertainment to the employee. The adage of "there's no such thing as a free lunch" generally rings true in the world of procurement. The recipient of a seller-provided gift should not be so naïve as to believe that a seller's representative is personally fascinated or enamored with the recipient such that the seller's representative feels compelled to provide a gift. Rather, the recipient should recognize that the primary objective of the seller's representative is to obtain, retain, or expand business with the project organization. With a gift, such as entertainment, the seller's representative wants to ingratiate himself or herself with the recipient and to extract as much influence or information as possible to advantage the seller in its primary objective. Project managers, buyers, and contract managers should look to their project organization's policy regarding seller-provided gifts for guidance on what is considered acceptable or not.

More and more, project organizations have a "zero tolerance" policy when it comes to accepting gifts from sellers. The rationale for such a policy is understandable: minimize a seller's influence on employees, remove the sense of obligation that an employee may have to a seller, and eliminate any appearance of influence or impropriety. Clearly, high-value gifts offered by sellers go beyond an ethical business relationship and should be prohibited. Further, there are points in a business relationship, such as during a competitive procurement, where seller-provided gifts should be prohibited and not be accepted. However, a zero tolerance policy employs a broad-brush approach that has the effect of eliminating the opportunity for a seller and a project organization's employees to have a closer business relationship in which trust can be established and cultivated. An entertainment setting, such as a lunch or a dinner, is an ideal venue for a buyer or contract manager and a seller to temporarily remove themselves from the workplace and get beyond the formalities and, in some cases, the "politeness" of the business relationship. Certainly, a buyer or contract manager and a seller can meet outside of a social setting, but such meetings are usually more formal and agenda-driven, thereby constraining casual conversation that may lead to better results for the project organization. Appendix III contains an example seller gift policy that strives to be flexible and reasonable but avoid any conflicts of interest.

Fraud

Fraud is an intentional non-violent act characterized by deceit, concealment, or a violation of trust that results in the fraudster achieving an illegal gain of money, property, services, or advantage and the victim suffering a loss. While fraud in the context of procurement most frequently involves an employee such as a buyer or contract manager defrauding a project organization on his or her own, an employee and a seller can conspire together to defraud the project organization (such as through kickbacks and bribes) or the seller alone can defraud the project organization. A project organization employee may also defraud a seller and not the project organization.

The factors that may cause a person to commit fraud are best illustrated by the "fraud triangle," first identified by sociologist Donald Cressey. The fraud triangle is a model for explaining the factors that, together, lead to fraudulent behavior: pressure, opportunity, and rationalization. Figure 8-1 depicts the factors which, according to Cressey, must be present at the same time in order for a person to commit fraud. When these three factors are present, there is a much higher than normal chance of an individual committing a fraud.

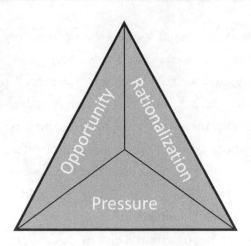

Figure 8-1. Fraud Triangle

The first factor, actual or perceived pressure, is the motive for committing the fraud. Most commonly, the pressure is a financial need brought on by, for example, greed, living beyond one's means, gambling or other vices, addiction, debt, actual or potential financial loss such as a divorce, job loss, or lawsuit, or unexpected expenses such as medical bills. The pressure is almost always "non-shareable" by fraudsters: They are typically embarrassed by the basis for their financial need, believe that others cannot help them with their financial need, or believe, for whatever reason, that their financial need must be addressed secretly. Consequently, "self-help" in the form of perpetrating a fraud is a plausible alternative in the minds of fraudsters.

Opportunity, the second factor, facilitates the ability to commit fraud and defines the method by which the fraud is perpetrated. Fraudsters do not want to be caught: They realize that being discovered would exacerbate their underlying pressure. Therefore, a fraudster must believe that he or she has a favorable or promising combination of circumstances to commit an undetectable fraud. Fraudsters have opportunity if they have access as a part of their position to information and assets that allow them to conceal the fraud. While employees may need such access to perform their job duties and responsibilities, that access can also provide employees with opportunity. Perpetrating fraud through the use of one's position commonly occurs when the circumstances surrounding the opportunity include poor management oversight and weak internal controls. Opportunities to perpetrate fraud can increase due to layoffs and staffing shortages when they weaken or eliminate internal controls. In exploiting the circumstances, a fraudster must have a certain level of technical or job skills to identify an opportunity, which is why fraud is most frequently perpetrated within the scope of the fraudster's job function—such as procurement or contract management.

Once an opportunity has been identified by fraudsters, they frequently test the opportunity to determine its effectiveness and then, if they believe that they are undetected, increase their exploitation of the opportunity. As a result, an initial fraud usually starts with a small amount of money or property being taken and then grows larger over time. A buyer or contract manager can perpetrate a fraud against the project organization by:

- Establishing a "ghost" seller that the buyer or contract manager controls and then directing fraudulent payments to that seller (which may include splitting purchases into smaller amounts in order to avoid detection)
- Taking over a legitimate but inactive seller account, changing the seller's payment remittance address to one that the buyer or contract manager controls, and then issuing false invoices for fraudulent payments
- Diverting the shipment of orders to an address controlled by the buyer or contract manager
- Directing a seller to provide services that benefit the buyer or contract manager and then charging the cost to the project organization

When a project organization employee and seller conspire together to defraud a project organization, their opportunities include:

- Inviting unqualified or unsatisfactory sellers to participate in a competitive procurement so as to limit competition and to provide a competitive advantage to the seller
- Bid rigging, such as drafting or falsifying requirements that favor or can only be met by the seller
- Providing the seller with information unknown to other sellers participating in a competitive procurement so as to provide that seller with a competitive advantage
- Drafting evaluation criteria that favor the seller
- The buyer using undue influence or manipulation on a seller selection committee or seller negotiation committee so as to favor the seller
- Sole sourcing a procurement to the seller for products, services, or results that can be provided by other sellers
- Making inappropriate changes to an awarded procurement agreement that reduces the seller's costs or otherwise increases the seller's profits
- Indicating receipt of products, services, or results that have not been received or that were received but are deficient in some way
- Inflating invoices, accepting falsified invoices, accepting duplicate invoices, or permitting false payments or over payments
- Extending a contract beyond its natural expiration without following a competitive procurement process

The third and final factor, rationalization, is crucial in that it allows the fraudster to reconcile his or her fraudulent behavior with the principles of trust and decency. The fraudster uses rationalization to convince himself or herself that the misdeed is justified and acceptable. Some common rationalizations for committing fraud include believing that:

- The money or property is a loan and intending that it will be paid back
- The project organization will not be adversely affected by the taking of the money or property
- There is no other way to relieve the pressure or that there is no one that can help
- The fraudster is owed something by the project organization or deserves more (such as not being paid enough)
- The money or property is needed to help or save a family member or loved one
- The fraudster will lose his or her family, home, car, or other coveted or important item if the money or property is not taken

Warning Signs of Unethical Conduct

While a fraud or undisclosed conflict of interest may be difficult to detect, there are warning signs that a project organization should be aware of which point to potential unethical conduct. Warning signs may indicate the risk is higher, but they are not evidence that unethical conduct is actually occurring. Typical signs that may indicate or warn of unethical conduct include employee traits and behaviors such as a buyer or contract manager who:

- Has a "wheeler-dealer" attitude
- Demonstrates a drastic change in personality or behavior
- Lives beyond his or her means
- Has financial difficulties
- Suddenly buys (and may brag about buying) high-cost items such as houses, cars, boats, jewelry, or travel
- Has creditors and collectors calling the employee at work or showing up at the workplace
- Exhibits signs of vices or addictions
- Complains about mistreatment at work, work issues, or other perceived inequities such as low pay
- Has an unusually close association with a certain seller
- Is unwilling to share duties, delegate, or collaborate
- Is unwilling to allow other staff to deal with certain sellers
- Works excessive overtime or starts coming in early or leaving late
- Refuses to take vacations or sick time, or, if taken, are taken in very short increments
- Refuses a promotion
- Is resistant to others reviewing his or her work, including audits, and can become unreasonably upset when asked about work activities
- Deviates from correct procedures

Other signs that may indicate or warn of unethical conduct include situations or practices such as:

- Frequent sole source or emergency procurements
- Repeated procurements from the same seller
- Multiple procurements from a seller that are below the threshold which requires a competitive solicitation (known as "split purchases" or "split bids")
- Excessive entertaining of an employee by a seller
- Overcharging by a seller
- Duplicate invoices and / or duplicate payments
- A seller paying travel and expenses for an employee to visit the seller's facilities
- Employment by a seller of an employee or a member of the employee's family
- A seller paying money to a business entity in which the employee or a member of the employee's family has an interest
- Poor record keeping or missing files
- Poor or no segregation of duties, such as an employee who receives products, services, or results being the same individual who makes payment
- Poor approval controls, such as only one employee being required to sign a procurement agreement on behalf of the project organization

Methods to Prevent and Detect Unethical Conduct

Strong prevention measures that deter unethical conduct are more important than detection: By the time most project organizations detect an undisclosed conflict of interest or fraud they have likely already suffered some sort of harm or loss. To avoid an actual or apparent conflict of interest in the context of competitive procurements, a project organization can undertake an employee awareness and training strategy, including a code of ethics, so that employees understand what constitutes a conflict. Additionally, a project organization can implement measures that identify and document actual or apparent conflicts. For example, it is a prudent business practice to have a buyer, seller selection committee, seller negotiation committee, and contract manager execute, in advance of a competitive procurement, a project organization-provided declaration and attestation that there is no conflict of interest with prospective sellers. This practice makes employees aware of the importance in avoiding conflicts, serves as a checklist for an employee to consider whether potential or actual conflicts exist, and, once executed, demonstrates the impartiality of the employee. As a part of awareness and training, employees involved in a procurement or who can influence the procurement must be required to maintain the highest standards of conduct so as to ensure the proper discharge of their duties and responsibilities. Such employees must avoid activities, relationships, and employment that reflect adversely on their objectivity, create conflicts of interest, impair their ability to make impartial decisions, or otherwise interfere with the proper performance of their duties and responsibilities. Additionally, to avoid an actual or apparent conflict of interest, a buyer or contract manager should:

- Immediately declare any potential or actual conflict of interest
- Not use information obtained for professional reasons for personal profit
- Not participate in or withdraw from any conflicting competitive procurement
- Obtain approval from the project organization for any secondary employment
- Notify the project organization if considering employment with an incumbent or prospective seller
- Strictly adhere to the project organization's policy regarding seller-provided gifts
- Avoid transactions such as seller-provided discounts that are or could be construed as a conflict of interest unless permitted by the project organization

In the case of fraud, a project organization can reduce risk by addressing each of the fraud triangle's three factors. Conversely, a project organization's failure to take measures to prevent fraud will increase the opportunity for fraud to occur. A project organization has the least amount of control over pressure and rationalization, and the greatest amount of control over opportunity. A project organization can create awareness about pressures and their warning signs. Rationalization can be reduced by promoting a strong sense of ethical behavior among employees and by creating a positive work environment. By implementing strong internal controls, a project organization can remove much of the opportunity for fraud to occur and can increase the chances of detecting it. As a part of its internal controls, a project organization can reduce the opportunity for fraud through:

- Employee background screening
- Mandatory vacation time
- A fraud detection program, including variance analysis and data mining
- A fraud reporting and whistleblower program
- Verification of a seller's ownership
- A robust vendor management program (which includes seller audits)
- Segregation of duties (breaking down tasks that might be completed by a single employee into multiple tasks so that no one employee is solely in control)
- Dual custody (where two employees are required to access the asset being controlled)
- Detailed procurement procedures, including limitations on sole source and emergency procurements
- Audits of the procurement function

- Matching an invoice to a receipt of products, services, or results and to the corresponding purchase order
- A system of financial authorizations and levels of authority
- Audit trails and other documentation and records
- Monitoring, including ongoing and periodic assessments
- An asset management and disposal program, which, separate from the procurement function, controls the receipt and storage of assets

Law of Agency

The law of agency is an area of commercial law dealing with a set of contractual, quasi-contractual, and non-contractual fiduciary relationships that involve an individual (the agent) who is authorized to represent or act on behalf of another individual or entity (the principal). Under agency, the principal entrusts the performance of certain activities to the agent, with the performance being transacted in the name of or on the account of the principal. The principal has the right to control the agent's conduct in matters entrusted to the agent. An agency relationship may be created orally, in writing, and, in certain cases, by conduct. A thorough examination of the law of agency is beyond the scope of this chapter; rather, the purpose of briefly highlighting the concept of agency here is to point out that, vis-à-vis the employer-employee relationship, the buyer or contract manager (agent) is entrusted to conduct or control procurements by his or her employer, the project organization (principal). As a result of this trust, an agency relationship is created between the buyer and project organization which thus imposes a fiduciary obligation on the buyer or contract manager. This fiduciary obligation and relationship between the employee and project organization is important in that, as an agent, the employee owes certain duties to the project organization in representing the project organization to sellers and in conducting or controlling procurements. Unless the duties are otherwise modified and agreed to between the employee and the project organization, the employee will have the following duties of loyalty, obedience, performance, accounting, and notification.

Duty of Loyalty

Loyalty is the most important duty owed by an employee to the project organization. The employee has the duty to act solely for the benefit of the project organization and not in the interest of any other party (including the employee). The employee cannot "self-deal," including benefiting in any way personally from the procurement or procuring any products, services, or results from himself or herself. The duty of loyalty also means that any knowledge or information obtained through the agency relationship is considered confidential between the employee and the project organization.

Duty of Obedience

A duty of obedience is placed on an employee, requiring that the employee follow all lawful and clearly stated instructions of the project organization. If a situation arises where the project organization cannot be consulted—such as in the middle of a negotiation—the employee may deviate from the project organization's instructions without violating this duty if the circumstances so warrant. Where instructions are not clearly stated, an employee can fulfill the duty of obedience by acting in good faith and in a manner reasonable under the circumstances.

Duty of Performance

Under the duty of performance, an agent implicitly agrees to use reasonable diligence and skill in performing the work. The degree of care or skill required is usually that expected of a reasonable person. However, the duty imposes a higher standard on those who are considered "specialists." Thus, buyers and contract managers, specialists in their vocation, are held to a higher degree of skill. This requires that a person who holds himself or herself out as a buyer or contract manager to fully exercise the skills claimed. Additionally, to claim the special skills associated with being a practitioner, a buyer or contract manager must make a reasonable effort to maintain those skills (such as through training and professional certifications).

Duty of Accounting

Because a buyer is committing money (the seller's price) and a contract manager is receiving something in return (products, services, or results) on behalf of the project organization, the buyer and contract manager have a duty of accounting. This requires the buyer and contract manager to keep track of money committed and spent as well as the receipt of the products, services, or results. The project organization and employee can agree that certain responsibilities under the duty of accounting be delegated to other individuals, such as a finance department or to a receiving department. In combination with the duty of loyalty and assuming that the project organization's seller gift policy requires it, a duty of accounting also requires that an employee report and turn over to the project organization all gifts received by the employee from sellers.

Duty of Notification

Simply, a duty of notification requires that all an agent knows, the principal must know. Therefore, a buyer or contract manager must notify the project organization of all matters that come to the attention of the employee that concern the subject matter of the agency (meaning procurement and contract management matters). Employees typically fulfill this duty by providing status reports and communicating metrics, such as negotiated savings, relating to procurements and contracts.

Professional Ethics

In the context of the Project Procurement Management Knowledge Area, there are at least three professional codes of ethics that are broadly applicable: The PMI's *Code of Ethics and Professional Conduct* applies to a project manager; the Institute for Supply Management's *Principles and Standards of Ethic Supply Management* apply to a buyer; and, the National Contract Management Association *Code of Ethics* applies to a contract manager. It is important to note that the *Code of Ethics and Professional Conduct* applies to all PMI members and non-members who meet certain criteria. In any case, whether the *Code of Ethics and Professional Conduct* applies or not, all project managers should adhere to the code as a matter of good and sound business practice. The *Code of Ethics and Professional Conduct* is divided into sections that contain standards of conduct which are aligned with the four values identified as being the most important to the project management community: responsibility, respect, fairness, and honesty.

Business Ethics

In addition to any professional ethics, employees of a project organization are also governed by that organization's (private, public, or governmental) code of ethics, which, in the interest of continued employment, has the effect of trumping all other codes of ethics. Thus, in the case of project managers, buyers, and contract managers, they must be familiar with both their professional code of ethics and that of their employer, the project organization.

Personal Ethics

While leading practices in procurement ethics begin with professional and trade association and project organization codes of ethics, an employee of a project organization such as a project manager, buyer, or contract manager must personalize applicable codes of ethics in order to properly discharge his or her duties and responsibilities. The reason that professional and business codes of ethics are typically written in broad conceptual terms is that it is impractical to attempt to describe expected conduct in very specific situational or descriptive terms: Regardless of how thorough, the drafter of a code of ethics will never be able to envision or include all of what is permitted or prohibited. Consequently, codes of ethics often seem ambiguous and leave room for interpretation. Project managers, buyers, and contract managers cannot abide merely by the "letter of the law" or the specific words in any code; rather, they must be guided by the spirit of the code or the broader concept that the code is intended to express and accomplish. This means knowing what caused the codes of ethics to be enacted, knowing why they are necessary, and interpreting and applying them in accordance with their intent. Considering the foregoing, it is therefore necessary for project managers, buyers, and contract managers to "translate" the lexicon and abstractions of their professional and business codes of ethics into a meaningful personal code of ethics that can guide one's behavior and conduct. Provided that it is no less stringent than the applicable professional and business codes of ethics, creating a personal code of ethics—essentially, "values"—helps to ensure being on the right side of an ethical dilemma. Some questions to consider as part of a personal code of ethics and when facing an ethical dilemma include:

- Is what I am doing or about to do in the best interests of my employer?
- Am I receiving any benefit that is more than the compensation or benefit that my employer provides?
- Am I placing myself in a position that would conflict with the interests of my employer?
- Are my actions consistent with what my employer and the law expect or require?
- Will I personally gain or benefit, indirectly or directly, from this?

- Am I performing the duties and responsibilities of my job to the highest standards of professionalism and consistent with the principles and qualities of honesty, integrity, fairness, impartiality, transparency, loyalty, and stewardship?

Appendix I ~ Sample Procurement Management Plan

[Project Organization]

[Project Name]

Procurement Management Plan[23]

Date First Created: [Creation Date]
Date Last Revised: [Last Revision Date]

---

[23] This Procurement Management Plan is only an example template for purposes of illustration. It may contain terminology different than that contained in the *PMBOK Guide*. Additionally, it may not contain all of the attributes / information necessary for a complete Procurement Management Plan.

Template Instructions

- *This template contains suggested boilerplate language and assumes that the project will make appropriate additions, deletions, and changes for specific needs.*
- *Insert information between [brackets] and then delete brackets.*
- *Additional template instructions in the document are noted in italics. Delete all italicized instructions.*
- *If the document is longer than five pages, insert a table of contents.*

Purpose

The Procurement Management Plan (PMP) identifies which project needs can be best met by procuring products, services, or results outside of [Project Organization]. The questions to be answered in this PMP are whether to procure, how to procure, what to procure, how much to procure, and when to procure it. The PMP communicates how all of the procurements and contracts will be managed from competitive solicitation planning, solicitation, source selection, contract management and administration, and contract closeout.

Document Change Activity

The following is a record of the changes that have been made to this document since its initial creation.

#	Change Description	Author	Date

1. [Project Name]'s PMP Activities

The following responsibilities should be adjusted based on procurement, type of contract(s), or based on numerous planned contracts.

a. The products, services, or results to be contracted are defined and planned according to the [Procurement Unit]'s documented procedures. The Sellers are selected, based on an evaluation of the Sellers' ability to perform the work, according to all requirements contained in the Request for Proposal.
b. The contractual agreement between the [Project Organization] and the Seller is used as the basis for managing the contract.
c. The Seller will provide a documented Work Plan to be reviewed and approved by the [Project Name] Project.
d. A documented and approved Seller's Work Plan will be incorporated into the [Project Name] Project Plan, which will be used for tracking the Seller's activities and communicating status.
e. Changes to the Seller's Statement of Work, contract terms and conditions, and other commitments are resolved according to the contract requirements and the [Procurement Unit]'s documented procedure.
f. The [Project Name] Project will conduct periodic status /coordination reviews with the Seller's management.
g. Periodic technical reviews and interchanges will be held with the Sellers.
h. Formal reviews to address the Seller's accomplishments and results are conducted at selected milestones according to the [Project Name] Project Plan's Schedule.
i. The [Project Organization] Quality Assurance Group monitors the Seller's quality assurance activities according to the Quality Assurance Plan.
j. The [Project Name] Project conducts acceptance testing as part of the delivery of the Seller's products, services, or results according to a written acceptance-testing plan.
k. The Seller's performance is formally evaluated on a periodic basis, and the evaluation is reviewed with the Seller.

2. PMP Inputs, Constraints, Assumptions

The following list should be changed to reflect the realities of a particular project.

The following are the basis or inputs for this procurement plan:

2.1 Project Result Description
[Enter a brief description of the intended result of the project. This is not a description of the products, services, or results to be contracted; it is a high-level description of the project result.]

2.2 Work Breakdown Structure (WBS)
[Briefly indicate what portion of the project's WBS will be performed under contract, products, or services. For example, if the entire requirement phase is intended to be delivered under contract, list that phase. If only specific portions of the phase are intended to be contracted, the activities or task should be listed. Leave the details in the referenced WBS. If a product is being purchased, e.g., software / hardware, reference the WBS element that relates to the purchase of the product.]

2.3 Constraints
[List any constraints such as cost (not to exceed) and schedule, quality plans, cash-flow projections, WBS, risks, staff plans, contracting process duration that will limit the contract or procurement options.]

2.4 Assumptions
[List factors that for procurement planning purposes are considered to be true, real, or certain.]

3. Procurement Considerations

3.1 Market Conditions
[List generically or if known, in detail, what products and services are available in the market place, from whom, and under what terms and conditions.]

3.2 Make or Buy Analysis
[Provide a brief analysis of the direct and indirect cost associated with either making or buying the products, services, or results. For example, the "buy" analysis should include costs for both out-of-pocket to procure and cost to manage the purchasing process. This may be the summary of a feasibility study when required.]

3.3 Internal Expert Judgment
[List any experts that will be required to participate as part of the procurement process. This may include consultants, technicians, business experts, or other.]

3.4 Contract Type Selections
[Provide the justification for the type of contract(s) selected as appropriate for this project.]

3.5 Standard Procurement Documents:
[List the standard procurement documents to be utilized to procure and contract. For example, contract request form, Request for Proposal Form, contract templates.]

4. PMP Staff Roles and Responsibilities

4.1 Procurement Staff
[List who or what group will be performing the following procurement-related activities as well as roles and responsibilities. The following table may be left high-level or very specifically detailed.]

#	Activity Description	Responsible
1.	**Procurement Planning** – Identifying which project should be bought.	[Name, Title]
2.	**Solicitation Planning** – Preparing of the documents to support the solicitation of responses from the Sellers: *[List the specific types of procurement documents to be used on this project and the name of the person responsible.]*	[Name, Title]
3.	**Solicitation and Source Selection** – Obtaining the information and receipt of documents from Sellers and the evaluation of this information against criteria to select a Seller.	[Name, Title]

#	Activity Description	Responsible
4.	**Contract Administration** – Organizing, tracking, filing, and modifications to ensure that the Seller meets the commitments and requirements of the contract and the project and management is kept aware of these commitments and contract time frames.	[Name, Title]
5.	**Contract Closeout** – Verifying that the requirements of the contract were met. Documenting the contracting lessons learned and archiving of information generated as a result of the procurement management.	[Name, Title]

5. Review and Approvals

[Indicate or list the reviews and approvals needed per contract or contract type. Indicate if the review and approval process is different or the same for a contract amendment, work order release, or exercising of a contract option.]

6. Contract Administration

[Indicate the process and templates that the project will use to organize, track, file, and modify contracts, as well as, to keep management aware of the contract commitments and contracted time frames.]

6.1 Contract Filing

The [Project Name] will file the project contract documents and related information in [Specify the server directory path here].

The project will also keep a hard copy binder, series of binders, or file for contract reference, audit or review purposes. The binder and table of contents represent the activity of one contract with a Seller. The minimum table of content for an auditable contract binder is as follows:

- Request for [Information, Proposals, Quotes]
- Contract(s)
- Contract Amendments
- Statements of Work, Work Orders, or Executed Options
- Change Requests
- Deliverables and Deliverable Approvals
- Contract Memos and Correspondence
- *[Contract Justification or Feasibility (Optional)]*
- *[Evaluation and Scoring (Optional)]*

6.2 Contract Change Management Process

Contract changes will follow the project's change management process as defined in the [Project Name] Change Management Plan document, however additional requirements for the review and approval process for all types of contract change is described in this PMP Plan and the contract requirements. *It is recommended that the project's Change Management Plan incorporate all additional requirements for contract changes via this plan and the contract requirements. This allows the project to refer to the project Change Management Process Plan as the governing document for all project changes including contracts.*

6.3 Contract Tracking

In order to ensure that the Seller meets the commitments and requirements of the contract and management is kept aware of these commitments and contract time frames, the project will perform the following tracking activities. The project will use a Contract Planning and Tracking Spreadsheet to track the project's contract progress and the Status Report template will be used to report summary level contract information to senior management. Contracting information to be tracked will be obtained by the project from several sources, the contract, and submitted invoices.

The following items will be tracked in spreadsheet format depending upon type of contract:

General / Master Contract
Contract #, Contract Term Dates, Days Remaining, Contract Administrator, Contract Not to Exceed Dollar Amount, Contract Not to Exceed Hour Amount, Contract Not to Exceed Travel and Expenses Amount, Amendment #

Per Statement of Work, Work Order, Option (if applicable)
Statement of Work #, Work Order #, Option #, Term Dates, Days Remaining, Contract Administrator, Not to Exceed Dollar Amount, Not to Exceed Hour Amount, Not to Exceed Travel and Expenses Amount

Per each Invoice
Invoice #, Invoice Date, Invoice Billing Period, Amount Billed, Hours Billed, Travel and Expense Billed, Balance Remaining. *Contracts that are not tracked by hours, but rather a fixed price deliverable, would not use the "Hours Billed or Travel and Expense Billed columns."*

Status Report (per contract per project)
Contract and Work Order or Option Term dates, 120/90/60/30 Day Warning of Expiration, Total Dollar Value, Total Dollar Remaining, % of Work Complete, Contract Status Comments

6.4 Contract Close-out and Archiving

The project will verify that the requirements of the contract were met and document the procurement / contracting lessons learned. The project will also archive the contract information generated as a result of the procurement management.

[Indicate what information the project plans to archive, how they will archive, and the length of time the records must be retained.]

Request for [Information / Proposal]
[Project name]

[Date]
[Project Organization]
[Project Number or Other Identifier]

RFx Template Instructions

- *This template contains suggested boilerplate language and assumes that the project will make appropriate additions, deletions, and changes for specific needs.*
- *Insert information between [brackets] and then delete brackets.*
- *Additional template instructions in the document are noted in italics. Delete all italicized instructions.*
- *If the document is longer than five pages, insert a table of contents.*

CONFIDENTIALITY

This document has been prepared by [Project Organization] and is being given to Seller, in consideration of Seller's agreement to treat the information contained within this document and related business discussions as confidential, to provide Seller with an opportunity to respond to [Project Organization]'s requirements as contained further herein. The information enclosed in this document is proprietary to [Project Organization]. [Project Organization] is not conveying any ownership to any party by disclosing this information. By accepting this document, Seller agrees that Seller will: (1) treat this information as confidential; (2) not allow any other person or entity to see it or use it; and, (3) not use it in any way other than to prepare the requested response.

1.0   INTRODUCTION

1.1   OBJECTIVE

The objective of this document is to solicit responses that will provide [Project Organization] with the [name/description of project] solution that best supports [Project Organization]'s requirements. Responses to this document are expected to propose a complete solution that meets all the stated requirements.

1.2   [PROJECT ORGANIZATION] OVERVIEW

[Insert Project Organization overview]

1.3   TIMETABLE

[Project Organization] expects to adhere to the timetable shown below. It should be noted, however, that the Target Dates are approximate and subject to change. [Select and modify the following activities as appropriate, subject to the RFx type]

Activity	Target Dates
Release of Request for [Information / Proposal]	[Target Date]
Intent to Bid Due	[Target Date]
Written Questions Due	[Target Date]
Responses to Written Questions	[Target Date]
Pre-Proposal Bidder Conference	[Target Date(s)]
Proposals Due	[Target Date]
Post-Proposal Bidder Conferences	[Target Date(s)]
Demonstrations [Proof-of-Concept Sessions]	[Target Date(s)]
Selection of Finalist Seller(s)	[Target Date]
Negotiations	[Target Date(s)]
Contract Award	[Target Date]
Start Date	[Target Date]

2.0   REQUIREMENTS

2.1   BACKGROUND

[Insert project-specific information background and any detailed objectives here]

2.2   FUNCTIONAL AND TECHNICAL REQUIREMENTS

Responses to this Section should concisely address the requirements as they are presented. If any of the requirements cannot be met by Seller, this must be identified in the response.

[Insert requirements here]

2.3   SELLER QUALIFICATIONS

2.3.1   SELLER OVERVIEW

Please provide information on the following:

Item	Seller Response
[Add / Modify / Delete items as needed]	
Main lines of business	
Organization and structure	
Locations - headquarters, implementation, and support	
Number of employees - total and by major department	
Number of contractors - total and by major department	
Company mission and vision statements	
Strategic relationships with other suppliers	
Total revenue	
Percent of revenue from solutions similar to those proposed by Seller	
Percent of revenue expended on research and development	
Audited financial statements for last five years	Attach as an appendix / separate file
Most recent annual report, if applicable	Attach as an appendix / separate file
If venture capitalist funded, provide information on investors	

Item	Seller Response
Dunn & Bradstreet Reports, if available	Attach as an appendix / separate file
Seller's performance over time (e.g., growth rate, stock performance)	
Demonstrated financial strength and the ability to perform on a long term basis	
Seller's account management approach	
Proposed organization chart of Seller's proposed account team	
Seller's method for managing account team turnover	
The turnover process when moving from pre-sales to sale to implementation to support	
Seller's tools / systems used to track and manage customer service issues	

2.3.2 REFERENCE INFORMATION

Provide an overview of two (2) references who are existing customers and two (2) references who are no longer customers. For each reference include the following:

Item	Seller Response
Customer Reference No. 1 – Existing	
Main Line of Business	
Principal Address	
Number of Employees	
Contact Name	
Contact Title	
Contact Telephone Number	
Contact Email Address	
Products / Services Provided by Seller	
First Date of Business Relationship with Seller	
Seller's rationale for including the specific reference	
Customer Reference No. 2 – Existing	
Main Line of Business	

Item	Seller Response
Principal Address	
Number of Employees	
Contact Name	
Contact Title	
Contact Telephone Number	
Contact Email Address	
Products / Services Provided by Seller	
First Date of Business Relationship with Seller	
Seller's rationale for including the specific reference	
Customer Reference No. 1 – Prior	
Main Line of Business	
Principal Address	
Number of Employees	
Contact Name	
Contact Title	
Contact Telephone Number	
Contact Email Address	
Products / Services Provided by Seller	
First Date of Business Relationship with Seller	
Basis for Which Reference is No Longer a Customer of Seller	
Customer Reference No. 2 – Prior	
Main Line of Business	
Principal Address	
Number of Employees	
Contact Name	
Contact Title	
Contact Telephone Number	
Contact Email Address	
Products / Services Provided by Seller	
First Date of Business Relationship with Seller	
Basis for Which Reference is No Longer a Customer of Seller	

Information to be requested by [Project Organization] and evaluated from each reference includes services performed, Seller's abilities, communication skills and timeliness, costs, accuracy, problems, overall performance, and whether or not the reference would rehire Seller. [Project Organization] reserves the right to check any other reference(s) that might be indicated through the explicitly specified contacts or that result from communication with other entities involved with similar requirements.

2.3.3   CONTRACT PERFORMANCE

If at any time during the past five (5) years, Seller has had a contract terminated for convenience, non-performance, or any other reason, describe fully all such terminations including the name and address of the other contracting party, and the circumstances surrounding the termination.

Seller Response

3.0   PRICING INFORMATION

Seller must provide the detailed price schedule(s), as described below, for the proposed solution. Pricing must be fully comprehensive, complete, and list any available discounts. Pricing information supplied with the response must be valid for at least 180 days from the response submission date. All one-time and recurring costs must be fully provided. [The Pricing Summary Schedule should always be present and can be elaborated upon if necessary. The remaining schedules can be modified or deleted as needed.]

- Pricing Summary – This schedule shall present the total price to perform all of the requirements of this document and the proposed solution. The Pricing Summary Schedule must be signed and dated by an authorized representative of Seller.

- Professional Services and Staffing – This schedule shall present Seller's total professional services and staffing costs for the proposed solution.

- Facilities and Supplies – This schedule shall present Seller's facility (office space, utilities, hardware, etc.) and supplies costs for the proposed solution. [Project Organization] reserves the right to secure facilities and supplies if it is cost justifiable to do so.

- Software and Tools – This schedule shall present Seller's costs associated with licensed software and/or tools proposed for the solution, as well as any maintenance costs.

- Hardware and Related Components – This schedule shall present Seller's costs associated with hardware and related components proposed for the solution, as well as any maintenance costs.

- Installation / Conversion / Implementation – This schedule shall present Seller's costs to install, convert, and / or implement the proposed solution in [Project Organization]'s environment.

- Training – This schedule shall present Seller's costs to train [Project Organization] technical staff and / or users on the applicable components of the proposed solution.

Any costs included in the solution price that are not covered in the Schedule(s) described above must be summarized in the Pricing Summary Schedule under the label of "Other Costs." The Seller must include details in the Cost Proposal supporting any and all other costs.

4.0   RESPONSE PROCEDURES

4.1   OVERVIEW

This document was developed to provide Seller with the necessary information to allow Seller to prepare a comprehensive response. This section contains solicitation information and procedures, response submission instructions, and general response format requirements. Seller is expected to carefully examine all requirements stipulated in this document and respond to each requirement in the format prescribed.

In the case that a response results in a procurement by [Project Organization], the provisions of this document and the winning response (each of which shall be incorporated by reference), and any additional clauses or provisions required by Federal, or State law, or regulations in effect at the time of the execution of a contract will be included in the same.

4.2   LIABILITY

The issuance of this document and the receipt of information in response to this document shall not in any way cause [Project Organization] to incur any liability or obligation to Seller, financial or otherwise. [Project Organization] assumes no obligation to reimburse or in any way compensate Seller for expenses incurred in connection with Seller's response to this document.

4.3   USE AND DISCLOSURE OF INFORMATION

4.3.1   SELLER INFORMATION

[Project Organization] reserves the right to use information submitted in response to this document in any manner it may deem appropriate in evaluating the suitability of the proposed solution. Materials submitted by Seller that are considered confidential must be clearly marked as such. In the event that confidentiality cannot be afforded, Seller will be notified and will be permitted to withdraw its response.

[Project Organization] reserves the right to use any and all ideas presented in any response unless Seller identifies such ideas as proprietary in the response. In no event will an objection be considered valid with respect to the use of such ideas that: are not the proprietary information of Seller and so designated in the response; which were known to [Project Organization] before submission of such response; or, properly became known to [Project Organization] thereafter through other sources.

4.3.2   [PROJECT ORGANIZATION] INFORMATION

The information contained in this document is proprietary to [Project Organization] as described in the Confidentiality section of this document.

4.4   COMMUNICATION WITH [PROJECT ORGANIZATION] STAFF AND AGENTS

From the date that this document is issued until a determination is made and announced regarding the selection of one or more finalist Seller(s), if applicable, contact between Seller and individuals employed or otherwise engaged by [Project Organization] is strictly prohibited. Following such selection, Seller is similarly restricted from communicating with [Project Organization] staff and agents until a contract is executed. The following exceptions to these restrictions are permitted:

- written communication with the [Project Organization] Contact as identified herein and related specifically to this document;
- contacts with [Project Organization] staff and agents which are approved in advance by the [Project Organization] Contact;
- those contacts made pursuant to any pre-existing obligation; and,
- contacts with [Project Organization] staff present at sessions specified by the Timetable, if any.

Violations of these conditions may be considered sufficient cause to reject a response and / or Seller selection irrespective of any other condition. Sellers are advised that only members of the [Project Organization] Seller Selection Committee, meeting in their official capacity, can clarify issues or render any opinion regarding this document. No individual member of [Project Organization], employee of [Project Organization], agent of [Project Organization], or member of the [Project Organization] Seller Selection Committee is empowered to make binding statements regarding this document.

4.5   RESPONSE PROTOCOL

Responses must be submitted no later than close of business on the date indicated on the timetable contained herein. [Project Organization], at its discretion, may elect to return responses received after the deadline.

[*Optional*: Seller must submit [XX] copies of its response on 8.5- by 11-inch paper, three-hole punched.] Responses that are less than 2 MB in size should be sent via email to the [Project Organization] Contact listed below. Responses that are greater than 2 MB in size must be received electronically through a secure Internet download site provided by Seller. Responses should be submitted in Microsoft® Word™ format unless otherwise specified.

[Insert Name of Project Organization Contact]
[Insert Project Organization Address]
[Insert Office Number] (Office)
[Insert Facsimile Number] (Facsimile)
[Insert Email Address] (Email)

[Project Organization] reserves the right to reject any responses or, at [Project Organization]'s discretion, to solicit additional responses. [Project Organization] may also accept or reject portions of a response.

The entire cost for the preparation of a response, the attendance at any subsequent conferences or sessions (as further described below), or participation in negotiations (if conducted) shall be borne by Seller.

This document represents the best estimate of [Project Organization]'s requirements. [Project Organization] reserves the right to adjust the specifications or scope of effort stated in this document. In the event that any modifications to the original document become necessary, all Sellers will be notified in writing by means of an addendum.

4.5.1   WRITTEN QUESTIONS AND ANSWERS

Any explanation desired by Seller regarding the meaning or interpretation of any provision contained herein must be submitted in writing, email, or via facsimile to the attention of the [Project Organization] Contact. [Project Organization] assumes no liability for receipt of letters or facsimiles, or assuring accurate or complete facsimile transmission.

4.5.2   PRE-PROPOSAL BIDDER CONFERENCE

Where the Timetable specifies a Pre-Proposal Bidder Conference, Seller is required to submit written questions prior to the conference. Seller will have an opportunity to ask questions at the conference, and [Project Organization] will make every reasonable attempt to answer those questions before the end of the conference. Oral answers shall not be binding on [Project Organization].

4.5.3   POST-PROPOSAL BIDDER CONFERENCES

Where the Timetable specifies Post-Proposal Bidder Conferences, Sellers may be requested to explain or clarify their responses in individual, confidential conferences with [Project Organization]. In such a conference, [Project Organization] may also question Seller's understanding of [Project Organization]'s requirements, its approach to providing the solution, and its account management style and philosophy. Sellers shall not be allowed to alter or amend their proposals or conduct negotiations during the conference.

4.5.4   DEMONSTRATIONS [PROOF-OF-CONCEPT SESSIONS]

Where the Timetable specifies Demonstrations [Proof-of-Concept Sessions], [Project Organization] may, at its sole discretion, invite individual Sellers determined to be in a competitive range to demonstrate ["prove out"] their responses. These sessions are also intended to allow the Sellers in the competitive range to make minor revisions to their responses based on clarified requirements from [Project Organization]. Note that [Project Organization] reserves the right to award a contract without conducting Demonstrations [Proof-of-Concept Sessions] with any Sellers.

4.6   EVALUATION CRITERIA

The [Project Organization] Seller Selection Committee will judge each response based upon their understanding of the responses. [Project Organization] will conduct a fair, impartial, and comprehensive evaluation of all responses. If applicable, a contract will be awarded, taking into consideration the best interests of [Project Organization]. The criteria for selecting a Seller may include the:

- demonstrated understanding of Seller of the requirements herein;
- responsiveness to the requirements herein, including the adequacy and creativity of the proposed solution;
- ability, capacity, and skill of Seller to perform the requirements herein;
- experience of Seller in providing a related solution and quality of services / product provided for other customers;
- character, integrity, reputation, judgment, experience, and efficiency of Seller;
- quality of Seller's services for other customers;
- proposed price and schedule; and,
- such other information that may be secured and that has a bearing on the decision to award the contract.

[Project Organization] reserves the right to make a contract award without any further discussion with the Sellers regarding the responses received. Therefore, responses should be submitted initially on the most favorable terms available to [Project Organization] from a price, contractual terms and conditions, and technical standpoint. [Project Organization], however, reserves the right to conduct discussions with Sellers who submit proposals that pass the initial screening process of this document. [Project Organization] is not under any obligation to reveal to a Seller how a response was assessed or to provide information relative to the decision-making process.

4.7   RESPONSE FORMAT

In order to assist in the fair and equitable evaluation of all responses, Sellers are being asked to adhere to the specific response format set forth below. Responses that deviate from the requested format may be classified as "non-responsive" at the discretion of [Project Organization] and may be subject to disqualification.

Emphasis should be concentrated on conformance to the instructions contained herein, responsiveness to requirements, completeness, and clarity of content. Responses should be tailored specifically to address the requirements set forth in this document. Seller should avoid broad, unenforceable responses. "Boilerplate" material should not be used within the body of the response. If desired, Seller may attach such material in a separate appendix. Elaborate responses are neither necessary nor desired. If Seller's response is presented in such a fashion that makes evaluation difficult or overly time consuming, it is likely that points will be lost in the evaluation process.

Section	Section Contents / Deliverables
Letter of Transmittal	The Letter of Transmittal must be ratified by an official authorized to legally bind Seller, and contain the name, address, email address, telephone number, and facsimile number of Seller's representative who is authorized to negotiate on behalf of Seller.
Table of Contents	(Self-explanatory)
Executive Summary	High-level summary of the most important aspects of the response, containing a concise description of the proposed solution and cost.
Seller Qualifications	A brief statement of Seller's qualifications related to the requirements described herein, as well as identification and qualifications of key personnel who will be responsible for the project.

Section	Section Contents / Deliverables

Detailed Description of Proposed Solution	• Detailed information of proposed solution to [Project Organization]'s specifications and requirements, including (where applicable):
	  − Narrative of solution activities.
	  − Scope of work.
	  − List of proposed deliverables.
	  − Time frame for implementation.
	  − Maintenance and support options, if applicable.
	
	• Provide a detailed schedule of activities and milestones that accomplish [Project Organization]'s requirements and the proposed solution, preferably in the form of graphic flowcharts.

Price Information	Provide detailed pricing in the format as further specified herein, such as a statement of total project costs, broken down by labor, materials, other expenses, subcontracted work, overhead, etc., with the proposed costs identified by task. Proposed costs should be accurate, realistic, and firm.
Terms and Conditions	Provide detailed comments, if any, in the form of redlines to [Project Organization]'s contract template included as a part of Appendix A, if included, and provide Seller's contract template.
Appendices	Provide the following, as applicable: • Annual report. • Financial statements (last five years). • Solution and / or product literature, maintenance, and support brochures. • Additional Seller information.

APPENDIX A - CONTRACT

The contract terms shall be defined by a written agreement that is not binding until fully executed by both parties. A copy of [Project Organization]'s contract template is attached as a part of this Appendix A. Where Seller does not currently have a contracted agreement with [Project Organization], Seller must submit, as part of the response, comments to the attached contract template in the form of redlines. [Project Organization] will assume agreement unless otherwise noted by Seller.

While [Project Organization] can show reasonable flexibility in contract terms and conditions, other factors being equal, preference will be given to Sellers who take minimum exceptions. While all contract terms and conditions in the attached contract template are important to [Project Organization], terms and conditions that are of particular importance to [Project Organization], and of which Sellers should carefully consider their redlines, follow:

- License Grants (if applicable)
- Termination Rights
- Acceptance (if applicable)
- Standards of Performance
- Representations and Warranties
- Rights and Ownership of Intellectual Property
- Indemnification
- Limitation of Liability
- Insurance
- Choice of Law

[Attach appropriate contract type as imbedded file icons. If not providing a contract template, delete this appendix in its entirety.]

Appendix III ~ Seller Gift Policy

The following is an example policy for employees regarding the acceptance of seller gifts, entertainment, and travel. It is intended to be short, flexible, and reasonable. It still, however, requires some degree of judgment in its application. When issuing competitive solicitations, it is recommended that the policy be included with the competitive solicitation so that prospective sellers are aware of the specifics of the policy as it relates to the competitive procurement.

GIFTS, ENTERTAINMENT, MEALS, AND TRAVEL FROM SELLERS

1 Policy

It is the policy of the Company that employees maintain ethical relationships with sellers, and negotiate, award, inspect, or audit contracts with the best interest of the Company uppermost in mind.

2 Guidelines

Subject to the following guidelines, employees are prohibited from receiving gifts, entertainment, meals, or travel from sellers that might directly or indirectly influence an employee's business judgment or decisions, or that might give the appearance of impropriety. In conducting Company business with sellers, employees must follow the following guidelines as they relate to receiving gifts, entertainment, meals, or travel from sellers.

(a) Business Gifts

    (1) In conducting Company business with sellers, sellers may offer employees business gifts. For the purposes of these guidelines, business gifts from sellers shall be defined to include any item or service of value. While gifts should be generally refused, employees may accept gifts, subject to the following guidelines:

        (i) If accepted, the cumulative value of gifts received from a seller should not exceed $100 in any 12-month period.

        (ii) Gifts exceeding the cumulative value may be accepted from sellers if the received gift will be used as a "give-away" or a shared item (e.g., food baskets) at a Company or departmental function.

        (iii) Gifts of cash or other negotiable instruments, including loans, are prohibited in all cases. However, donations provided by the seller to a charitable organization on behalf of Company are permissible.

        (iv) The gift is not made during a time period when bids are being sought to establish a new contract or renegotiate an existing contract with the seller.

(v) Gifts won from sellers as a part of a contest or "give-away," where other individuals have an equal chance of winning, shall be excluded from this policy.

(b) Business Entertainment

(1) In conducting Company business, employees may be invited by a seller to attend a sporting event, cultural activity, or other entertainment event. It may be appropriate for employees to accept such offers, subject to the following guidelines:

(i) The seller is in attendance.

(ii) Business will be conducted at the event.

(iii) The value of the entertainment is reasonable and not excessive.

(iv) The entertainment offer is not made during a time period when bids are being sought to establish a new contract or renegotiate an existing contract with the seller.

(c) Business Meals

(1) In conducting the Company's business, employees may find it appropriate to do so in conjunction with meal times. While employees should not routinely plan business meetings around meal times in order to receive meals from sellers, it may not be inappropriate for employees to accept such a meal from sellers. The following guidelines should be observed:

(i) The seller is in attendance.

(ii) Business will be conducted at the meal.

(iii) The value of the business meal is reasonable and not excessive.

(iv) Offers for business meals should not be accepted with routine frequency; for example, no greater than four business meals per year with any one seller.

(d) Business Travel

(1) In conducting Company business that requires out-of-town travel, employees may receive offers from sellers to pay for transportation, lodging, and meals. For the purposes of these guidelines, Company business shall be defined to include an employee's service on a board, speaking at an event, or evaluating the seller. It may be appropriate for employees to accept such offers according to the following guidelines:

(i) The seller is in attendance or will be at the travel destination.

(ii) Business is the sole reason for the travel.

(iii) The value of the business travel is reasonable and not excessive.

Appendix IV ~ Activity Cross-References

Activities Sorted by Reference

Type	Reference	Activity	Process
Inputs	12.1.1.1	Project Charter	*Plan Procurement Management*
Inputs	12.1.1.2	Business Documents	*Plan Procurement Management*
Inputs	12.1.1.3	Project Management Plan	*Plan Procurement Management*
Inputs	12.1.1.4	Project Documents	*Plan Procurement Management*
Inputs	12.1.1.5	Enterprise Environmental Factors	*Plan Procurement Management*
Inputs	12.1.1.6	Organizational Process Assets	*Plan Procurement Management*
Tools & Techniques	12.1.2.1	Expert Judgment	*Plan Procurement Management*
Tools & Techniques	12.1.2.2	Data Gathering	*Plan Procurement Management*
Tools & Techniques	12.1.2.3	Data Analysis	*Plan Procurement Management*
Tools & Techniques	12.1.2.4	Source Selection Analysis	*Plan Procurement Management*
Tools & Techniques	12.1.2.5	Meetings	*Plan Procurement Management*
Outputs	12.1.3.1	Procurement Management Plan	*Plan Procurement Management*
Outputs	12.1.3.2	Procurement Strategy	*Plan Procurement Management*
Outputs	12.1.3.3	Bid Documents	*Plan Procurement Management*
Outputs	12.1.3.4	Procurement Statement of Work	*Plan Procurement Management*
Outputs	12.1.3.5	Source Selection Criteria	*Plan Procurement Management*
Outputs	12.1.3.6	Make-or-Buy Decisions	*Plan Procurement Management*
Outputs	12.1.3.7	Independent Cost Estimates	*Plan Procurement Management*
Outputs	12.1.3.8	Change Requests	*Plan Procurement Management*
Outputs	12.1.3.9	Project Documents Updates	*Plan Procurement Management*
Outputs	12.1.3.10	Organizational Process Assets Updates	*Plan Procurement Management*
Inputs	12.2.1.1	Project Management Plan	*Conduct Procurements*
Inputs	12.2.1.2	Project Documents	*Conduct Procurements*
Inputs	12.2.1.3	Procurement Documentation	*Conduct Procurements*
Inputs	12.2.1.4	Seller Proposals	*Conduct Procurements*
Inputs	12.2.1.5	Enterprise Environmental Factors	*Conduct Procurements*
Inputs	12.2.1.6	Organizational Process Assets	*Conduct Procurements*
Tools & Techniques	12.2.2.1	Expert Judgment	*Conduct Procurements*
Tools & Techniques	12.2.2.2	Advertising	*Conduct Procurements*
Tools & Techniques	12.2.2.3	Bidder Conferences	*Conduct Procurements*
Tools & Techniques	12.2.2.4	Data Analysis	*Conduct Procurements*
Tools & Techniques	12.2.2.5	Interpersonal and Team Skills	*Conduct Procurements*
Outputs	12.2.3.1	Selected Sellers	*Conduct Procurements*
Outputs	12.2.3.2	Agreements	*Conduct Procurements*
Outputs	12.2.3.3	Change Requests	*Conduct Procurements*
Outputs	12.2.3.4	Project Management Plan Updates	*Conduct Procurements*
Outputs	12.2.3.5	Project Documents Updates	*Conduct Procurements*
Outputs	12.2.3.6	Organizational Process Assets Updates	*Conduct Procurements*
Inputs	12.3.1.1	Project Management Plan	*Control Procurements*
Inputs	12.3.1.2	Project Documents	*Control Procurements*

Type	Reference	Activity	Process
Inputs	12.3.1.3	Agreements	*Control Procurements*
Inputs	12.3.1.4	Procurement Documentation	*Control Procurements*
Inputs	12.3.1.5	Approved Change Requests	*Control Procurements*
Inputs	12.3.1.6	Work Performance Data	*Control Procurements*
Inputs	12.3.1.7	Enterprise Environmental Factors	*Control Procurements*
Inputs	12.3.1.8	Organizational Process Assets	*Control Procurements*
Tools & Techniques	12.3.2.1	Expert Judgment	*Control Procurements*
Tools & Techniques	12.3.2.2	Claims Administration	*Control Procurements*
Tools & Techniques	12.3.2.3	Data Analysis	*Control Procurements*
Tools & Techniques	12.3.2.4	Inspection	*Control Procurements*
Tools & Techniques	12.3.2.5	Audits	*Control Procurements*
Outputs	12.3.3.1	Closed Procurements	*Control Procurements*
Outputs	12.3.3.2	Work Performance Information	*Control Procurements*
Outputs	12.3.3.3	Procurement Documentation Updates	*Control Procurements*
Outputs	12.3.3.4	Change Requests	*Control Procurements*
Outputs	12.3.3.5	Project Management Plan Updates	*Control Procurements*
Outputs	12.3.3.6	Project Documents Updates	*Control Procurements*
Outputs	12.3.3.7	Organizational Process Assets Updates	*Control Procurements*

Activities Sorted by Activity

Type	Reference	Activity	Process
Tools & Techniques	12.2.2.2	Advertising	*Conduct Procurements*
Outputs	12.2.3.2	Agreements	*Conduct Procurements*
Inputs	12.3.1.3	Agreements	*Control Procurements*
Inputs	12.3.1.5	Approved Change Requests	*Control Procurements*
Tools & Techniques	12.3.2.5	Audits	*Control Procurements*
Outputs	12.1.3.3	Bid Documents	*Plan Procurement Management*
Tools & Techniques	12.2.2.3	Bidder Conferences	*Conduct Procurements*
Inputs	12.1.1.2	Business Documents	*Plan Procurement Management*
Outputs	12.1.3.8	Change Requests	*Plan Procurement Management*
Outputs	12.2.3.3	Change Requests	*Conduct Procurements*
Outputs	12.3.3.4	Change Requests	*Control Procurements*
Tools & Techniques	12.3.2.2	Claims Administration	*Control Procurements*
Outputs	12.3.3.1	Closed Procurements	*Control Procurements*
Tools & Techniques	12.1.2.3	Data Analysis	*Plan Procurement Management*
Tools & Techniques	12.2.2.4	Data Analysis	*Conduct Procurements*
Tools & Techniques	12.3.2.3	Data Analysis	*Control Procurements*
Tools & Techniques	12.1.2.2	Data Gathering	*Plan Procurement Management*
Inputs	12.1.1.5	Enterprise Environmental Factors	*Plan Procurement Management*
Inputs	12.2.1.5	Enterprise Environmental Factors	*Conduct Procurements*
Inputs	12.3.1.7	Enterprise Environmental Factors	*Control Procurements*
Tools & Techniques	12.1.2.1	Expert Judgment	*Plan Procurement Management*
Tools & Techniques	12.2.2.1	Expert Judgment	*Conduct Procurements*
Tools & Techniques	12.3.2.1	Expert Judgment	*Control Procurements*
Outputs	12.1.3.7	Independent Cost Estimates	*Plan Procurement Management*
Tools & Techniques	12.3.2.4	Inspection	*Control Procurements*
Tools & Techniques	12.2.2.5	Interpersonal and Team Skills	*Conduct Procurements*
Outputs	12.1.3.6	Make-or-Buy Decisions	*Plan Procurement Management*
Tools & Techniques	12.1.2.5	Meetings	*Plan Procurement Management*
Inputs	12.1.1.6	Organizational Process Assets	*Plan Procurement Management*
Inputs	12.2.1.6	Organizational Process Assets	*Conduct Procurements*
Inputs	12.3.1.8	Organizational Process Assets	*Control Procurements*
Outputs	12.1.3.10	Organizational Process Assets Updates	*Plan Procurement Management*
Outputs	12.2.3.6	Organizational Process Assets Updates	*Conduct Procurements*
Outputs	12.3.3.7	Organizational Process Assets Updates	*Control Procurements*
Inputs	12.2.1.3	Procurement Documentation	*Conduct Procurements*
Inputs	12.3.1.4	Procurement Documentation	*Control Procurements*
Outputs	12.3.3.3	Procurement Documentation Updates	*Control Procurements*
Outputs	12.1.3.1	Procurement Management Plan	*Plan Procurement Management*
Outputs	12.1.3.4	Procurement Statement of Work	*Plan Procurement Management*
Outputs	12.1.3.2	Procurement Strategy	*Plan Procurement Management*
Inputs	12.1.1.1	Project Charter	*Plan Procurement Management*
Inputs	12.1.1.4	Project Documents	*Plan Procurement Management*

Type	Reference	Activity	Process
Inputs	12.2.1.2	Project Documents	*Conduct Procurements*
Inputs	12.3.1.2	Project Documents	*Control Procurements*
Outputs	12.1.3.9	Project Documents Updates	*Plan Procurement Management*
Outputs	12.2.3.5	Project Documents Updates	*Conduct Procurements*
Outputs	12.3.3.6	Project Documents Updates	*Control Procurements*
Inputs	12.1.1.3	Project Management Plan	*Plan Procurement Management*
Inputs	12.2.1.1	Project Management Plan	*Conduct Procurements*
Inputs	12.3.1.1	Project Management Plan	*Control Procurements*
Outputs	12.2.3.4	Project Management Plan Updates	*Conduct Procurements*
Outputs	12.3.3.5	Project Management Plan Updates	*Control Procurements*
Outputs	12.2.3.1	Selected Sellers	*Conduct Procurements*
Inputs	12.2.1.4	Seller Proposals	*Conduct Procurements*
Tools & Techniques	12.1.2.4	Source Selection Analysis	*Plan Procurement Management*
Outputs	12.1.3.5	Source Selection Criteria	*Plan Procurement Management*
Inputs	12.3.1.6	Work Performance Data	*Control Procurements*
Outputs	12.3.3.2	Work Performance Information	*Control Procurements*

Activities Sorted by Type and Reference

Type	Reference	Activity	Process
Inputs	12.1.1.1	Project Charter	*Plan Procurement Management*
Inputs	12.1.1.2	Business Documents	*Plan Procurement Management*
Inputs	12.1.1.3	Project Management Plan	*Plan Procurement Management*
Inputs	12.1.1.4	Project Documents	*Plan Procurement Management*
Inputs	12.1.1.5	Enterprise Environmental Factors	*Plan Procurement Management*
Inputs	12.1.1.6	Organizational Process Assets	*Plan Procurement Management*
Inputs	12.2.1.1	Project Management Plan	*Conduct Procurements*
Inputs	12.2.1.2	Project Documents	*Conduct Procurements*
Inputs	12.2.1.3	Procurement Documentation	*Conduct Procurements*
Inputs	12.2.1.4	Seller Proposals	*Conduct Procurements*
Inputs	12.2.1.5	Enterprise Environmental Factors	*Conduct Procurements*
Inputs	12.2.1.6	Organizational Process Assets	*Conduct Procurements*
Inputs	12.3.1.1	Project Management Plan	*Control Procurements*
Inputs	12.3.1.2	Project Documents	*Control Procurements*
Inputs	12.3.1.3	Agreements	*Control Procurements*
Inputs	12.3.1.4	Procurement Documentation	*Control Procurements*
Inputs	12.3.1.5	Approved Change Requests	*Control Procurements*
Inputs	12.3.1.6	Work Performance Data	*Control Procurements*
Inputs	12.3.1.7	Enterprise Environmental Factors	*Control Procurements*
Inputs	12.3.1.8	Organizational Process Assets	*Control Procurements*
Outputs	12.1.3.1	Procurement Management Plan	*Plan Procurement Management*
Outputs	12.1.3.2	Procurement Strategy	*Plan Procurement Management*
Outputs	12.1.3.3	Bid Documents	*Plan Procurement Management*
Outputs	12.1.3.4	Procurement Statement of Work	*Plan Procurement Management*
Outputs	12.1.3.5	Source Selection Criteria	*Plan Procurement Management*
Outputs	12.1.3.6	Make-or-Buy Decisions	*Plan Procurement Management*
Outputs	12.1.3.7	Independent Cost Estimates	*Plan Procurement Management*
Outputs	12.1.3.8	Change Requests	*Plan Procurement Management*
Outputs	12.1.3.9	Project Documents Updates	*Plan Procurement Management*
Outputs	12.1.3.10	Organizational Process Assets Updates	*Plan Procurement Management*
Outputs	12.2.3.1	Selected Sellers	*Conduct Procurements*
Outputs	12.2.3.2	Agreements	*Conduct Procurements*
Outputs	12.2.3.3	Change Requests	*Conduct Procurements*
Outputs	12.2.3.4	Project Management Plan Updates	*Conduct Procurements*
Outputs	12.2.3.5	Project Documents Updates	*Conduct Procurements*
Outputs	12.2.3.6	Organizational Process Assets Updates	*Conduct Procurements*
Outputs	12.3.3.1	Closed Procurements	*Control Procurements*
Outputs	12.3.3.2	Work Performance Information	*Control Procurements*
Outputs	12.3.3.3	Procurement Documentation Updates	*Control Procurements*
Outputs	12.3.3.4	Change Requests	*Control Procurements*
Outputs	12.3.3.5	Project Management Plan Updates	*Control Procurements*
Outputs	12.3.3.6	Project Documents Updates	*Control Procurements*

Type	Reference	Activity	Process
Outputs	12.3.3.7	Organizational Process Assets Updates	*Control Procurements*
Tools & Techniques	12.1.2.1	Expert Judgment	*Plan Procurement Management*
Tools & Techniques	12.1.2.2	Data Gathering	*Plan Procurement Management*
Tools & Techniques	12.1.2.3	Data Analysis	*Plan Procurement Management*
Tools & Techniques	12.1.2.4	Source Selection Analysis	*Plan Procurement Management*
Tools & Techniques	12.1.2.5	Meetings	*Plan Procurement Management*
Tools & Techniques	12.2.2.1	Expert Judgment	*Conduct Procurements*
Tools & Techniques	12.2.2.2	Advertising	*Conduct Procurements*
Tools & Techniques	12.2.2.3	Bidder Conferences	*Conduct Procurements*
Tools & Techniques	12.2.2.4	Data Analysis	*Conduct Procurements*
Tools & Techniques	12.2.2.5	Interpersonal and Team Skills	*Conduct Procurements*
Tools & Techniques	12.3.2.1	Expert Judgment	*Control Procurements*
Tools & Techniques	12.3.2.2	Claims Administration	*Control Procurements*
Tools & Techniques	12.3.2.3	Data Analysis	*Control Procurements*
Tools & Techniques	12.3.2.4	Inspection	*Control Procurements*
Tools & Techniques	12.3.2.5	Audits	*Control Procurements*

Activities Sorted by Type and Activity

Type	Reference	Activity	Process
Inputs	12.3.1.3	Agreements	*Control Procurements*
Inputs	12.3.1.5	Approved Change Requests	*Control Procurements*
Inputs	12.1.1.2	Business Documents	*Plan Procurement Management*
Inputs	12.1.1.5	Enterprise Environmental Factors	*Plan Procurement Management*
Inputs	12.2.1.5	Enterprise Environmental Factors	*Conduct Procurements*
Inputs	12.3.1.7	Enterprise Environmental Factors	*Control Procurements*
Inputs	12.1.1.6	Organizational Process Assets	*Plan Procurement Management*
Inputs	12.2.1.6	Organizational Process Assets	*Conduct Procurements*
Inputs	12.3.1.8	Organizational Process Assets	*Control Procurements*
Inputs	12.2.1.3	Procurement Documentation	*Conduct Procurements*
Inputs	12.3.1.4	Procurement Documentation	*Control Procurements*
Inputs	12.1.1.1	Project Charter	*Plan Procurement Management*
Inputs	12.1.1.4	Project Documents	*Plan Procurement Management*
Inputs	12.2.1.2	Project Documents	*Conduct Procurements*
Inputs	12.3.1.2	Project Documents	*Control Procurements*
Inputs	12.1.1.3	Project Management Plan	*Plan Procurement Management*
Inputs	12.2.1.1	Project Management Plan	*Conduct Procurements*
Inputs	12.3.1.1	Project Management Plan	*Control Procurements*
Inputs	12.2.1.4	Seller Proposals	*Conduct Procurements*
Inputs	12.3.1.6	Work Performance Data	*Control Procurements*
Outputs	12.2.3.2	Agreements	*Conduct Procurements*
Outputs	12.1.3.3	Bid Documents	*Plan Procurement Management*
Outputs	12.1.3.8	Change Requests	*Plan Procurement Management*
Outputs	12.2.3.3	Change Requests	*Conduct Procurements*
Outputs	12.3.3.4	Change Requests	*Control Procurements*
Outputs	12.3.3.1	Closed Procurements	*Control Procurements*
Outputs	12.1.3.7	Independent Cost Estimates	*Plan Procurement Management*
Outputs	12.1.3.6	Make-or-Buy Decisions	*Plan Procurement Management*
Outputs	12.1.3.10	Organizational Process Assets Updates	*Plan Procurement Management*
Outputs	12.2.3.6	Organizational Process Assets Updates	*Conduct Procurements*
Outputs	12.3.3.7	Organizational Process Assets Updates	*Control Procurements*
Outputs	12.3.3.3	Procurement Documentation Updates	*Control Procurements*
Outputs	12.1.3.1	Procurement Management Plan	*Plan Procurement Management*
Outputs	12.1.3.4	Procurement Statement of Work	*Plan Procurement Management*
Outputs	12.1.3.2	Procurement Strategy	*Plan Procurement Management*
Outputs	12.1.3.9	Project Documents Updates	*Plan Procurement Management*
Outputs	12.2.3.5	Project Documents Updates	*Conduct Procurements*
Outputs	12.3.3.6	Project Documents Updates	*Control Procurements*
Outputs	12.2.3.4	Project Management Plan Updates	*Conduct Procurements*
Outputs	12.3.3.5	Project Management Plan Updates	*Control Procurements*
Outputs	12.2.3.1	Selected Sellers	*Conduct Procurements*
Outputs	12.1.3.5	Source Selection Criteria	*Plan Procurement Management*

Type	Reference	Activity	Process
Outputs	12.3.3.2	Work Performance Information	*Control Procurements*
Tools & Techniques	12.2.2.2	Advertising	*Conduct Procurements*
Tools & Techniques	12.3.2.5	Audits	*Control Procurements*
Tools & Techniques	12.2.2.3	Bidder Conferences	*Conduct Procurements*
Tools & Techniques	12.3.2.2	Claims Administration	*Control Procurements*
Tools & Techniques	12.1.2.3	Data Analysis	*Plan Procurement Management*
Tools & Techniques	12.2.2.4	Data Analysis	*Conduct Procurements*
Tools & Techniques	12.3.2.3	Data Analysis	*Control Procurements*
Tools & Techniques	12.1.2.2	Data Gathering	*Plan Procurement Management*
Tools & Techniques	12.1.2.1	Expert Judgment	*Plan Procurement Management*
Tools & Techniques	12.2.2.1	Expert Judgment	*Conduct Procurements*
Tools & Techniques	12.3.2.1	Expert Judgment	*Control Procurements*
Tools & Techniques	12.3.2.4	Inspection	*Control Procurements*
Tools & Techniques	12.2.2.5	Interpersonal and Team Skills	*Conduct Procurements*
Tools & Techniques	12.1.2.5	Meetings	*Plan Procurement Management*
Tools & Techniques	12.1.2.4	Source Selection Analysis	*Plan Procurement Management*

Index

CPSIA information can be obtained
at www.ICGtesting.com
Printed in the USA
LVHW051600101222
734842LV00008BA/682